Visions of Virtue in Popular Film

Thinking Through Cinema

Thomas E. Wartenberg, Series Editor

VISIONS OF VIRTUE IN POPULAR FILM

Joseph H. Kupfer

Westview Press
A Member of the Perseus Books Group

Thinking Through Cinema

Copyright © 1999 by Westview Press, A Member of the Perseus Books Group

Published in 1999 in the United States of America by Westview Press, 5500 Central Avenue, Boulder, Colorado 80301-2877, and in the United Kingdom by Westview Press, 12 Hid's Copse Road, Cumnor Hill, Oxford OX2 9JJ

Find us on the World Wide Web at www.westviewpress.com

Quote on page 13 excerpted from "The Dry Salvages" in *Four Quartets*, copyright 1941 by T.S. Eliot and renewed by Esme Valerie Eliot, reprinted by permission of Harcourt, Inc.

Library of Congress Cataloging-in-Publication Data
Kupfer, Joseph H.
    Visions of virtue in popular film / Joseph H. Kupfer.
        p.   cm.—(Thinking through cinema)
    Includes bibliographical references and index.
    ISBN 0-8133-6720-4 (hc)—ISBN 0-8133-6721-2 (pbk).
    1. Motion pictures—Moral and ethical aspects.   I. Title.
    II. Series.
PN1995.5.K87   1999
791.43'653—dc21   99-23485
                                                        CIP

The paper used in this publication meets the requirements of the American National Standard for Permanence of Paper for Printed Library Materials Z39.48-1984.

10   9   8   7   6   5   4   3   2   1

For my wife, Lu

Contents

Photos

Acknowledgments

I benefited from Iowa State University's generosity in providing me with a leave of absence during which this book was begun. I would like to thank Tom Wartenberg for his insightful, constructive criticism of my early efforts on the project—it has made all the difference. I am also indebted to my colleague, Lee Honeycutt, who showed uncommon patience and discernment in capturing the film stills for me. Above all, I am grateful to my wife, who eagerly read everything I wrote. Her wonderful suggestions for clarity, emphasis, and organization made every chapter better.

Joseph H. Kupfer

Introduction:
Visions of Virtue
in Popular Film

The idea for this book began to take shape some time ago, when I noticed what I was thinking about in the weeks after seeing the film *Jaws*. I was preoccupied with the fact that the men with technical expertise fail to kill the monstrous shark and that the successful Chief Brody has little more than his virtuous character to recommend him for the task. Thinking about the variety of Brody's virtues led me to look more thoughtfully at other popular Hollywood films. I found that close viewing revealed many of the movies contained much more than met the eye and that taking note of the philosophical ideas in these films made them more enjoyable. Since that time, my attention has gravitated to popular films with a decidedly moral content, especially movies in which virtue appears to be the crux of the story.

The films discussed here were made primarily to entertain and only secondarily, if at all, to edify their audiences. However varied in tenor, style, or genre, the films are of a piece in endorsing a salutary conception of the virtues. I do not analyze films that focus on antiheroes or the failure of virtue or the failure of people to be virtuous. These are important topics in their own right, but they are for a different book. I also avoid such classics as *It's a Wonderful Life* or *Mr. Smith Goes to Washington*, as well as more recent biographies that are testaments to people of stellar moral character. *Beckett, Gandhi*, and *Schindler's List*, for instance, seem designed to illustrate virtues and vices, if not moral theories about them.

This book addresses movies that have not received the philosophical interpretation classic American films have received, or that do not lend themselves as readily to moral analysis as such foreign gems as *La Strada* and *Babette's Feast*. The interpretations offered here deal with films that range over a wide array of genres: comedy and science-fiction/horror, historical and romantic adventure, and realistic social drama. The characters in these movies are pushed and pulled within engrossing plots. We enjoy the story first and wonder about the moral strengths of the characters later.

Film and Philosophy

Although I use films to illustrate philosophical views or theories, the views they illustrate have not been fully articulated prior to the interpretations of the films. I approach the films with a provisional conception of the virtues, which includes my adaptations of relevant ethical theory. Because the films have something new to show about virtue, the process of interpreting them modifies and extends my theory-laden thinking.

The philosophical view of virtue that emerges from interpreting a particular film is sketched at the beginning of each chapter. This treatise-in-a-nutshell situates the film, and the reader, within a perspective on virtue and indicates why that position is important. Subsequent comments on virtue and vice then make more sense, as they elaborate on and concretize the initial expression of the view. As the movie fiction is interpreted, the opening matrix should keep the interpretation in sharp philosophical focus.

But why use movies to exemplify philosophical views of virtue? The films help reformulate and elaborate virtue theory in the way that interpreting novels, of Dostoevsky and Melville, for instance, has long invigorated philosophical analysis of such subjects as evil, forgiveness, or love. The richness of developed, nuanced narrative examples extends reflection on moral life. For instance, the idea of someone taking responsibility for harm that could reasonably be denied is given texture and complexity in the person of Police Chief Brody, in the film *Jaws*. Examining his character leads me to reflect more deeply on what taking such responsibility indicates about an individual's character. Artistic narratives provide us with quasi-biographies, which can help us see possibilities for modifying existing moral generalizations or for formulating new ones.

As Aristotle notes, ethics concerns contingent events. Facts make a difference. In their details, and twists and turns, stories provide the particulars necessary for actual as well as hypothetical moral judgments. It is possible for a story to capture the shape and substance of human character in a way that eludes more analytic histories and reports or everyday accounts of people. We witness particulars situated in an overall pattern as experienced by a keen observer's mind. What Anne Lamott says about novels also applies to films. She claims that novels help us understand who we are: "An author *makes* you notice, makes you pay attention" to the details that we might otherwise ignore in the course of a day.[1]

However, film fictions may play a more integral role in moral reflection than serving as useful complements to abstract philosophical formulations. Alasdair MacIntyre persuasively argues that narrative, in general, is necessary for moral thinking. For actions to be intelligible in terms of intentions, plans, and dispositional properties, we require "a concept of a self whose unity resides in the unity of a narrative."[2] In Chapter One, I discuss MacIntyre's position in greater depth. But the gist of his argument is that without reference to some form of biographical story, describing the conduct of individuals can amount to little more than enumerating a collection of behavioral events. The concept of personhood or agency is unintelligible without an historical field within which to articulate a self responsible for action. It follows that ascriptions of virtue and vice to individuals also presuppose construction of a relevant narrative for them.

If MacIntyre's position is on the right track and the intelligibility of human conduct requires narrative, then stories are more than just one way among many for getting closer to comprehending human nature and virtue. Rather, artistic narratives, such as fiction films, mirror the form of people's lives, or at least the form needed for us to find those lives meaningful. Stories can serve as paradigms not simply of moral exemplars but of imaginative constructs essential to moral inquiry.

Interpreting the stories presented in movies can give us practice in fitting the pieces of actual people's lives into coherent accounts. No one interpretation of moral character, occurring in fiction or reality, is ever exhaustive, authoritative, or comprehensive. Our experience of the freedom to select among possible threads of intelligibility in interpreting fictional characters can further our appreciation for the complexity and creativity of ascribing virtue and vice to people in everyday life. Consequently, we may come to a more fine-grained understanding of the nature of moral assessment in general.

Just as interpreting the narrative aspects of film fleshes out a fuller view of virtue, approaching film with a theory of virtue deepens our cinematic appreciation. Elucidating the visions of virtue expressed in the films enables a fresh appreciation of their plots, characters, images, and cinematic structures. My appropriation of film is much like that well-worn approach taken by philosophers to literature, which has proved to wear so exceptionally well. Consequently, I draw on a few literary-minded philosophers to make clear the role of philosophy in film.

Morris Weitz claims that literary works contain philosophical themes or ideas dealing with "morality, knowledge, human purpose, and reality."[3] Therefore, an important task for literary criticism is to "state and clarify these themes, show how they are presented, and relate them to the other aspects of the work."[4] Philosophical ideas may be presented explicitly through dialogue or commentary, but the more interesting ideas are usually implicit in the art work. For example, consider David Ross's observation about *The Brothers Karamazov*. He argues that Dostoevsky contrasts Alyosha's successes with Ivan's failures to show that goodness is always particular and never abstract. Consequently, the novel is thought by Ross to embody, but nowhere states, the following claim: "Rational principles are not wrong; they are simply beside the point in human life."[5]

In discussing the films chosen for this book, I focus on the way they imply or embody philosophical themes through characterization, plot, dialogue, and cinematic features. The ideas uncovered in philosophical explication of films increase our appreciation because they make important aesthetic contributions to the film's story. Through their embodiment of philosophical themes, the narrative and cinematic aspects of film are deepened and creatively related to one another. The philosophical perspective on love and virtue in *The African Queen,* for instance, positions the shave Charlie Allnut gives himself as a symbolic harbinger of his moral transformation. Subsequent details of incidence, character, and conversation are connected through the philosophical viewpoint on his action.

This book symbiotically undertakes film criticism and a philosophical exploration of virtue. The form of the interpretive chapters reflects the interplay between the two enterprises. The initial outline of the philosophical view of virtue embodied in the film helps me articulate the themes of the story and also helps to organize aspects of plot, character, and cinematography. At the same time, exposition and interpretation of the film are woven into discussion of virtue and vice. The opening perspective on virtue grows and is refined through the analysis of the film. The pedagogical benefits of the book for both film study and moral philosophy flow from this interplay between film criticism and philosophical theorizing.

Philosophical Underpinnings

I have written a book that explores philosophy in film rather than one that offers a philosophy of film. Although I do not tackle theory of film explicitly, all interpretation and criticism operate within some theoretical perspective, however unsystematically defined or deployed. Let me begin by saying that I do not take my bearings from the contemporary mainstream of academic film studies. From strands of semiotic linguistics, Marxism, and psychoanalytic theory, academic film critics have fashioned their conceptual nets. Simplifying what unites these conceptual schemes, one can say that they understand cinema as socially constructed, ideologically driven, coded text.

The semiological-Marxist-psychoanalytic theories, and their variants, have been the most dominant form of academic criticism for several decades. Scholars working within these theoretical perspectives tend to look through or past the movie text to its ideological function in society. Thus, these theories emphasize how and why films "position" or manipulate viewers—in terms of class, gender, consciousness, or with regard to subjectivity itself. Commentary on the film stories, therefore, usually reverts to the central issue of philosophy of film. I hardly have the space or expertise needed to explicate or evaluate the family of theories mentioned above. I wish only to indicate what my film analyses are *not* trying to accomplish.

The approach I take centers on the story told by the film, the film fiction. It is viewed as a tale about people and events that are more or less like real people and events and, as a result, can shed light on the human situation. The story illustrates philosophical generalizations or themes that can be cognitively grasped and stated. In particular, I am concerned with inferring moral truths about people and their behavior from the narrative and cinematic aspects of films. Hidden or implicit meaning is to be found in the details and connections within the story, as well as in the way the film tells the story, rather than through the categories of a specialized theory about language, class, or mind.[6] Because such special knowledge is not needed to grasp the story's meaning, I assume that audiences respond to the conceptual content examined here, although often unconsciously, and that they sometimes even think about it.

Stanley Cavell's interpretations of Hollywood cinema in *Pursuits of Happiness* are paradigms of the sort of philosophical exegesis of film I aspire to in my film interpretations. Cavell's ability to blend philosophical insight with cinematic sensitivity is showcased, for example, in his discussion of George Cukor's *The Philadelphia Story* (1940). Cavell views C. K. Dexter Haven's triumph over George Kittredge as championing the distinctively American idea of a natural aristocracy—one that is compatible with egalitarianism. "The expulsion [of George] is . . . a promise to be rid of classes as such, and so to be rid of George as one wedded to the thoughts of class division."[7] Cavell's interpretation places the complications of marriage and divorce within larger issues of human value and sociopolitical stratification, resulting in a deeper appreciation of a fine popular film.

Philosophical interpretation of film may even uncover perspectives on philosophy itself. For instance, Richard Gilmore interprets John Ford's *The Searchers* (1956) as "structurally and allegorically like the very best philosophical texts."[8] He takes the search of the protagonist, Ethan Edwards, to be a quest to discover something he does not quite understand he is seeking. Finding in Ethan an illustration of Nietzsche's (or Wittgenstein's) conception of the philosopher, Gilmore sees him as "one who necessarily stands outside of society."[9] In interpreting *The Searchers* as a story about the philosophical attempt to overcome self-deception and also provide society with a perspective on itself, Gilmore posits a relationship between the philosophical search and the good of society. The philosophical angle taken on Ethan Edwards's quest provides a provocative new mode of appreciating a much-analyzed movie classic.

Thinking philosophically about screwball romantic comedies and westerns, Cavell and Gilmore reveal how complex and profound popular movies can be. Beneath the entertainment these movies provide, audiences may be glimpsing perspectives on human dignity, social structure, even the philosophical quest for knowledge. In some respects, it is harder for films to be philosophically rewarding while entertaining than to address philosophical questions in the studied manner of the art film. I believe that the popular films that have become classics, such as *The Philadelphia Story* and *The Searchers,* endure because their underlying philosophical views inform audiences' experience and enjoyment of the story. I think the films chosen for examination in this book have a good chance of becoming "popular philosophical classics" as well.

My interpretations should speak to the popular culture in a way more sophisticated semiological analyses cannot because these interpretations develop out of experience that is typical of mass audiences for movies. Working outside the mainstream of academic film studies has two other advantages. Since typical film studies proceed from theories whose primary domain is noncinematic, such as psychoanalysis, they tend to employ specialized, technical vocabularies. Furthermore, to the extent that the technical theories make claims that are questionable as applied within their own fields, film criticism derived from these theories may be correspondingly compromised.

I avoid both the technical language of specialized theories as well as dependence on their noncinematic credibility. I suppose my approach is a kind of popular-philosophical hybrid. It is popular in eschewing the prevalent academic theoretical frameworks, but philosophical in pressing the film's narrative surface for moral truths. Perhaps also because so much recent criticism has been done in the semiological-Marxist-psychoanalytic vein, the approach I take actually provides a new alternative in interpreting movies, traditional as it is.

Emphasizing the conceptual or propositional content of the film's story as I do is clearly a didactic perspective, one that suits my philosophical interests. But it is not didacticism in the narrow sense of claiming to have cornered the only meaning or value film can have—philosophical or otherwise. My perspective is not reductionistic. I simply work at the didactic end of the interpretive spectrum and readily acknowledge a varied palate of interpretive interests available for explaining or evaluating film.

Overview

Before examining the particular films, in Chapter One I present the philosophical conception of virtue with which I work and an explanation of how I undertake the philosophical interpretation of film. The conception of virtue I bring to the films is a classical one, originating with the ancient Greeks, and modified within the major traditions of Western thought. This conception of virtue has had the greatest influence in Western daily life and philosophical thought. The outlook of most of the audience for this book, and the films discussed in it, therefore, has also been shaped by this understanding of the virtues.

I augment the traditional understanding of virtue with contemporary thought on autonomy, feminist ethic of care, and ideal speech theory. I also delineate particular virtues, absent from the traditions, through examination of such contexts as family and moral community. The outline of virtue theory includes an explanation of different kinds of virtue and their personal and social value.

As indicated, philosophical interpretation of film involves explicating the moral themes and theses implicit in film and articulating their relationship to other cinematically rendered aspects of the story. The attribution of particular thematic meanings is justified by their ability to unify and further define such elements as visual portrayal of incident, character motivation, and narrative form. Interpretive claims occur at different levels, with higher-level claims supported by those at lower levels. All interpretive arguments must be supported ultimately by direct reference to the movie text.

The films that are analyzed present a variegated, yet integrated, view of the virtues and virtuous character. The chapters on the specific films can be read in isolation from one another, with or without the theoretical précis on virtue and interpretation contained in Chapter One. However, the film chapters are united by a broad thematic background and several smaller, foregrounded motifs or subthemes. In the foreground, running in and out of the discussions to different degrees, to different effect, is the motif of vice. In all the films, protagonists must overcome vices. Sometimes the vices are their own, sometimes they belong to adversaries. The subject of virtue is also amplified by the subthemes of self-knowledge, the nature of moral growth, and the role of such auxiliary, nonmoral virtues as cheerfulness and playfulness.

The background for the corpus of film interpretations is woven from the relationships (or their lack) between the virtuous characters and other individuals in the story. From film to film, this pervasive theme of social relationship is realized in an expanding, balloon-like shape. The virtues are developed and exercised by the films' protagonists in a context of gradually enlarging, meaningful interpersonal relationships until the social fabric finally bursts, giving way to a depersonalized socioeconomic order. Beginning with emphasis on the development of the virtuous individual *(Groundhog Day)*, the discussion proceeds to romantic friendship as an interpersonal context for mutual moral education *(The African Queen)*. Romantic friendship naturally leads into family *(Parenthood)* and then to cooperative community *(Rob Roy)* as the social milieu in which the virtues are nurtured and given particular definition.

I conclude with films about virtuous individuals who must act in societies in which they are practically isolated. In these societies, family and community have been weakened or undermined *(Fresh)*, or they have been eclipsed by economic forces and interests *(Jaws* and *Aliens)*. We seem to have come full circle, returning to the individual per se, except that we are not back where we began with *Groundhog Day*. *Groundhog Day* portrays an individual whose virtuous maturation readies him for romantic friendship and the fellowship of community. Our concluding movies present virtuous individuals in depersonalized societies dominated by commercial interests. The thematic shape of an ever-enlarging framework of social meaning and cooperation, therefore, culminates in the breaking of the bonds that constitute that framework.

Analysis of *Groundhog Day* emphasizes virtue, and virtuous activity, as essential to human happiness. The fanciful conceit of reliving the same day over and over demonstrates how a life of egoistic hedonism is incapable of bringing lasting happiness. Only when Phil Connors engages in moral and artistic pursuits for their own sake can he enjoy life and experience genuine friendship.

The African Queen depicts romantic friendship as the context of shared moral education. The film shows how romantic love first inspires us to see ourselves becoming morally better with the beloved and then enables us to realize our potential for virtuous growth. Rose Sayer and Charlie Allnut encourage the virtuous development of one another in collaborating to keep the African Queen afloat and headed downriver. The work of love is fulfilled in the mutually encouraged moral growth found in working together.

Parenthood expands the context for the cultivation of virtue in the individual to the family. It reveals how family relationships, support, and difficulties provide a complex environment for acquiring virtues and their correlative vices. The film looks with humor, yet serious purpose, at the parent-child relationship during three stages of the child's development: in early childhood, as a teenager, and as an adult. I examine how parents, rather than their children, are morally influenced, for better and worse, by the practice of child-rearing.

Rob Roy sharpens the contrast between virtue and vice by situating family within cooperative community and the still wider world of the political-economic state. The central virtues explored are those which are constitutive of a community of trustworthy language users. Truth telling, promise keeping, and reciprocity of respect are shown to be necessary to the functioning of moral community. The distinctive evil of the antagonists in the film is exhibited in their treatment of language simply as a tool, which renders them incapable of friendship, love, or community.

In the film *Fresh*, community is corrupted and family is seriously attenuated. The hero, Michael, must act within social networks that are dominated by the power relations and commerce of inner-city drug markets and racketeers. Michael's family is socially marginalized and personally fragmented by these economic forces. Although Michael lacks the grandeur of Rob Roy and the completeness of virtue exemplified by the heroes in *Jaws* and *Aliens*, his character provides an opportunity to explore a singular virtue in depth. Practical wisdom, or phronesis, may be the most difficult virtue to achieve and the most elusive to define. Articulating the complexity of Michael's practical wisdom in *Fresh* is also an occasion for putting in perspective discussions of the extent to which characters in other films possess this crown of the virtues.

The last interpretive chapter deals with virtuous individuals for whom the erosion of supportive communal relations is complete. In *Jaws*, the setting is a resort town built on the loose ties of shared mercantile aims. What little community remains is distorted by economic interests, and in *Aliens*, community has been swallowed up by corporate interplanetary power. The two films depict how virtue enables civic-minded individuals to triumph over the evil engendered by economic greed. The virtues of Brody and Ripley are the most complete of the characters examined, but they are exhibited and fully realized only in response to the predatory creatures they must vanquish.

Stepping back from the individual film interpretations, the conclusion sketches some affinities among the films. The films in the first three interpretive chapters, for example, are humorous, and virtue is explored within close personal relationships. The films in the latter half of the book involve their protagonists in violent confrontations in a wider, harsher social milieu. The conclusion explores the themes shared by the movie stories, including obstacles to a realistic perspective on the world, why individuals fail to listen to wise counsel, and the place of pleasure in a life of virtue. Rounding out the conclusion is a discussion of the way the movie stories themselves conclude with their protagonists paired with another individual. In ending their stories with a return to a partner or with a new (or renewed) pairing, the films emphasize the social nature of human life and moral virtue.

The book's analysis of virtue in movies does not simply proceed from film to film looking for provocative characters or shining character. Instead, the films are organized to illustrate the value of virtue within ever-widening social contexts. Arranged in this way, the book has an internal structure that should carry the reader through an increasingly more comprehensive account—analogous to the way a film's plot unfolds the virtues of its characters. Readers see the influence of social relations on virtues, as well as how virtues, in their turn, are instrumental in sustaining relations of love, family, and community.

In addition to the film interpretations fitting together as a whole, the six chapters divide into two halves, each with a tone and orientation common to the movies within it. The first three chapters cover films that are comic, if not comedies proper. What little humor is to be found in the films of the latter three chapters tends to be grim, morbid, or ironic. In the first group of films, the protagonists are shown developing their virtues—overcoming vices and character flaws, or flawed outlooks on life. Their major conflicts are with themselves, situated in the private sphere of romantic friendship and family. Larger political-economic realities play very little part in the movie stories, and money is practically irrelevant to the characters. In contrast, the heroes of the second set of films possess characters that are well established. Their stories are about how their virtues are brought to full expression in struggles with external foes, within monolithic political economies. Money motivates the enemies of the protagonists and moves the plot within which they must fight for survival.

These essays in film criticism are flexible in their reading and use. Even though the essays are unified as a whole, each is self-contained and can be read independently. Thus, readers can pick and choose according to their interests or movie preferences. Casual and academic cineasts alike can enjoy the ethical interpretation of popular films they originally found simply funny or charming, frightening or exciting. Readers with theoretical interests, in either film or ethics, should appreciate the extent to which narrative and cinematic features of film can extend our more abstract, philosophical understanding of morality. And film buffs might be surprised at how much moral content can be embodied in films they had previously enjoyed without much systematic thought. Creating cinematic entertainments within which are embedded substantive moral views is no mean feat, and to do it justice is challenging. I intend this book to be philosophically rich but readable, the way the films examined are morally insightful but enjoyable to watch.

Notes

1. Anne Lamott, *Bird by Bird* (New York: Pantheon, 1994), p.15.
2. Alasdair MacIntyre, *After Virtue* (Notre Dame, Ind.: Univ. of Notre Dame Press, 1981), p.191.

3. Morris Weitz, *Philosophy in Literature* (Detroit: Wayne State University Press, 1963), p.9.

4. Ibid., p.91.

5. David Ross, *Literature and Philosophy* (New York: Appleton-Century-Crofts, 1969), p.170.

6. Noel Carroll has this to say about the theoretic independence of cinematic experience: "Such [cinematic] images could be recognized by untutored spectators without the necessity of training in processes of symbol reading, decoding, deciphering, or inference." *Mystifying Movies: Fads and Fallacies in Contemporary Film Theory* (New York: Columbia University Press, 1988), p.210.

7. Stanley Cavell, *Pursuits of Happiness: The Hollywood Comedy of Remarriage* (Cambridge: Harvard University Press, 1981), p.156. Cavell does theorize about the nature of film as artistic medium and our relationship to it. However, he finds theory of film *within* the films themselves rather than importing theoretical considerations from other disciplines, such as linguistics or psychoanalysis. Cavell points out that "each of the films in the genre of remarriage essentially contains considerations of what it is to view them" and then probes the issue of viewing (p.159). This is to pursue the presence of philosophy in film, however sophisticated and self-referential that philosophy may be.

8. Richard Gilmore, "John Ford's *The Searchers* as an Allegory of the Philosophical Search," *Film and Philosophy* 3 (1996):61–76, 65.

9. Ibid., p.69.

1
Film Criticism
and Virtue Theory

Before interpreting the films for their insights into the nature of virtue, I should explain briefly the assumptions I bring to film criticism and the view of virtue with which I operate. Each of these topics is complex enough to warrant a chapter or book in its own right, but a serviceable understanding of my conception of them seems adequate in a nontheoretical work devoted to analyzing particular films. A number of gaps and unanswered questions, therefore, should be expected in an explanation suited to the practical aim of orienting readers in the ensuing discussions of film.

Film Criticism

We had the experience but missed the meaning,
And approach to the meaning restores the experience . . .

—T. S. Eliot, *Four Quartets*

Interpretive Levels and Assumptions

I am concerned with fiction films, films that tell stories in the colloquial sense that novels, theater plays, and raconteurs tell stories. The stories told in these films, then, are film fictions or movie stories. Fiction films are distinguished from other films such as documentaries, advertisements, travelogues, instructional or educational films, and artistic (non-narrative) explorations of the medium. The term director or filmmaker is used when referring to the team of people responsible for making the film, which is typically headed by the director.

I approach interpretations of movie fictions as a layered structure or edifice. At the base of the interpretive structure are the first-order descriptive claims that refer directly to perceptual images and sounds. These descriptions tend to pick out discrete, discriminable images and scenes in a relatively uncontroversial way. Topping off the structure are comprehensive claims about the story's meaning that encompass the lower-level statements. The comprehensive assertions are supported by the lower-level statements but, in turn, organize and make sense of them. In between the top and bottom levels are numerous strata of inferences and construals of meaning. Let's start at the foundation.

Interpretations are grounded in more or less indisputable descriptions of what happens in the story. As these statements refer directly to what is observable, they are basic, or first-order, descriptions. The first-order account of *Psycho,* for example, includes the claims that Norman Bates runs a hotel and that he watches a hotel patron, Marion, through a peephole. We take the cinematic depiction of character and events as providing uncontestable story data. The cinematic depiction is like reading that Captain Ahab had lost a leg pursuing a great white whale.

The assumption of narrative facticity is a basic convention for reading novels and viewing fiction movies. Imagine the oddness of someone challenging basic descriptive claims, saying: "Yes, we see Norman apparently running the Bates motel and spying on Marion, but how can we be sure? Maybe we are mistaken." Such a challenge to basic, first-order descriptive claims is to miss how the convention of facticity is necessary for readers or viewers to make sense of a story. It would be like thinking that evidence exists outside the fictional presentation that might change our minds about what we see. The basic content of what we see or are told just does constitute the narrative facts.

However, conventions do exist for exceptions to the assumption of facticity. There may be cinematic or narrative clues that an unreliable narrator is telling a story, such as the storyteller in Ford Maddox Ford's novel *The Good Soldier.* A classic way for films to generate uncertainty about what actually takes place in the story, one that is self-reflective about storytelling, is to present multiple, incompatible versions of the tale, as in Akira Kurosawa's *Rashomon.* Films that are open-textured, or open-texted, in this way usually trade on this feature. Ambiguity or uncertainty about what really occurs is essential to interpreting the film. The films I consider, however, are of the prosaic variety—straightforward narratives for which numerous uncontestable descriptions can be asserted. For instance, the statement "Carter Burke tries to kill Ripley" is a first-order description of the story told by *Aliens*.

As we leave the foundational descriptions of the story, we initially make inferences, which can be considered immediate because they are made directly from first-order descriptions and because they, too, tend to be unproblematic. In *The African Queen*, Rose Sayer manages a weak smile and offers more tea and bread in response to Charlie Allnut calling attention to his loud gastric rumblings. We immediately infer that she wishes to change the subject to something more pleasant. When the boy Kevin grimaces as he maneuvers to catch a fly ball during a baseball game in the film *Parenthood*, we are justified in making the immediate inference that he is tense and unsure of himself.

We do not always make inferences from first-order descriptions and subsequent immediate inferences in a one-to-one, atomistic fashion. Instead, we often derive implications from clusters of scenes, collages of images, and counterpoints of dialogue. Thus, we combine our immediate inference about Kevin's nervousness with the inference that his father, Gil, suffers an excessive sense of parental responsibility for Kevin's welfare. Together, these inferences imply that Gil's attitude and the behavior it produces are probably contributing to Kevin's insecurity.

When we make a case for our interpretations of movies to other people, we typically marshal evidence and inferences so as to ground higher-level claims in lower-order inferences and, finally, in descriptive statements about the movie text. Although we may begin a piece of criticism with summary generalizations stating what the film is about, a hierarchical structure of argument is usually discernible within the discussion. As with scientific hypotheses, however, the order of discovery or creativity tends to be quite different from the format we use to present or justify our interpretation of a film.

Our intermediate and higher-order meaning statements frequently dawn on us as a result of unexpected concatenations: Disparate scenes appear to fit together; seemingly unrelated intermediate inferences suggest an overarching theme; a striking image draws diverse moments in the film to itself and to each other like a magnet. Even when our exposition proceeds neatly from description to immediate inference to intermediate inference, stage by stage, it is a reconstruction for clarity of communication from a more rough-and-tumble process of discovery and ordering, and re-ordering upon yet further discovery.

Moreover, as we offer intermediate-level conjectures about such aspects of the story as character motivation and symbolic weightiness, we must necessarily tie together different portions and dimensions of the film. It is as if we are backing away from the film, trying to see a variety of images and scenes in relationship to one another. In the movement away from basic description and immediate inference, we see connections between and among them and higher-level interpretive claims. In this movement also lie the most creative and interesting features of interpretation.

As we well know, the same movie fiction is subject to different and diverging interpretations; nevertheless, ordinary moviegoers and critics alike assume a common referent for these interpretations. For our purposes, the common referent of interpretation is that which is picked out by first-order descriptions and immediate inferences. I use the term text to mean an object available for public inspection. Interpretive claims find their eventual support in textual referents. However, citing the text rarely resolves interesting interpretive disagreements or indicates which interpretations are better than others.

We assume movie fictions are purposive, that the cinematically rendered tale has a point, without necessarily assuming that the filmmaker actually had these particular (or any) purposes in mind. The point or meaning of a film is indeterminate because the text is amenable to different construals of meaning. Consequently, viewers of movie fictions have a degree of freedom in interpreting them. The overall meaning of the film is captured in comprehensive, summary generalizations that are supported by the interpretive edifice. Exercising interpretive freedom responsibly and convincingly involves tethering the contestable intermediate and summary ascriptions to the text by means of first-order descriptions and immediate inferences. How well the contestable or summary ascriptions are textually grounded depends on the number of such foundational supports and the plausibility of the inferences drawn.

No movement beyond the basic descriptions and the immediate inferences from them would be possible without a backdrop of other conventional assumptions for making sense of movie fictions. Of course, most of these conventions are taken for granted in viewing and interpreting films. Only in such self-conscious reflection as this do we make them explicit. For example, we typically take the sequence of events as they are presented in the film to be identical with the temporal sequence of events in the story being shown. Conventions and contexts, such as those suggesting flashbacks, indicate the movie's departure from the linear directionality of time, which we habitually transfer from the real world.

In fact, we naturally assume a rough resemblance between the world portrayed in the fiction movie and the real world. Assumptions of reality resemblance include temporal and spatial uniformity, object individuation and continuity, and causal linkage among events. We operate with these assumptions unless we are cinematically cued to see the world of the movie fiction as different from our own. Similarly, familiar conventions let us know when we are seeing the world through a character's eyes (in contrast to an objective camera point of view), when time has elapsed, or when place has changed.

In *Groundhog Day*, for example, we are given ample evidence that the people in Punxsutawney, Pennsylvania, are reliving the same day and that only Phil Connors remembers what occurs from one "same" day to the next. But aside from this big exception to the laws of spatio-temporal uniformity and temporal directionality, everything else in the world of this movie fiction resembles the real world.

No matter how bizarre the tale of fantasy or science fiction, a good deal of resemblance is necessary for viewers to find the fictional world intelligible. The requirements of intelligibility always constrain the extent to which the fictional world can deviate from reality as we conceive it. If the fictional world departs too much from the actual one, viewers simply cannot make sense of it. Of course, that can be the point of a film. In such cases, the meaning of the film is not going to be found primarily within its story but will be discovered in how the unintelligibility of the events portrayed is cinematically constructed.

Critical Perspectives

Interpretations are appropriations of movie texts, and all are from a perspective or viewpoint. No interest-free, or nonperspectival interpretations are possible. As John Dewey points out, "Critic and artist alike have their predilections."[1] Because criticism is judgment, Dewey tells us, critics reveal themselves in their criticisms.[2] The particular approach a critic takes may tell us as much about the critic's tastes or concerns as it does about the film being examined.

Films can be interpreted from many viewpoints, reflecting various values and interests. As noted in the Introduction, the dominant trend in recent academic film studies has been to interpret films from a linguistic, Marxist, or psychoanalytic perspective or some combination of those perspectives. Interpretation in this vein tends to underplay the importance of the story for the sake of placing the film in a social or psychological context of creation and reception. Critics who are concerned with the significance of the story, as I am, are hardly of one mind. Their interests can range over narrative style, social commentary, religious symbolism, metaphysical or psychological outlook, and historical placement.

The point of a story is not always obvious, and where obvious, further meanings or complexities may be enfolded within the central idea that require creative viewing and reflection. Critical creativity includes resourcefulness and decisionmaking because the movie fiction is indeterminate. Not only is it open to the panorama of interpretations resulting from the many perspectives from which a film can be approached, but within a given perspective, a film is amenable to different interpretations. Different interpretations can be justified by reference to the text because, as noted earlier, film fictions underdetermine their interpretations, allowing for indefinitely many implications to be drawn from a movie text. As Peter Jones writes of the texts of novels: "There are no formal limits to the ways in which texts may be taken."3

Because the movie fiction is open to competing interpretations, critics view films and think about them creatively. Creative freedom is necessitated by textual indeterminacy of meaning and significance. Critics vary in their powers to discriminate parts and nuance, as well as in their abilities to discern thematic threads with which to weave these elements into a meaningful whole. According to Dewey, "This unifying phase, even more than the analytic, is a function of the creative response of the individual who judges. It is insight . . . It is at this point that criticism becomes itself an art."4

The danger lurking in critical creativity is that critics can make more of the text than is warranted and ground too little of their interpretation in it. They then use the movie fiction as a springboard for their own flights of fancy instead of fitting their inventiveness more faithfully to the story. Dewey again astutely observes how "sometimes critics of the better type substitute a work of their own for that they are professedly dealing with. The result may be art but it is not criticism."5 For Dewey, the more creative the critics, the more susceptible they are to this temptation. Critics cannot overreach unless they are blessed with ingenuity and aesthetic acuity.

The diversity in viewpoints from which movies are interpreted probably accounts for the most striking differences among interpretations.

Interpreters naturally emphasize those components of the story and propose organizational schemes that are consonant with their specific backgrounds and interests. From various interpretations, we infer diverse meanings about life. For example, my interpretation of *Rob Roy* stresses features of the film that coalesce around themes of moral language use.

In contrast, a Marxist perspective would produce an interpretation whose unifying thrust and points of accent would be very different. The meaning of the story would tend to be cast in terms of control over the means of production and the economic stratification that limits Rob Roy's options, including his inability to see natural allies in the impoverished tinkers. A more historically minded critic would probably emphasize the decline of the Scottish clans as a consequence of the centralization of politico-military power or as the product of changes in the political economy, such as those due to technological innovation.

The interpretations of film offered in this book, of course, are framed by the theme of virtue and my interest in virtue theory. In contemporary critical language, I "thematize" the films, although the thematization is typically ascribed directly to the films, not to my thought processes. Thus, I speak of Patty's lack of autonomy as represented in the film *Parenthood*, even though I am the one seeing it there. This locution is typical of interpretations for two reasons. For critics to qualify all of their comments as the result of their interpretive efforts is distracting. More importantly perhaps, interpreters are trying to get readers and viewers to see their interpretations fleshed out in the features of the text. To call attention to one's own thematic agenda easily interferes with bringing the reader into that thematic perspective.

I do not mean to suggest that interpretations are exclusively the result of a perspective that viewers bring to the film. This may be more prevalent in academic film studies, and it certainly describes the way my interpretations are presented here. However, there are times when the film itself draws us to particular features of the narrative and orients us in one way rather than another in its viewing. Whether we subsequently fit those features or that orientation into a previously existing framework of significance or are led to an unanticipated vantage point is an open question. For example, I was struck by the role played by Chief Brody's virtuous character in his triumph over the shark in *Jaws*. The movie seemed to direct my attention to this feature, but I may have been prepared to fasten on the contrast between moral and technical excellence by my background and interests.

We can learn from movie fictions because the construals we make of them have reference to the world in which we live. Indeed, the viewpoint from which we fashion an understanding of the film already reflects our everyday interests, beliefs, and values. We do not perform our interpretive activity in a vacuum and then happily discover that the interpretation speaks so incisively to our life! Our life's interests filter our movie perception, especially when we seriously scrutinize the movie for purposes of systematic interpretation.

In addition, the interpretive viewpoint we bring to the text can be modified by it. In the course of interpreting the film, our views about real life can deepen, expand, narrow, shift, or even do an about-face. Before viewing the film *Fresh*, for example, I had some ideas about the nature of practical wisdom. Watching the film's protagonist apply advice about playing chess to the people who wield power over him prompted me to rethink an aspect of this rare and stunning virtue. In particular, I thought about a particular agility of mind, which I now believe is inherent in practical wisdom.

Movie fictions can be a basis for a new understanding of the world. Even when we look at them from an established viewpoint or ideology, the resulting interpretation can apply to actual experience in promising ways. The interplay between my prior understanding of virtue and my experience of the film *Rob Roy* yielded an interpretation that revolves around the theme of moral standards of language use. In leading me to connect virtue with language and moral community, the emergent theme also enabled me to explain the particular virulence of the evil characters in *Rob Roy*. Generalizations about moral communities and the evil that opposes them seem to me now to apply to everyday life, although not usually with the clarity with which they inform this film.

Were the interests or perspectives we bring to the interpretation of film inviolate or static, movie-going would soon become monotonous. One of the pleasant surprises of watching and discussing films is the way an interpretive angle favored at one viewing of a film can be modified or supplanted by a different approach at a later time. The change in interpretation may be caused by alterations in ourselves that occurred between the two movie experiences, but it can be wrought by the film itself—by relationships and meanings in the film that we now happen to notice but missed on earlier viewing. What critics find important depends on their interpretive outlooks, but what strikes critics as salient in the movie can also determine the interpretive strategy.

Successful Interpretations

When I say that interpreting movie fictions assumes that they have a purpose or point, I do not imply that the purpose is the filmmaker's. Even where ascertainable, the filmmaker's intentions or goals are not authoritative in constructing or assessing interpretations of films. As with all art, once a film is made, it is a public object open to interpretation according to conventions of intelligibility and the interpreter's creative response.

What a filmmaker tries or intends to accomplish in making a film is distinct from what interpreters take the film to mean. For one thing, not all intentions of filmmakers are realized in the film. For another, some unintended cinematic effects are indeed realized in the finished product. Problems of intentionality in art have been well articulated, and I do not wish to unreel the arguments here.[6] I mention a few of the more glaring difficulties with intentionality in interpretation to allay any concerns that my talk of a film's purposes may arouse.

Among the more blatant problems with deferring to the artist's intentions as definitive of interpretation is the consequence that artists could not discover new things in their work nor could they change their interpretation of their work once they were finished. Some artists explain that they do not know what they intend until they actually make their art, and this is incompatible with giving authority to intentions of the artist that exist prior to the creative process. As if these difficulties were not enough to undermine the attractiveness of intentionality in criticism, consider the problem of deciding the intention, or even a consistent set of intentions, operating in works of collective creativity such as we find in film. How is a critic to ascertain which are the relevant or authoritative intentions among the writers, producers, editors, actors, cinematographer, and director?

It is precisely to avoid such monumental detective work and subsequent adjudication that some film critics turn to the plans and intentions of directors alone. But recourse to only the director's state of mind seems ad hoc, and it still leaves open the slew of other difficulties, even if otherwise acceptable. Of course, rejecting intentionality as a procedure for assessing or deriving interpretations does not preclude looking to the director, or others involved in making the film, for suggestive lines of interpretation. What a director had in mind, like a writer's drafts or a producer's projected goals, may or may not prove helpful in a critical construal of a movie fiction. But this is an altogether different tack to take, one that gives no special privilege to the director's purposes.

My approach to film interpretation clearly works better for some films than for others. For instance, some films seem to cry out for historical or social interpretations. The film *Matewan* (1987), by John Sayles, is about the first coal miner's strike in the United States, which took place early in the twentieth century. Situating the movie fiction within the country's nascent labor movement and European emigration to the United States is probably a more fruitful approach than looking at the film after my fashion, as a self-contained moral fable. Other films lend themselves to psychoanalytic exploration, such as Hitchcock's *Vertigo* (1958). As mentioned, films whose form undermines narrative continuity are perhaps best interpreted on a metanarrative level. When films depart radically from the storytelling structures characteristic of most movies, we should think first of interpreting them as commenting on filmmaking or the film medium rather than primarily as telling stories whose significance is paramount.

Different kinds of criticism reflect different questions asked and different aims. No one interpretive approach can respond to the spectrum of questions or tangle of interests that movie-goers and critics may have. As I understand it, interpretation stands in between the movie text and the viewer's experience. The text and the experience determine an interpretation's value, but in different ways. As I have been arguing, the text supports or justifies the interpretation, from intermediate inferences through subsequent building of meaning, to summary statements of the film's overall themes and views.

On the other hand, the experience of viewers vindicates the creative work of interpretation. Interpretations are vindicated when they help viewers see more in the film—more details, more significance in those details for the overall work, more connections among the parts and aspects of the film, more meaning altogether in the story. Sometimes an interpretation gives viewers a complete perspective for viewing the film more rewardingly. But perhaps more edifying are interpretations that stimulate viewers to think about films more vigorously for themselves, using the remarks of the critic as a guide to create their own interpretations.

On a smaller scale, movie-goers may simply find a view that a critic claims is implied in a movie is indeed in it. Such corroboration is not the same thing as agreeing with the view that is implied. Consider the conclusion of the film *An Officer and a Gentleman* (1982). Dressed in Navy whites, Zack Mayo (Richard Gere) marches into the factory where Paula Pokrifki (Debra Winger) toils and sweeps her up into his arms. Zack carries Paula out of the factory life, and out of the film, amid the cheers of her former coworkers. It seems reasonable to construe this finale as expressing the view that a woman's salvation is to be found in a close relationship with a successful man. Finding that construal plausible, and therefore helpful in appreciating the meaning of the movie, does not commit us to agreeing with it.

The difference between finding interpretive claims borne out by movie fictions and finding them true of our actual world leads me to comment further on the interpretations I make in this book. I have chosen films whose visions of virtue seem to me to be right. Interpreting these movie fictions has amplified my understanding of virtue and vice, as well as the place of various virtues in our social lives. The moral generalizations that I propose, therefore, have a double reference—to the film fiction and to the real world. Taken as referring to the movie fiction, the generalizations purport to enhance movie appreciation. Taken as referring to reality, the general claims are supposed to capture truths about human life.

The correctness or plausibility of the general moral claims taken in one sense is independent of the claims taken in the other. Readers need not agree with me that the claims implied by a movie are true of the real world in order to find them fruitful in their experience of the movie. The reverse could also be the case, that readers find the generalizations true or plausible of the real world but not very satisfying when it comes to interpreting a film. In either event, I hope readers will take up the gauntlet and think of a more accurate understanding of moral life or develop more illuminating interpretations of the movies.

Unlike much very good, instructive criticism, I have chosen to examine only films I find worthwhile. Consequently, readers will find little in the way of evaluative judgments in my commentaries. My capsule evaluation of the films is that they are all very good. They have their flaws, but I hope I will be forgiven for not paying much attention to them. As an acid test of my judgment, I suggest the reader compare the films I discuss with other popular movies in their respective genres. Compare *The African Queen,* for instance, to other romantic adventure films such as *Romancing the Stone* (1984) or the Indiana Jones series of movies.[7] These more recent films are filled with attractive characters, well-paced plots, and settings replete with ambience and invention. But do they explore anything comparable to the transformative power of romantic friendship with the subtlety or depth found in *The African Queen?*

As with all interpretation, the crucial question is whether the interpretations I offer lead viewers to a richer appreciation of the films than they would have had otherwise. In Dewey's terms, the value of criticism lies in furthering the "reeducation of perception of works of art."[8] My movie interpretations are guided by Dewey's conception of the value of criticism, yet another topic worthy of full-scale discussion in its own right. He maintains that criticism fulfills its educational office by directing "the perception of others to a fuller and more ordered appreciation of the objective content of works of art."[9]

Because the emphasis of this book is on moral views I find implied in the films, I have focused on the larger meanings and themes of movie fictions. But good interpretation also leads to an appreciation of detail, in the service of the larger meaning to be sure, but also for its own sake. In constructing an interpretation, critics are occasionally struck by a moment that at first seemed unimportant but that on subsequent viewing appears laden with meaning. Sometimes the first glimmer of significance is the result of nothing more than the fact of the detail catching our eye. Charlie Allnut kicking the boiler aboard the African Queen is one such detail for me. He says, "I kinda like kicking her. She's all I've got." Just because the incident snagged my attention, I lingered over it and wondered how it fit into the bigger picture.

No claims are made here about the possible or likely effects on audiences of the visions of virtue I find portrayed in the films. Exposure to images of virtue alone is not likely to alter people much, although such exposure could inspire us to reexamine our lives. The popularity of the films examined here, however, might indicate the concern of audiences for moral character or their attraction to the struggle between virtue and vice. I now turn to the concept of virtue with which I approach the films.

Virtue Theory

Give me that man/ That is not passion's slave, and I will wear him/ In my heart's core, ay, in my heart of heart.

—Shakespeare, *Hamlet*

Types of Virtue

Thanks to Alasdair MacIntyre's lucid and provocative *After Virtue* and the impetus supplied by several other prominent philosophers, the virtues have returned to center stage as a lively topic among academic philosophers, educators, and people of letters. But interest in the virtues has never really been far from the thoughts of mass audiences whenever they read novels, watched plays, or viewed movies.[10] Narrative arts have always emphasized the character of their characters, whether the protagonist be a Scrooge or a Ulysses, an Othello or a Huck Finn. Audiences, elite and popular, are drawn to questions of virtue and vice perhaps because so much of our welfare depends on our own character and because we prosper and suffer at the hands of other people on account of their moral traits.

Virtues are excellent qualities of individuals that make them valuable to themselves and to other people. They are relatively settled dispositions to act, feel, desire, and think in specifiable patterns. These dispositions can be manifested in indefinitely many ways.[11] Thus, the same behavior can indicate different virtues (or vices), and a particular virtue (or vice) can be expressed in very different, even opposite, behaviors. For example, waiting for someone to give us a gift might exhibit friendship, patience, generosity, or forgiveness. On the other hand, the virtue of kindness can be shown by refraining from commenting on another person's behavior, as well as by offering constructive criticism of someone's behavior.

As excellent traits, virtues naturally make those individuals who possess them more attractive and desirable than people who do not have them. Virtues can be classified according to the different sorts of strengths people have. Intellectual virtues, for example, are responsible for success in problem solving or theorizing, especially in mathematics or science. Moral virtues can also be distinguished from aesthetic virtues, such as nobility and wit, and the meliorating virtues, such as gentleness and unpretentiousness.[12] Meliorating traits make life more pleasant, cooperation more likely, and difficult situations more tolerable. James Wallace finds in the distinctively moral virtues the qualities that enable individuals to flourish.[13] Just as biological abilities, such as a hound's olfactory sense, enable animals to flourish, moral virtues are crucial to human thriving.

Some moral virtues are "executive," enabling the execution of actions, strategies, and projects. Executive virtues are instrumental to our carrying out plans and realizing our ends.[14] Not only do these virtues enable us to perform successfully in general, but they are often critical to moral action. Because doing what we believe is right may be difficult for us, they can also be described as virtues of willpower or self-mastery.[15] Virtues such as determination, patience, and resourcefulness enable us to overcome obstacles to acting on our moral beliefs and values, and so have a distinctive bearing on moral life.

Courage seems to be an especially important and dramatic virtue of execution or willpower. We must be courageous when moral conduct is risky, and courage can be essential to the expression of other virtues. Individuals may need courage to keep their integrity, to be patient, or to maintain their loyalty. In the film *Rob Roy*, Rob most obviously displays courage in risking his life for the sake of his clan and his honor. But he is also courageous in remaining steadfast to his good friend McDonald when all his kinsmen believe the worst of McDonald. In maintaining McDonald's innocence, Rob not only risks the lives of his family and the clan's survival, but he risks looking like a fool.

In contrast to the executive virtues of self-mastery are the substantive virtues that motivate our action. They supply our ends, including particular ethical patterns of behavior, emotion, or judgment.[16] The substantive virtues include compassion, generosity, loyalty, justice, and humility. For example, generosity prompts us to look for occasions to give what we value to others, for their own sake. Loyalty motivates us to believe the best of our friends and to stand by them when they are in trouble. Justice also supplies us with action-guiding ends. When the reconnaissance expedition learns that Burke has tried to kill Ripley and Newt, in the movie *Aliens,* Ripley's sense of justice moves her to urge returning Burke to stand trial rather than be executed on the spot.

Executive and substantive virtues complement one another. Executive virtues are the means by which we perform the actions motivated by the substantive virtues. We do not act out of courage or patience, for instance, but by means of these virtues. But we do act out of loyalty or compassion and not by means of them. Executive virtues without the substantive are morally directionless; substantive virtues without the executive are without efficacy. Although nonmoral virtues, such as wit and friendliness, are interesting, keeping to the moral virtues in the analyses of the films in this book is work enough. When nonmoral virtues are discussed, their relevance to moral virtue is the purpose.

Edmund Pincoffs argues that what makes (substantive) virtues moral is that "they are forms of regard . . . for the interests of others."[17] The substantive virtues mentioned do seem to motivate individuals to pay attention to, and act for, the welfare of other people. Therefore, the egoism exhibited by Phil Connors in *Groundhog Day* is not just one vice among many. Rather, it is a wholesale renunciation of the moral enterprise, which sometimes requires sacrificing one's personal interests for the sake of other people.

Pincoffs appears to be at odds with James Wallace in what he sees as the definitive dimension of moral virtue. Whereas Pincoffs takes regard for other people as individuating the moral virtues, Wallace understands virtue in terms of human flourishing. However, the two views can be seen as different emphases, which dovetail in the social nature of human well-being. Strong social relations are needed for human flourishing, and the virtues promote social life through their regard for the welfare of others. The substantive virtues supply a regard for other people's needs and interests, and the executive virtues increase the likelihood that those needs will be met and their interests satisfied. Speaking of the conventions that inescapably govern social life, Wallace points out the importance of the virtues: "Whatever variations this [conventional] form of life admits of, such things as . . . conscientiousness, benevolence, restraint, and courage tend in their ways to foster it."[18]

The best societies are conspicuous by what the virtues free their members from worrying about concerning other individuals—deception, violence, corruption, indifference, and capricious or stifling governance. The virtues are the necessary attributes for happy common life because we need to be able to rely on others, as well as to count on ourselves, in order to flourish. For Alasdair MacIntyre, the best communities are built on a shared concept of the good. The members of such a community are held together not merely by mutual advantage. Rather, they agree on an ideal of living.[19]

The virtues that members of a healthy community esteem facilitate achieving the ideal way of life, but they are also ingredient to it. For example, the character traits of peacefulness and cooperativeness, which the Amish hold in high regard, not only promote the ideal of living shared by the Amish people, but these virtues are also part of that ideal. We see a community governed by a shared concept of the good in the film *Rob Roy*. The bonds of good character, and mutual awareness of it, sustain the MacGregor clan. In sharp contrast are the social organizations depicted in *Jaws* and *Aliens*, in which people are connected almost exclusively by economic interest rather than by a moral ideal of communal life.

Aristotle's Heritage

Because the virtues, of whichever stripe and in whatever combination, are necessary to social life and individual flourishing in society, every culture has some conception of valuable character traits. However vague their definition or boundaries, some traits are promoted in a society's members, while others are discouraged. It seems plausible that all cultures subscribe to some version of courage, justice, honesty, and wisdom, as it is difficult to imagine how a culture could survive, let alone prosper, without these particular virtues. As Alasdair MacIntyre argues, courage is a virtue because "the care and concern for individuals, communities and causes . . . requires the existence of such a virtue."[20] Care and concern for one's community are necessary for social success. Since threats to a community and its members inevitably arise in the course of events, the willingness of individuals to risk harm to themselves for the greater good seems to be necessary and valuable to all societies.

Cultural differences in how particular virtues are defined or ordered exist, but such variations are compatible with the broad claim that virtues exist in all societies and that particular virtues likely cross cultural borders. Regardless of how truthfulness, justice, or kindness are precisely understood, or what their scope of application includes, versions of these attributes of character seem to be prized universally.

Although I believe the virtues possess some form of cultural universality, the purposes of this book hardly require it. The films examined here are popular Hollywood movies and so are heavily influenced by, if not firmly embedded in, the Western tradition of the virtues. According to MacIntyre, the Western tradition, which includes the Judeo-Christian heritage, is deeply ingrained with appropriation of and response to "Aristotle, whose account of the virtues decisively constitutes the classical tradition as a tradition of moral thought."[21]

Without necessarily subscribing to Aristotle's biology, metaphysics, or view of the ideal political state, we in the West operate within Aristotle's conception of virtue. We do so in part because he writes so extensively and insightfully about virtue itself, as well as about the particular virtues. We are also influenced by Aristotle's understanding because of the widespread impact of classical thinking on Western culture and because of the Aristotelian philosophy passed down by Aquinas.

According to Aristotle, virtues are necessary for personal and social goods, but they are not merely a means for attaining them. The virtues help constitute these valuable aspects of life. For example, both social cooperation within a community and trust in friendship demand truthfulness. But truthfulness is not simply a means to cooperation or trust; rather, it is constitutive of communal harmony and the bonds of friendship. Similarly, within friendship, openness is not just an instrument for the attainment of intimacy. Self-disclosure is part of the fabric of intimacy.

Thus, although it is true to say that virtues enable people to live well, we cannot think of a good life as specifiable independent of the virtues. Acting on the virtues is what we mean by a good life. We describe the action itself as acting virtuously. The entwinement of virtue, activity, and well-being can be seen within the narrower confines of specific activities. The virtues are necessary for technical success, such as Phil Connors's piano playing and ice sculpting in *Groundhog Day*. However, "the enjoyment of the activity and the enjoyment of the achievement are not the ends at which the agent aims, but the enjoyment supervenes upon the successful activity in such a way that the activity achieved and the activity enjoyed are one and the same state."[22]

Virtues are qualities that promote attainment of those goods that are internal to activities. When values are internal to an activity, we delight in the activity itself, and the goods of which we partake cannot be described, understood, or experienced apart from the activity. The goods internal to playing a team sport are found in the playing—the exertion of muscle, the competition, the way different individuals jell as a team, and the freedom (and need) to improvise. On the other hand, goods external to such an activity might be praise, fame, status, or payment, valued and achievable apart from the playing of the sport.

MacIntyre goes into detail in explaining the structure of a practice, how values are internal to it, and why the virtues are necessary to participating in the practice so as to realize those internal values. We need only note here the integral role of the virtues in engaging in the panoply of practices that make up the domains and disciplines of life: technical and theoretical work, family and community, arts and games, hobbies and avocations. Virtues enable us to locate ourselves in the reigning traditions and to subject ourselves to the standards that govern the relevant practices. As a result of such virtues as honesty and justice, we are able to communicate with people who are similarly engaged as well as gauge our relative progress. By means of traits such as diligence, discipline, and even courage, we can develop the capacities and skills germane to the practices.

What MacIntyre seems to overlook is that virtues are also needed when we perform activities simply for their instrumental benefits. When we treat a social or technical practice merely as a means to an end, we must nevertheless exhibit certain excellences of character. Should we play baseball for money, perform surgery for glory, or work with a political party in order to be elected, success is likely to require tenacity, self-confidence, moderation, or resourcefulness. Most of these virtues are executive. To realize the values internal to a practice, however, substantive virtues seem additionally required. Put simply, then, a web of virtues is needed to derive the values that are both external and internal to practices. The virtues are essential to living well, in all its aspects.

Even though the virtues promote practical success, we should act virtuously irrespective of anticipating it in specific situations. In discussing *Groundhog Day*, I argue that the goods internal to a practice can be had only when ignored, or looked past, for the sake of engaging in the activity itself. The irony for Phil Connors is that he receives the adulation of the townspeople of Punxsutawney, for both his good deeds and his piano playing, only when he undertakes the ethical and musical endeavors for their own sakes.

Internal to exercising the virtues is a vital value. Whether we are engaged in technical or ethical pursuits, we find value in the virtuous activity itself. This is because the virtues are the forms by which people realize their human potential. Inherent in developing our distinctively human potential is the most fundamental of internal goods. The good is vital because it defines a life truly and fully human. In Aristotelian terms, we are most alive when realizing our human natures, and this is one and the same thing as acting virtuously. Success in achieving moral and technical ends also flows naturally from putting the virtues into practice. Consequently, Aristotle finds the virtues central in a human life that, taken as a whole, can be called good. Our lives are deficient and therefore incomplete insofar as they are lacking the virtues—in number and degree.

The virtues themselves, moreover, are incomplete without judgment. Judgment is essential because concrete circumstances enter into the requirements and constituents of virtuous (and vicious) conduct. The same action that would be courageous in one situation may be rash in another. Whereas compassion in one circumstance may commend leaving someone alone, in another context providing consolation or diversion may be the compassionate thing to do.

People with practical wisdom, phronesis, exercise good judgment in particular situations. In the midst of people's diverse interests and purposes, mingled and merged, individuals with practical wisdom are able to estimate how much to do and when to do it. Moral matters necessarily are concerned with "more or less," hence, Aristotle's claim that the virtue lies in the mean between the extremes of more and less—the vices. Knowledge about ethics, including the virtues, consists in imprecise generalizations, which cannot cover all contingencies. Moral knowledge therefore has a large empirical component, and practical wisdom involves being able to learn from one's own experience, as well as the successes and setbacks of other people.

The Virtue of Narrative

In MacIntyre's view, in order to make sense of human action we have to situate the behavior within a historical understanding of the individual. The meaningful construal of behavior as having this rather than that intention, or as pursuing one goal rather than another, requires a temporally extended account of a subject capable of responsible choice. A relatively unified conception of self is needed to find human conduct intelligible, and such unity is supplied by a narrative account of the life of an individual. To make sense of action by reference to the purposes of an agent with enduring character traits, we require "a concept of a self whose unity resides in the unity of a narrative which links birth to life to death as narrative beginning to middle to end."[23] Obviously, I cannot do justice here to questions of personhood or the intelligibility of human behavior, but I hope that sketching MacIntyre's response to them points to a potential value of movies.

The argument made by MacIntyre is that if we wish our descriptions of human conduct to be more than a list of disconnected, discontinuous behaviors, we must provide some form of biographical account. Since the concept of personhood, or responsible agency, demands a narrative of a human life, ascribing virtue and vice to individuals also presupposes constructing the appropriate stories for them. Discussions of moral character make sense only if we conceive of people as having histories.

Because of the presuppositions of intelligibility, MacIntyre claims that "narrative history of a certain kind turns out to be the basic and essential genre for the characterisation of human actions."[24] If MacIntyre's approach is roughly correct, either by itself or as an integral component of a larger theory, then looking to stories such as movie fictions is most appropriate in the exploration of the virtues. The narrative arts are not merely ancillary to understanding human nature and the many ways it can go right or wrong. Rather, stories uniquely capture formal aspects of the lives of individuals, real and imagined, needed for us to make sense of them.

Martha Nussbaum further specifies a MacIntyrean position by stressing the importance of narratives to the moral imagination and the virtues that especially depend upon it. The forgiveness or mercy we show wrongdoers, for example, depends on inquiry into and appreciation for the details of their individual histories. Nussbaum notes how the merciful attitude "entails regarding each particular case as a complex narrative of human effort in a world full of obstacles."[25]

As with entering into the lives of fictional characters, the merciful attitude toward actual people requires putting ourselves in their place, with their histories of misfortunes and mistakes. A supple, energetic imagination vivifies for us a wrongdoer's social milieu, distorted experience, and destructive options. Nussbaum's description of how imagination and feeling are wed by the structure of the novel applies to the form of film as well: "It is a form of imaginative and emotional receptivity," in which the life of another penetrates "into one's own imagination and heart."[26] Because the trajectory of narrative underlies the appreciation of the lives of both fictional characters and actual people, our experience of movie fictions can inform our understanding of real individuals—in general outline or in particular situations.

In providing detailed, complex pseudo-biographies, movies augment more abstract philosophical analysis. Film fictions are like case studies in law, filled with the subtlety and messiness that naturally elicit attention to those loose ends of life so easily lost on the clean edges of academic theory. As mentioned above, practical judgment deals with particular situations, and when it is effective, judgment alights on what is morally important in the particular. The concrete particular "must be seized in a confrontation with the situation itself."[27] Movies present simulacra or representations of actual and possible particular situations and can thereby clarify what exactly practical judgment is supposed to grasp.

In contrast to the particularity of narrative, philosophers must generalize, even when championing the irreducible significance of particularity in moral judgment. Thus, Martha Nussbaum generalizes about the limits of generalization. She points out that practical wisdom is the capacity to deal with novelty and contextual variety with a "responsiveness and yielding flexibility . . . that could not be adequately captured in any general description."[28] The film *Fresh*, however, is able to depict concretely how extrapolating from one particular situation to another takes a nimble imagination, abetted by insight into the vagaries of human desire and fear. The cinematic rendering not only illustrates Nussbaum's necessarily general observation but also elaborates on it.

The films I examine extend and modify the Aristotelian moral tradition—in general and in its particulars. We in the West take our bearings
from this tradition in part because we have been shaped by it, yet our lives
interrogate and redefine its perspective. Our culture and the Aristotelian
heritage that it reflects are as narratively figured as the lives of actual individuals or the characters in movie fictions. Changes in family and social
conditions, for example, narratively reshape the development and exercise
of virtuous character.

The conception of virtue with which I work, therefore, should be understood as situated within "a tradition which always sets itself in a relationship of dialogue with Aristotle, rather than in any relationship of simple assent."[29] This book is an effort to participate in that dialogue by
reinterpreting the Aristotelian perspective in light of popular American
movies, which confront it with a contemporary sensibility. The wisdom
and resiliency of the Aristotelian view of virtue are confirmed in its practical relevance to modern life.

Notes

1. John Dewey, *Art as Experience* (New York: Minton, Balch, 1934), p.313.

2. Ibid., p.308.

3. Peter Jones, *Philosophy and the Novel* (Oxford: Oxford University Press,
1975), p.191.

4. Dewey, *Art as Experience*, p.313.

5. Ibid., p.314.

6. A locus classicus of trenchant criticism of intentionalism is the essay by W.
K. Wimsatt and Monroe Beardsley, "The Intentional Fallacy," *Sewanee Review*
54 (1946): 468–488.

7. This series, starring Harrison Ford in the title role, begins with *Raiders of the
Lost Ark* (1981), continues with *Indiana Jones and the Temple of Doom* (1984), and
concludes with *Indiana Jones and the Last Crusade* (1989). *Jewel of the Nile* (1985),
the sequel to *Romancing the Stone,* again pairs Michael Douglas with Kathleen
Turner, providing a romantic continuity missing from the Indiana Jones series.

8. Dewey, *Art as Experience*, p.324.

9. Ibid.

10. Hence the recent success of William Bennett's anthology *The Book of
Virtues,* as well as the children's cartoon show based on it.

11. For strong reasons to think of virtues and vices as dispositions rather than
as habits, see Edmund Pincoffs' *Quandaries and Virtues* (Lawrence: University
Press of Kansas, 1986), pp.79–80.

12. Ibid., p.85.

13. James Wallace, *Virtues and Vices* (Ithaca: Cornell University Press, 1978), p.19.

14. See David Pears, "Aristotle's Analysis of Courage," *Midwest Studies in Philosophy* 3 (1980): 274–285.

15. See Andreas Eshete, "Character, Virtue, and Freedom," *Philosophy* 57 (October 1982): 495–513; and Robert C. Roberts, "Will Power and the Virtues," *Philosophical Review* 93 (April 1984): 224–247.

16. Roberts, "Will Power and the Virtues," p.228.

17. Pincoffs, *Quandaries and Virtues*, p.89.

18. Wallace, *Virtues and Vices*, p.36.

19. Alasdair MacIntyre, *After Virtue* (Notre Dame, Ind.: Univ. of Notre Dame Press, 1981), pp.146–147.

20. Ibid., p.179.

21. Ibid., p.138.

22. Ibid., p.184.

23. Ibid., p.191.

24. Ibid., p.194.

25. Martha Nussbaum, "Equity and Mercy," *Philosophy and Public Affairs* 22 (Spring 1993): 83–125, 103.

26. Ibid., p.108.

27. Martha Nussbaum, *The Fragility of Goodness* (Cambridge: Cambridge University Press, 1986), p.301.

28. Ibid., p.304.

29. MacIntyre, *After Virtue*, p.154.

2
Virtue and Happiness in Groundhog Day

How, if some day or night a demon were to sneak after you into your loneliest loneliness and say to you, "This life as you now live it and have lived it, you will have to live once more and innumerable times more; and there will be nothing new in it, but every pain and every joy and every thought and sigh and everything immeasurably small or great in your life must return to you. . . ." If this thought were to gain possession of you, it would change you, as you are, or perhaps crush you. . . . How well disposed would you have to become to yourself and to life to crave nothing more fervently than this ultimate eternal confirmation and seal?

—Friedrich Nietzsche, *The Gay Science,* Aphorism 341

Virtuous Living Versus Egoistic Hedonism

In the passage quoted above, Nietzsche's thought experiment entertains the idea of the eternal return of our way of life to prompt us to reflect on whether we are living the good life.[1] The question of the good life recurs throughout history, receiving a variety of responses. The ancient Greek philosophers Plato and Aristotle argued that living virtuously is the good life. Although virtuous action cannot guarantee well-being or happiness (eudaimonia), acting virtuously is central to it and is the only thing within our power to secure our happiness. Both philosophers take great pains to distinguish goodness from pleasure, partly because they see the life of self-centered pleasure seeking (egoistic hedonism) as the perennial rival to the

Groundhog Day: The new
and improved Phil nour-
ishes the aged derelict.

moral life they champion. Harold Ramis's film *Groundhog Day* (1993) interprets and adapts the philosophy that living virtuously is the good life.
The film dramatizes its philosophical adaptation, moreover, by means of a
humorous version of Nietzsche's idea of the eternal return.

We live most happily when we do things that develop our distinctively
human abilities. These abilities are our natural potential, which virtuous
activities enable us to realize or perfect. Exercised and developed in these
activities, the virtues are themselves human excellences and also make
possible the perfecting of our natural gifts. Plato proposed that the virtue
of justice, for example, is psychic order—reason, emotion, and appetite
working in harmony. Not only is such an ordered soul itself the realization
of our potential, but it facilitates the overall flourishing of the individual.
We enjoy engaging in activities that bring our natural endowments to
fruition and choose to perform them for their own sake. Aristotle considered the life of virtue happiest because virtuous activities are intrinsically
good.[2]

Virtuous activities also include intellectual pursuits, as the intellect has
virtues of its own. Intellectual virtues are cultivated in the abstract reasoning demonstrated in mathematical proofs, scientific theories, and philosophical reflections. We also need the intellectual virtue that is concerned
with moral action—practical wisdom. It enables us to see what virtuous
response is called for by a particular situation and how to make the response effectively. In *Groundhog Day*, for example, Phil Connors routinely
sees how to help people without embarrassing them or making them feel
indebted to him.

Groundhog Day suggests that aesthetic potential is another aspect of our nature, the realization of which contributes to happiness. The film includes among the activities we intrinsically value those that deepen our capacities for artistic appreciation, as well as those that develop talents for creating art. We realize our human nature not only in playing the piano but also in discerning the nuances of poetry or painting. Although the intellectual and aesthetic are nonmoral dimensions of human nature, the moral virtues of discipline, resourcefulness, and tenacity are needed for their cultivation. The natural results of the various intrinsically enjoyable activities are also good—such as health, knowledge, artistic beauty, and justice. We find these diverse activities worthwhile in themselves because all of them develop our inherent abilities, and the beneficial results of the activities reinforce this development.

The goodness of life, then, is found in activity: in the moral doing, the artistic making, the rational thinking. Pleasure is not the reason for engaging in the activities, but we naturally take pleasure in them. The pleasures of the activities are woven into them and are generated by the demands they make on us. As Alasdair MacIntyre points out, we cannot even specify the particular pleasure apart from the relevant activity.[3] It is not as if all the pleasures in the world are floating freely and just happen to be experienced by participating in this enterprise rather than by doing something else. Because these activities are intrinsically worthwhile, moreover, they are self-sustaining; we do not have to look beyond them for pleasure. As Aristotle observes, "Actions which conform to virtue are naturally pleasant. . . . The life of such men has no further need of pleasure as an added attraction, but it contains pleasure within itself."[4]

Groundhog Day tries to show why a life of egoistic hedonism is necessarily self-defeating and filled with ironies. Egoistic hedonists look at actions merely as the means to pleasure, their own pleasure in particular. The goal in life is to maximize pleasure—itself a passive state, not an activity. As a consequence, hedonists miss out on the enjoyment of activities that are done for their own sake. They are thereby also deprived of the delight found in realizing their moral, intellectual, and artistic potential in those activities. The irony is that a life of hedonism is actually much less pleasant than a virtuous one.

In the Platonic dialogue *Gorgias,* Callicles says that the point of life is to have great desires and then to be able to satisfy them.[5] Indeed, power is the ability to dominate other people so as to better gratify one's appetites. Socrates' rejoinder is that a life of egoistic hedonism is like filling a leaky vessel. No sooner are an individual's desires satisfied than they require replenishment.[6] Selfish pleasure seekers cannot make progress because their current appetites increase in strength and new appetites indefinitely multiply. The hedonists' flurry of activity to quench their desires in effect leaves them standing still, or worse off, because they are always left wanting more.

To make matters even worse for hedonists, there is no way for them to figure out which new desires could crop up or what is likely to please them in the future. By its nature, pleasure is contingent and variable.[7] What pleases different people, or one person at different times, cannot in principle be known, which makes long-term planning for pleasure a practical impossibility. Instead of defining pleasure as the good, the correct approach is to seek what is good, for it is necessarily pleasant.

In order to seek what is good, we must think about it. The Socrates of Plato's dialogues is famous for saying that the unexamined life is not worth living.[8] Unless we rationally reflect on how we live, we cannot disabuse ourselves of false beliefs that undermine our happiness, such as mistaken opinions about pleasure and power. Examining ourselves enables us to recognize the general lineaments of human nature and, with that, the human good. In *Groundhog Day*, self-knowledge includes knowing ourselves, and what is good for us, in our individuality. When Phil Connors is thoughtful of others and acts for their welfare, he exemplifies the universally valuable virtue of kindness. However, when Phil perfects his talent for playing the piano and his receptivity to poetry, he is achieving a good born of his individuality.

We cannot carry out our self-investigation with equanimity unless we have rational control over our appetites and emotions.[9] Otherwise, we will be so influenced by them that we are likely to make mistakes about what is really in our interest. Once we understand how realizing our human potential in worthwhile activities is good for us, self-control will then enable us to perform those activities well. Desire and emotion should yield gradually to the promptings of reason until they habitually complement it in the choice and performance of the right things to do. For example, kindness involves the confluence of the desire to help other individuals, an emotional sensitivity to notice and respond to their needs, and the cognitive ability to see how best to meet those needs.

As self-absorbed as hedonists are, they do not really know themselves and so cannot know what is actually good for them. The quest for pleasure funnels the individuals' attention outward, toward opportunities for gratification, distracting hedonists from themselves. Because they are ruled by their appetites, self-indulgent people are never freed from the immediate attractions of pleasure long enough to think about whether they are truly happy with the life they lead or with the pleasures they happen to be seeking at the time.

Hedonists cannot even do the best for themselves in striving after what they mistakenly think is ultimately in their interest—pleasure. They lack the self-control provided by reason to pause in their reaching for pleasure and ponder what might give them the most pleasure—overall or in the long run. Under the sway of their strongest desires of the moment, hedonists are incapable of properly assessing which cravings to appease and which to leave unsatisfied. Apart from being plagued by their inability to evaluate actual or potential desires, hedonists cannot answer the multitude of urges that are liable to move them at any particular time. Acting on the most urgent impulses of the moment, they are blown about by competing feelings and conflicting appetites, unable to act consistently so as to maximize their pleasure.

All the pleasures hedonists would ever need to be happy are to be found in performing worthwhile activities. In artistic, intellectual, and moral pursuits, hedonists would enjoy developing their natural potential. Instead, the repetitive hunt for greater and newer pleasures leaves their abilities and sensitivities largely uncultivated. The performance of intrinsically valuable actions depends mostly on the abilities of the people doing them; therefore, the foundation of genuine happiness lies in the individuals themselves.

Our characters and minds are most permanent because they are most independent of life's vicissitudes. Aristotle notes that "no function of man possesses as much stability as do activities in conformity with virtue."[10] Without these inner resources of character and intellect, hedonists are at the mercy of external conditions to provide them with either more of what they already want or the means to satisfy new appetites. The desirability of hedonism is revealed as illusory once individuals are deprived of novelty of situation or circumstance. The sweetest things in their novelty must become tedious when indefinitely repeated.

Of course, the good life is not lived alone; it also includes friends. According to Aristotle, friendships based on utility and pleasure are inferior types of friendship. The only genuine friends are those who love each other's virtuous character.[11] True friends take pleasure in doing virtuous things for and with each other, and they value one another for their own sakes. Because moral character is long-lasting, these friendships are the most enduring and also the most beneficial.[12]

However, what is loved seems to be the other person's virtuous character and not the individual proper. The person merely instantiates the universal complement of virtues, which correspond to the essential features of human nature and well-being. *Groundhog Day* takes the object of virtuous friendship to be the unique individual. Embedding the virtues of the friends in their particular personalities, the film presents an image of virtuous friendship blended into romantic love. *Groundhog Day* does not explore this interesting hybrid, what we might consider romantic friendship, but in illustrating a concept of romantic love enriched by virtue, the film is suggestive about an important component of the good life.

As should be expected, egoistic hedonists are incapable of genuine friendship and are therefore deprived of its enduring benefits and joys. At best, they can form useful friendships because they view other people simply as providing the means to their own pleasures. Friendships of utility are not based on who the individuals are but on what the parties can do for one another at a particular time; therefore, these friendships are shallow and tend to be transient.[13]

The lesson taught by Plato, Aristotle, and *Groundhog Day* is that egoistic hedonism must fail because individuals cannot successfully pursue their happiness directly. Happiness comes about only as the indirect result of realizing our human potential in activity that is intrinsically valuable—primarily, virtuous activity. The implication is that happiness is achieved only when we forget about ourselves. Having examined our lives and thought through the importance of virtue and self-development to the good life, we must put aside concern for ourselves. Following Ecclesiastes, we might say there is a time for self-scrutiny and a time to stop thinking about ourselves.

No philosophical argument can demonstrate once and for all that a virtuous life is better than its hedonistic counterpart. For this reason, Plato and Aristotle offer narrative support for their view with fables, myths, and stories of famous people. In *The Republic*, Plato cites the tale of Gyges whose magic ring makes him invisible. The invisible Gyges is able to please himself at the expense of others, with apparent impunity.[14]

Groundhog Day constructs its fable around the Nietzschean conceit of the eternal return. It is similar to the story of Gyges, however, in that Phil Connors alone remembers what has transpired from one recurring day to the next. Phil is rendered figuratively invisible in that other people cannot "see" what he has done the day before. Phil is able to satisfy his desires without seeming to pay the price, just as Gyges appears to escape retribution. However, even as Phil and Gyges cannot be seen by other people, so do they not see the harm they inflict on their moral character by their self-indulgent way of life. We turn now to the film to see how it illustrates and develops the view that the good life is a virtuous one.

All the Pleasures of Punxsutawney

Groundhog Day extends Nietzsche's idea of imagining our actual lives as recurring eternally by giving Phil Connors (Bill Murray) the chance to re-live any way of life he can imagine over and over. Of any pattern of living he thinks is ideal, Phil will have to ask whether he would choose it if he had to live it always. The result of imaginatively enlarging Nietzsche's question is also to put our own actual lives in perspective, just as Nietzsche originally intended. Envisioning our actual or idealized pattern of living as recurring forever can liberate us from the cramped, selfish habits into which we have fallen willy-nilly, with neither thought nor care. Imagining ourselves locked into a particular way of life can vivify for us, as perhaps nothing else can, the meaningfulness or meaninglessness of that life.

The theme of repetition is figured from the beginning of the story when television weatherman Phil Connors and his crew return to Punxsutawney, Pennsylvania, to film the town's annual celebration of Groundhog Day. Just as the town reenacts the festivities that commemorate the anticipation of seasonal change, Phil must repeat his coverage of the event for the fourth consecutive year. He yearns for a big-time network job and hates the small-town hoopla of the celebration. Phil is unaware of how small his own life and outlook are. Phil will learn just how much his life can expand and he can grow by having to relive the same Groundhog Day until he sees the light and begins living virtuously.

Before that happens, however, the film has great sport with Phil's egoistic hedonism. Once Phil realizes that he is the only person who knows the same day is repeating and has memory of all of them, he goes to work grabbing for all the pleasurable experiences he can cram into the ever-present Groundhog Day. *Groundhog Day* telescopes what we surmise is an extended period of Phil's life into a series of hilarious vignettes in which he eats what he wants, steals money, watches movies, plays with people like a puppeteer, and seduces women. All but Rita (Andie MacDowell), who is impervious to Phil's wily ways.

Eventually, Phil tires of his life of pleasure and, bored beyond endurance, tries to kill himself. In rapid, giddy succession, we watch as Phil tries every way at his disposal to dispose of himself—all to no avail. With the dawn, a new Groundhog Day awaits Phil, in which he despairs once again at his meaningless existence. Only when Phil shows concern for other people and starts developing his own talents does he begin to enjoy life. Only when he stops looking at Rita as a sexual conquest does he come to appreciate her as a potential lifetime companion. Virtuous living and genuine regard for other people and himself free Phil from his despair and, as providence would have it, from the eternal return of Groundhog Day.

The film's introductory camera shot of a blue sky filled with billowing clouds segués to Phil, gesturing and talking in front of an empty blue backdrop. Meaning accrues to his behavior only when a weather map is electronically superimposed on the studio image of Phil and the backdrop.[15] The television monitor registers Phil's huffing and puffing as causing the image of a storm front to move from west to east. The show's new producer, Rita, is delighted by the technological trompe l'oeil, as well as by the accompanying glib patter Phil provides. We soon see a darker side to the humor of the televised illusion, and Phil's performance within it. Phil's cocky on-screen style reflects his inflated self-image. Phil is sarcastic and supercilious, thinking he is too good for everyone, including Rita and the cameraman, Larry (Chris Elliott). Using Phil's condescending humor to express his lack of self-understanding and perspective, *Groundhog Day* makes Phil the unintentional butt of his own smart-alecky remarks.

The comedic narrative effect to which the plot puts Phil's delusions of grandeur turns on his smug prediction that the approaching snowstorm will veer off and miss the Pittsburgh area. In Punxsutawney the next morning, before Phil leaves to cover the Groundhog Day celebration, he reprises his weather forecast spiel and pantomime for the proprietor of the bed and breakfast. The film thereby harkens back to the earlier studio shot, just as Phil will have to turn back to Punxsutawney.

As Phil, Rita, and Larry head down the highway toward Pittsburgh, they are greeted by the onset of the blizzard Phil promised would not hit the vicinity. Phil exclaims, "What is going on?" Of course, this foreshadows Phil's (and our) reaction to the repetition of Groundhog Day. But the phrase is also emblematic of what Phil does not ask of his everyday life. He does not ask Nietzsche's crucial question or any approximation to it in self-questioning. Phil exclaims, "This is impossible," and then, "No, no," as if an error on his part is inconceivable. The accompanying music of light-hearted, mischievous flutes and fairy-like swirling strings suggests playful otherworldly forces at work. Just as the tornado in *The Wizard of Oz* marks the beginning of Dorothy's lesson in life, the Pennsylvania blizzard is the beginning of Phil's fabulous journey of self-discovery.[16]

The very snowstorm that Phil had predicted would not affect him inaugurates his moral quest. The laugh is again on Phil as he protests the possibility of the storm to a policeman. Shivering with cold, he says, "I make the weather," and amidst the gusting snow, he again ridiculously repeats his erroneous television forecast. Phil is compelled to reiterate his whole performance, just as he mindlessly must try to satisfy his selfish desires and just as he will have to recapitulate each Groundhog Day. Upon their return to Punxsutawney, Phil tells Rita and Larry he will go back to his room and take a hot shower. He is treated to a cold blast of water from the shower head instead, but he still has not awakened to his true predicament. *Groundhog Day* seems to say that we set ourselves up to look foolish when we cannot see ourselves in the right perspective.

The film depicts several changes in Phil's response to reliving Groundhog Day. He moves from fear and confusion at repeating the same day, to delight at the opportunity to indulge himself, and then to despair over his deadening life of hedonism. Only when Phil is committed to improving himself and the lives of other people can he affirm a way of life he chooses. Overshadowed by Phil's glaring error in weather prognostication is his long-standing, mistaken forecast about what would bring him lasting happiness. He had thought that a life of pleasure, generated by money and fame in television, would satisfy him, and he disparaged Rita, saying that she was "not [his] kind of fun." By story's end, Phil will have changed his mind about the nature of the good life and Rita's role in it.

On what should be the day after Groundhog Day, Phil awakens to the same rock song that awakened him on Groundhog Day, "I Got You Babe," and the same disc jockey chatter. He is unnerved by the duplication, fearing for his sanity. When he arrives at the site of the Groundhog Day ceremony, he asks Rita to slap his face, as if to bring him to his senses or wake him from a nightmare. In Rita's hands, the slap will become a comic trope. We will watch her slapping Phil over and over as she figures out, again and again, that his behavior is not that of genuine friendship but only calculated to seduce her.

The repeated, unrequested slapping will bring Phil to his senses part of the way—he will realize that he cannot succeed in fooling Rita. But it will not fully awaken him to his deepest moral failure. The film intimates that we cannot be brought fully to our senses by something someone else does to or for us, such as a literal or figurative slap in the face. Understanding the right way to live necessarily requires a self-revelation, as we are struck by what is wrong with how we live.

The endless repetition of Groundhog Day dictates that no one can initiate new behavior because no one can remember what has happened on the previous, identical day—except Phil. For everyone but him, each Groundhog Day is experienced anew. Once he realizes the fantastic conceit on which his subsequent life rests and that he alone remembers what has occurred during the previously repeated Groundhog Days, Phil adapts to his situation with aplomb. Recalling what has transpired and acting without physically suffering the consequences the next day, Phil benefits at the expense of other people.

Day after repeated day, Phil ferrets out and stores information about his unsuspecting victims. Chronicling the lives of attractive women, for example, he uses the information to romance them. Attuned to the inattentiveness of the drivers of the armored car, he steals money in their keeping. The behavior is a logical extension of Phil's selfish pleasure seeking.

Phil's self-indulgence is filled with humor. For example, he highlights his freedom from physical worries by saying, "I don't even floss." He also exclaims, "I'm not gonna live by their rules anymore," after driving down railroad tracks toward an oncoming train. But even these moments of levity have serious reverberations. Not flossing can be viewed as a miniature, physical representation of Phil not taking care of his spiritual self. He ignores the possible decay of his character, which is not precluded by the repetition of Groundhog Day. And flouting the rules of the road indicates that Phil conceives of rules only as constraints on doing what he wishes. He misses the way rules can be positively action-guiding, for example, in making art or behaving morally.

The film also weaves moments that will prove portentous into Phil's more comic antics and comments. For example, Phil is told by a man in the diner to "look out for [his] shadow," again taking Phil's physical representation as an image of his inner nature. Punxsutawney Phil, the groundhog, is another weatherman who is called upon to see his shadow to discover whether winter will be prolonged. The film offers Phil Connors seeing his own shadow as a metaphor for his noticing whether the winter of his discontented life will continue, and perhaps figuring out why his life is lacking in warmth.

The image of Phil behind jail bars is a further serio-comedic touch. Although played by Phil for laughs, since he knows he will be sprung by morning when he will wake up in bed, the image does indicate the way Phil is trapped. His most significant entrapment is not within the recurrence of Groundhog Day; indeed, that is the avenue of liberation from the stultifying normal life he led prior to Groundhog Day. Rather, he is trapped by the narcissistic pleasures that keep him from examining himself.[17]

Even in its playful references to other films and actors, *Groundhog Day* takes sensitive stock of Phil's moral nature. Standing with his latest girlfriend in front of a movie theater showing "Heidi II," Phil is dressed as the character played repeatedly by Clint Eastwood in the famous "Spaghetti Westerns" directed by Sergio Leone—such as *A Fistful of Dollars*. As Phil imitates Eastwood's speech and wields a facsimile of his familiar little stogie, we hear the signature Spanish guitar and whistle from Leone's western movies. The irony of Phil seeing a Heidi film "over a hundred times" is that the Heidi story is about love, family, and friendship, whereas the Eastwood character Phil impersonates is a rugged loner.

Despite the comic incongruity between Heidi and Eastwood's solitary gunslinger, *Groundhog Day* aligns its Heidi movie with the much-sequeled westerns by inserting the "II" after the Heidi title. Just as Eastwood repeated his role as the no-name drifter in several Leone films, Phil repeats his self-scripted role of seducer and play-actor. Moreover, Phil's behavior is portrayed as an imitation, or shadow, of an actor playing a movie character. He even asks his girlfriend of the moment to call him Bronco.[18] Phil is so lost in layers of disguise from himself that the thought of self-reflection cannot even cross his mind. The character Eastwood plays is a friendless stranger who always leaves town at the movie fiction's conclusion. Phil is also without friends, and he is a stranger to himself who would like nothing more than to leave Punxsutawney.

Futile Pursuit

The only real challenge for Phil is Rita, the producer of Phil's weather program. She represents all that Phil is not: gentle, unassuming, caring, and considerate of the needs of other people. Whereas Phil is sarcastic and wisecracking, Rita is genuine, open, and sincere. She relishes life's ordinary joys and ordinary people, including Punxsutawney's corny celebration of Groundhog Day. Even though Phil has months of repeated Groundhog Days to perfect his seductive ploys, he gets nowhere with Rita.

Rita seems impervious to Phil's charming chicanery. No matter how much he emulates her tastes in literature, social causes, or family life, he cannot get to her. The suggestion is that Rita's moral character unwittingly protects her from Phil's veneer of goodness. It is as if she sees through his charade, her virtue providing a touchstone for its likeness in others. Rita illustrates Aristotle's observation that virtuous individuals find their greatest pleasure in the good character of other people. She cannot be fooled because her true metal responds only to the sterling character of other individuals and not its imitation.

Groundhog Day conveys the futility of Phil's conniving with cinematic repetitions. Phil repeatedly meets Rita at the hotel bar, reviewing her taste in drinks and toasts until he has them down pat. In swift succession, we see the recurring scenes of Phil talking about and reciting nineteenth-century French poetry with Rita and playing in the snow with her. And, of course, we also see the rapid-fire sequence of goodnight slaps Rita administers to Phil's face.

During a pivotal conversation about what she wants from life, Rita tells Phil that her perfect guy would be too humble to know he's perfect. As Rita then ticks off her ideal man's traits—intelligent, supportive, funny, romantic, courageous—Phil punctuates the naming of each virtue with "me," "me," "me." Phil's self-referential counterpoint is funny, but again the larger joke is on him. Not only is he deficient in these moral traits, but humility, supportiveness, and courage require forgetting or subordinating the "me" with which Phil is completely occupied. The variety of virtues cited by Rita contrasts cleanly with the simple unity of Phil's hedonistic outlook.

Rita says that her beloved will have a great body but will not have to look in the mirror. The reference to looking at oneself in a mirror, which reflects light, subtly revisits the theme of seeing one's shadow, an inky projection of one's self that nevertheless is created by light. Not looking in mirrors indicates the self-forgetfulness characteristic of such virtues as humility. However, the mindful counterparts of self-forgetfulness—self-examination and self-knowledge—are also virtues. We hear hints of them in the recurring snow scenes.

As Rita and Phil lie quietly in the snow, panting and laughing from their exertions, the romantic mood is underscored, and commented on by the lyrics of the song "You Don't Know Me" on the soundtrack. Rita does not (yet) know what Phil is up to, but Phil also does not (yet) know himself or the value for him of the Nietzschean recurrence. The song includes the phrase "You give your hand to me," which echoes the lyric "So put your little hand in mine," from the morning wake-up song "I Got You Babe." Rita will not give her hand to Phil, he will not "get" her, until Rita trusts him. She will not trust him until he is genuinely good.

Phil must understand himself well enough to see what is wrong with his self-centered pleasure seeking. Once he sees this, he will be able to forget himself by immersing himself in artistic, intellectual, and virtuous activity. Until he sees, and then ignores himself, the you of "I Got You Babe" refers ironically to Phil himself. He has only himself, and in his present condition that is not nearly enough to make his life meaningful.

The song "You Don't Know Me" also plays during the series of repeated slaps Rita bestows on Phil's face. The irony is that Rita does know Phil in the sense that she sees through him, through his manipulative strategies. She fathoms his true nature without understanding the advantage he has in the recurring scheme of things. As mentioned, the repetition of slaps fails to bring Phil to his senses. The cinematic device of showing them in quick succession makes Phil's failure not only comic but also makes it appear inevitable. Stringing the stinging rejections together in frame after repeated frame creates a sense of fated frustration, which reinforces the self-defeating nature of Phil's self-centeredness. Even when Phil is apparently successful in getting what he wants, such as other women and money, he must fail to make himself truly happy.

The film connects the themes of knowledge and love in the conversation Phil has with Rita about what she wants from life. After their last snow scene, and the playing of "You Don't Know Me," Phil takes Rita back to his apartment. When Phil tells Rita that he loves her, she becomes annoyed and replies, "You don't even know me." Rita tells him that what he feels is not love and demands that Phil stop saying he loves her. Of course, Phil knows Rita better than she can realize, but I interpret the film as raising the question of what knowing someone well enough to love truly involves. The exchange indicates that Phil is mistaken in thinking that such knowledge is equivalent to accumulating information about the person, just as he is mistaken in thinking that happiness is found in accumulating pleasures. We are left to speculate that perhaps knowing another person well enough to love involves working together and sharing the joys and tragedies that mark the stages of life.

Rita persists, saying that she could never love anyone like Phil because he loves only himself. Phil insightfully responds, "That's not true. I don't even like myself." Phil's heedless grabbing for pleasures is not genuine self-love. Self-love involves seeking what is truly good for ourselves, and we cannot do that unless we meet the Platonic challenge to know ourselves. The story implies that if we seek our good based on that self-knowledge, we will work for our moral improvement. Moreover, self-improvement requires extending ourselves on behalf of other people. We cannot simply or directly improve our moral character the way we can simply and directly perfect our golf swing or our facility in French.

Phil will achieve what is genuinely good for himself in the course of becoming more virtuous. He will grow in virtue as the result of performing virtuous actions, and his virtuous actions will aim at the welfare of other people. But to achieve what is good for himself, to love himself, Phil must stop striving for pleasure and examine his life. Phil will duly reflect and pursue his true good only after taking his egoistic hedonism to its limits. Only by grace of the repeated Groundhog Day can Phil exhaust the allure of his hedonism and begin to acquire the self-knowledge necessary for self-love. By linking Phil's doubtful claim to love Rita with his confessed lack of self-love, *Groundhog Day* also suggests that we cannot love another person until we truly love ourselves. Therefore, the self-knowledge that is needed to love ourselves may also be a prerequisite for loving another person.

Having experienced what will be his last slap of the film, Phil walks away from Rita's hotel, past ice sculptures. "You Don't Know Me" is repeated for the last time, played by a somber, solo saxophone. The movie metaphor of coldness is insinuated here with frozen imagery. It signifies not only the freezing of time for Phil but that Phil is frozen as a person. He is frozen inside an uncaring, cold heart, and his capacities for moral, artistic, and intellectual growth are immobilized.

However, the icy image also points positively to the reformed person Phil is to become. When Phil turns over a new leaf, his talent development includes teaching himself to sculpt ice! The film will therefore repeat the ice sculpture symbol, but with inverted meaning, especially as Phil will use the sculpture to express Rita's beauty and his genuine affection for her.

From Despair to Virtue

The morning after Rita's last slap, a close-up of Phil's digital clock shows the numbers flipping to the accompaniment of a loud, ominous, industrial turning sound. We hear and feel the oppressiveness of the daily repetition for Phil before we see him express it. When the disc jockeys repeat the phrase, "It's cold out there, today," we sense just how chilling Phil's existence has become for him. Phil corroborates the diagnosis in his daily television coverage of Groundhog Day, saying: "It's gonna be cold. It's gonna be grey. And it's gonna last you for the rest of your life." His despair is overt. He is ground down, as if by big industrial-strength gears, by the endless repetition of the life he first thought so delicious in its promise of limitless pleasure.

The film humorously repeats itself by again using the technique of repeated, quick takes—this time, to express the pointlessness of Phil's attempts at suicide. It takes several failed attempts, however, for Phil to realize he cannot kill himself: hurtling a truck into a gorge, jumping off a building, or taking a bath with an electric toaster (with the toast still in it!). The film poses the philosophical question, Why has Phil's life of self-indulgence become an intolerable burden? He is bored with seducing women, stealing money, eating to excess, and driving recklessly. The novelty and delight of doing whatever he wishes without negative repercussions wear off. The sameness of the recurring days becomes, in Nietzsche's phrase, crushing.

The larger implication is that an ordinary life of egoistic hedonism would also be homogeneous and stagnant, regardless of how the pleasures were procured. Variations in incidents and diversions might hide the repetition and emptiness of such an existence, but only because we were not living it endlessly. The pleasures of his hedonistic life cease once Phil becomes used to his situation. Actions that are done merely for the pleasure they bring must become tedious when indefinitely repeated. Only when Phil engages in activities for their own sake does he properly experience pleasure—as the natural concomitant of those activities. He enjoys bringing his human nature to fruition in moral conduct and in intellectual or artistic activity.

From one same day to the next, Phil never exerts himself in such ways as develop his human endowment. Artistic talents, intellectual abilities, and social capacities are neither prompted nor promoted by Phil's behavior. The literal predictability of Phil's life is a metaphor for the dullness of an ordinary life spent without the challenges needed for the individual to grow in the distinctively human ways he or she can. Phil's boredom, and subsequent despairing of his existence, are inevitable for someone who is capable of a full human life but is living only for momentary satisfactions.

Phil has no genuine friends, although his relationship with Rita might be described charitably as an incipient friendship of pleasure and virtue.

She is the only one whose company Phil enjoys and whose character stirs a vague sense of decency or admiration in him. Phil's lack of true friends contributes to the torpor of his life. He has no one with whom to share his aspirations and fears, his ideas and talents. His loneliness compounds his despair. A virtuous friendship can help us through bleak periods and point us to the moral activity in which our happiness lies.

As a consequence of his lack of meaningful activity and friendship, Phil finds his life of self-centered pleasures unendurable. His only recourse is to end it—by death or change. When he discovers he cannot kill himself, Phil undertakes virtuous activity as a practical necessity. He is driven to a morally salutary life by the natural human desire to live well.

As a model of a good person, Rita is a catalyst for Phil's change. He sees what he could be and that he would have to be virtuous, as Rita is, in order to be worthy of her friendship. Rita provides Phil with a moral alternative to the tedium of unsatisfying pleasure seeking and an incentive to the moral life. Phil eventually convinces Rita of the recursive loop of Groundhog Days by telling her about everyone in the diner and then predicting exactly what is about to happen. He does not show off his knowledge, as we would expect him to on the basis of his previous, cocky weather forecasting, but instead describes everything in a matter-of-fact way. He is totally honest about the daily repetition, and Rita replies: "Maybe it's not a curse. It depends on how you look at it." Nietzsche's point, exactly.

Back in his room that evening, Phil is relaxed and natural with Rita as he shows her how to pitch cards into a hat. We soon realize that perfecting this routine presages Phil's disciplined pursuits of piano playing and ice sculpting. The desultory pastime will be replaced by serious, but playful, artistic development. The quiet evening ends with Rita falling asleep in Phil's bed after they cuddle tenderly. When Phil wakes up from his honest, unmanipulative night with Rita, he begins to change. He gives the old derelict money, instead of giving him the usual brush off. At the Groundhog Day festival, Phil brings Rita and Larry refreshments, helps with the equipment, and treats them with professional respect.

The piano music Phil hears while reading in the diner continues on the soundtrack as Phil goes to take his first piano lessons. Instead of mocking Phil, as the earlier tunes did, the piano music becomes a motif of his growth. With the melody playing on, Phil takes the derelict to the hospital, calling him "Father," where the old man dies. He will die over and over, whether Phil feeds him extra bowls of soup or applies mouth to mouth resuscitation—urging him, as "Dad" and "Pop," to breathe.

In trying to rescue the aged tramp, and calling him by paternal names, Phil appears to be adopting the old man. The behavior is radically different from Phil's former pretense of wanting to adopt the children with whom he and Rita repeatedly have snowball fights. Failing to save the derelict humbles Phil by teaching him his limitations, even within his privileged knowledge of the recurring Groundhog Days. Some things even he cannot change, and this contrasts with the opportunity the relived Groundhog Day gives Phil to change the morally decaying course his life had been taking. The irreversibility of the old man's sickened condition suggests that Phil was lucky to have caught his life's downward spiral at the moment he did. Later, it might have been too late for Phil to change.

Phil's kindness to the derelict, and avowed kinship with him, situate Phil within a human family and within the intergenerational matrix of life's replenishment. The next morning, instead of his usual, dispirited coverage of Groundhog Day, Phil substitutes an affectionate, poetic speech about the warmth of the Punxsutawney people in the middle of a long winter. Phil extrapolates from the old man's death, transforming it artistically into the winter of every person's existence—"another step in the cycle of life." As Phil speaks about the return of the seasons, the old man's death is a reminder that the existence of each person is nonetheless linear. The irony of winter as the season of Phil's personal rebirth is heightened by the warmth of his wintry encomium to Punxsutawney.

Phil's moving commentary prompts Rita to tell him that he surprises her. Phil's answer, that he surprises himself sometimes, points to important connections between engaging in worthwhile practices, developing ourselves, and self-knowledge. Once we begin developing our intellect, moral sensibility, and appreciation for the arts, we tap abilities and sensitivities in ourselves we did not know we had. We are new to ourselves, as we become known to ourselves. Phil is making a small, quiet joke, not exactly at his own expense, but it plays on his erstwhile lack of self-knowledge.

Phil delivers this line about himself thoughtfully, in welcome departure from his former, typically sarcastic style. We are reminded of the recent scene in which Phil convinces Rita of the recurrence of Groundhog Day. Rita concludes that the recurrence offers the only plausible explanation of Phil's ability to predict what everyone is going to do. Phil concurs with Rita, saying that there is no other way he could know so much because he is "not that smart." The softening of Phil's humor accompanies the stirrings of his self-awareness. Moreover, the movie stops harvesting laughs at Phil's expense, a device through which it perversely showed toward Phil the same superior attitude he had taken toward other people. Instead, *Groundhog Day* smiles with Phil as he uses humor to poke fun at himself or to be considerate of other people.

Phil's behavior illustrates how the nonmoral virtue of humorousness or wit can be incorporated into such moral virtues as considerateness and kindness.[19] When the wife of the mayor (Brian Doyle-Murray) tells a group of people at the evening party how Phil saved the mayor's life by expelling a chunk of beef from the his throat, Phil suggests that next time the mayor not try to swallow the whole cow. Instead of feeling foolish and beholden, the mayor can laugh along with Phil and the other partyers. Phil also uses humor to deflect praise from himself, a way to foster humility without calling other people's attention, or even his own, to it. For example, Phil is thanked by a woman for straightening out her husband's back and told that the husband can now help her around the house. Phil replies to the husband, "Sorry to hear that, Felix," as if Phil had done the husband more harm than good!

The film even changes the import of its humorously repeated, comic signature of quick-paced repetitions. Recall the succession of slaps from Rita, information gatherings by Phil, and suicide attempts by him. The compressed repetition in those cases conveyed Phil's futility. The new Phil is presented performing a batch of good deeds in short order: catching a boy falling from a tree, helping ladies with a flat tire, saving the mayor from choking. Now the suggestion is of fertility rather than futility. The repetitions imply still more virtuous actions to come for as long as Phil relives Groundhog Day.

Practice Makes Perfect

The reformed Phil undertakes long-term, arduous projects that require discipline and fortitude. Phil enjoys life because he grows through the efforts he expends. He grows artistically, as a pianist and ice sculptor, intellectually, as a lover of literature, and morally, as a performer of good deeds. Only by committing himself to far-reaching goals is Phil required to exert himself in the activities that develop his human capacities. Although Phil embarks on his self-improvement in order to win Rita's love, he comes to enjoy the activities for their own sake. The result is a life made meaningful by activity that is intrinsically valued. Piano playing, poetry reading, lifesaving—all are undertaken by Phil as ends in themselves. At the same time, Phil comes to value people for their own sakes, not for what they can provide him.

The underlying truth is that some good things cannot be sought directly. We can achieve happiness, for example, only by trying to do good for others. In pursuing moral ends we do virtuous things; becoming more virtuous, we forget ourselves and enjoy life. The ironic converse of this truth is that the more we strive for pleasure, as Phil initially does, the less we please ourselves—although it may take a Nietzschean eternal recurrence to teach us the truth of this relationship.

Some pursuits may be self-defeating because our selves get in the way. Virtues such as humility and compassion, for instance, cannot successfully be sought directly. Trying to be humble or compassionate is self-defeating because when we attend to our selves, humility and compassion are obstructed. To take a nonmoral example, working at being graceful usually results in movement that is overly studied, lacking in grace. Similarly, people tend to worry more about something the more they consciously strive to stop worrying about it.

After he turns over a new leaf, Phil stops focusing on himself. His actions are directed toward things that are worthwhile independent of him. To appreciate literature, an individual cannot be concerned about what he is getting out of the study. Instead, he must pay attention to the aesthetic features of the literary works and work to understand what they have to offer. To become skilled at playing the piano, Phil must concentrate on the music and what he has to do to evoke it from the instrument. To benefit people, Phil must notice their needs and figure out ways to help the individuals meet these needs.

The consequence of not worrying about what he is getting out of the disciplined artistic or moral endeavors is that Phil is enriched. His interior life, in all its emotional, intellectual, and moral complexity, is enhanced in ways impossible for his self-centered behavior to achieve. Absorbed in himself, Phil missed out on what the world of art, thought, and other people had to offer. In the cultivation of his artistic talents and in his moral habituation, Phil exemplifies an Aristotelian view of how people realize their human potential.

Groundhog Day illustrates that artistic and moral activities are causally connected and also resemble one another. For example, developing his artistic talents requires that Phil exhibit discipline, a moral virtue. Until his disciplined behavior becomes habitual, moreover, Phil needs self-control to give up the easy pleasures he enjoyed before his change of heart. Before he can take pleasure in doing virtuous or artistic things, Phil must be able to withstand the tugs of appetite or the shoves of emotion. As with morality, the arts have an objective structure and standard. Playing the piano is not a matter of private desire or approval, like finding some clothing attractive or some foods tasty. To make good music, individuals must learn the structure of sounds and fit their senses and motor skills to it. Phil's love of music and devotion to it represent a recognition of a value that does not depend on him or his appetites. Instead of valuing something because he wants it, Phil now wants something because he appreciates its value.

Affirming the value of an objective order is also a condition of developing virtues. To be just, for example, we must recognize a standard of distributing benefits and burdens independent of our personal preferences. Honesty or truthfulness require subordinating what we wish to be the case to respect for criteria of objective judgment. Even virtues that flow from refinement of our subjectivity, such as compassion and kindness, require perceiving the actual needs and difficulties of people different from ourselves. Because virtue and art have objective standards of performance, both admit of degrees of excellence and perfection.

Phil develops morally as his virtues become second nature, and he habitually helps others without ulterior motives.[20] His virtues also expand in scope. For instance, his generosity enlarges into magnanimity when he buys huge amounts of insurance from an old classmate and when he treats young newlyweds to a honeymoon trip. In repeatedly helping the old derelict, Phil extends himself to his moral, emotional, and physical limit. Tactful responses blossom into friendly wit, as Phil unflaggingly helps people out of trouble with a cheering word.

Phil seems to appreciate his artistic and moral growth, but in contrast to his former self, he has neither the inclination nor the leisure to rejoice in his accomplishments. He is too busy with the activities themselves. Exhibiting the self-forgetfulness that is a facet of virtuous character, Phil tends not to notice his achievements, and when they are called to his attention he seems genuinely unimpressed with himself.

Just as Phil's humor is incorporated into morally virtuous action, so his artistic abilities are put to generous use. Phil makes beautiful music and ice sculptures for other people to enjoy instead of using his talent to further his own interests. In the scene in which he sculpts Rita as a gift to her, *Groundhog Day* again infuses warmth into cold. The beauty of Rita's face, which Phil depicts in ice, not only captures her good heart but also reveals his own. Giving through our artistic creations is giving of ourselves, not only in the sense of sharing our talents and energies but also in giving our sensibility and feelings.

Love and Virtue

Where Phil used to see other people as opportunities for his personal advantage, he now views himself as a resource for the benefit of others. Rather than demean people, Phil goes out of his way to spare people's feelings, including sparing them the embarrassment of being grateful to him. He works to improve the lives of his neighbors at his own expense instead of exploiting them for his own ends. Phil no longer amuses himself by slighting Punxsutawney. His arrogance is replaced by humility—a subtle effect of respecting the value things possess without reference to himself.

Rita's moral goodness is the first thing Phil understands and values for its own sake, apart from his self-interest. Rita's virtue is the impetus for his moral transformation, and by movie's end, Phil has begun a friendship of virtue with Rita. Phil is more motivated by furthering Rita's happiness than by how happy she can make him. As Aristotle remarks of the highest form of friendship: "Those who wish for their friends' good for their friends' sake are friends in the truest sense."[21] Over months of Groundhog Days, Phil's character has matured to a level comparable to Rita's, so that they are "alike in excellence" and therefore capable of a friendship of virtue.

Only when Phil no longer strives to seduce Rita but regards her good character as worthy of emulation, does he begin to win her over. The surest way to a virtuous person's heart is through virtue, because good character provides virtuous people with the most pleasure.[22] To become sexually intimate with Rita, Phil must forget sexual conquest. It is significant that on the evening of the final Groundhog Day, Phil kisses Rita tenderly, not passionately. He does not have sex with her, even though he could have, because genuine love has replaced lust—by itself, another appetite whose satisfaction yields personal pleasure.

In *Dangerous Liaisons,* the moral complexion of another character undergoes a comparable transformation. In this Stephen Frears (1989) film, a pure, sweet woman is seduced by a man for whom sexual acquisition is a contest. Valmont is a callous, sexual sportsman. He is so decadent that he does not want to destroy Madame de Tourvel's virtue, because he wants "the excitement of watching her betray everything that's most important to her"—God, virtue, and the sanctity of marriage. Valmont manipulates the morally superior Madame de Tourvel in the only viable way, by claiming to be attracted to her virtuous character and transformed by it.

The irony is that Madame de Tourvel is indeed having the salutary effect on him that Valmont pretends to experience. Even as Valmont's liaison with Madame de Tourvel endangers her virtuous character, so does it jeopardize his vice. Valmont is unsuspectingly made more sensitive and caring because of the relationship he enjoys with his lovestruck victim. Madame de Tourvel's virtue does not protect her nearly as well as Rita's virtue shields her from amorous subterfuge. But Valmont is more practiced and formidable than Phil, even without the advantage conferred by the recurrence of Groundhog Day. Moreover, Valmont is actually evil. He enjoys destroying virtue, whereas Phil's self-absorption bespeaks moral immaturity rather than depravity.

Valmont never becomes truly virtuous, as Phil Connors does, but he is crippled as a sexual competitor and predator. Valmont's cynical view of love is shaken, and he becomes so unmoored by Madame de Tourvel's unanticipated moral effect on him as to allow himself to be killed in a duel over her honor. As he lies dying, Valmont asks his opponent to tell Madame de Tourvel that her love was the only real happiness he had ever known. Valmont confirms the Aristotelian insight into the proper object of love and the source of human well-being—virtuous character. Virtuous character has power over those who fall within its orbit. For Valmont and his ilk, the radiance of a person's virtue can deflect them from further corruption, and even illuminate their lives, however fleetingly.[23] For people like Phil, another individual's virtue can inspire transformation.

Inspired by Rita to become more virtuous, Phil is finally worthy of her love. The film thereby suggests a conception of romantic love as including a friendship of virtue, thereby creating a romantic friendship. Such a reconception of romantic love is more robust than popular notions. The suggestion of a morally invigorated view of romantic love, however, is inconsistent with the dénouement of *Groundhog Day*. In particular, the film is inconsistent in its implications about the relevance of knowledge to romantic friendship.

Recall the scene in which Rita tells Phil that he cannot love her because he doesn't know her. I interpreted this as meaning that the knowledge necessary for the love of romantic friendship involves more than simply acquiring biographical information about the other person, however extensive that information might be. Even if we grant that the repeated Groundhog Days enable the reformed Phil to know Rita as profoundly as needed for romantic friendship, what about Rita? How could she know Phil well enough to love him in just the one day her memory-deprived existence permits, even if it is a wonderful day with a virtuous man?

I think that here *Groundhog Day* lapses into a more popular notion of romantic love, one that does not incorporate virtuous friendship or the deep sense of mutual knowledge it entails. The lapse is forgivable, however, since love is subordinate to Phil's virtuous development in a way it is not subordinate, for example, to the moral growth of the protagonists in *The African Queen*. As we shall see in the next chapter, Charlie Allnut and Rose Sayer minister to one another's moral growth within a romantic friendship. For Phil, Rita functions more as an idealized love object who inspires Phil to his virtuous labors but does not participate in them. Phil grows because of Rita but not by means of her. Phil becomes more virtuous largely through his own individual efforts, not by means of interacting with Rita. Phil's moral development is also unilateral in that Rita herself does not change.

In a similar way, the townspeople of Punxsutawney provide the opportunity or material for Phil's virtuous actions, but they do not connect with him as real friends. How could they, since the Punxsutawney folk have but one day's experience of Phil? My conclusion is that *Groundhog Day* is primarily about one individual's moral transformation and that the idea of situating a friendship of virtue within romantic love—a romantic friendship—is a brief, interesting grace note to a song about living well by living virtuously.

At the evening party of the final Groundhog Day, Rita walks into the ballroom only to discover that the vibrant piano playing she hears is Phil's. Rita's wonderment at the hidden dimensions of Phil grows as she witnesses the admiration and affection the people of Punxsutawney have for him. Rita finally has to ask Phil, "What is goin' on? . . . There is something goin' on with you." Her question is a variant of Phil's own perplexed query the first morning he relives Groundhog Day. It is also a colloquial way of expressing the self-questioning Nietzsche urges us to undertake periodically in order to steer our lives on the right course. Before Phil can answer Rita, the Bachelor Auction begins.

After the bidding for Phil, Larry, the cameraman, bounds up on the auction block. Humiliatingly, Larry goes for a laughable two bits. *Groundhog Day* uses the low bid for Larry's company to reflect his moral stature. Just moments before, Larry comically reminds us of what Phil used to be when he crudely attempts to pick up Nancy over drinks in the hotel bar. The scene reflects the "old" Phil in that Nancy was one of his original romantic conquests and the hotel bar was the recurring site of Phil's wooing of Rita. Just as Rita rebuffed the old, unreformed Phil, so Nancy will have none of Larry's sleazy come-on. Like other women in town, Nancy has her sights set on prevailing in the auction and spending the evening with the sweet and affectionate Phil.

Phil is so well liked, in fact, that Rita wins him only after spirited bidding against a flock of eager women, who are sorely disappointed to be outspent in the auction. Rita wins Phil for $339.88. The exact figure is important because it comes right after a $60 bid, indicating that Rita probably could have had Phil for less. But she offers all the money she has, down to the last penny, and the film thereby impishly uses money to stand for giving all we have in love. Rita will hold nothing back to be with the person who, just the day before Groundhog Day, she rightly thought was an unmitigated jerk. Phil's last exhausting day of giving of himself, completely and for the sake of other people, rounds into its homestretch with Rita symbolically emptying her checking account to vouchsafe her time with him.

Phil has been blessed by a benign Nietzschean demon, who bestows on him the gift of experiencing his usual life in distilled, exaggerated form. He is thereby spared a failed life. Phil's egoistic hedonism becomes intolerable as it might not otherwise have become, because in ordinary life, selfish pleasures can themselves conceal what is wrong with devoting oneself to their pursuit. *Groundhog Day* shows Phil freed by the eternal return to experience and understand his self-absorbed life for what it is, and change before it is too late.

Just as Phil finally gains the love of the woman he wants by relenting in his seductive enterprise and becoming more virtuous, so too does his endless repetition of Groundhog Day end when he finds meaning, and therefore joy, in living each repeated day. When he enthusiastically embraces the people of Punxsutawney, Phil's moral character evolves and he finds life fulfilling. The town Phil Connors began by reviling has become the place in which he wants to settle down with Rita, although they will "just rent" at first. The creature Phil Connors once found so cloyingly stupid, the groundhog named Punxsutawney Phil, has become his namesake. By film's end, Phil Connors is truly Punxsutawney Phil—the town's most caring, civic-minded citizen.

Notes

1. The view that Nietzsche's notion of eternal recurrence is practical rather than cosmological or metaphysical is supported by several recent interpretations. For example, Maudemarie Clark writes, "We can avoid thus making Nietzsche's doctrine [of eternal recurrence] dependent on cosmological support if we inter-

pret his doctrine of recurrence as the [practical] ideal of affirming eternal recurrence," *Nietzsche on Truth and Philosophy* (Cambridge: Cambridge University Press, 1990), p.252; see also pp.245–286.

2. Aristotle, *Nicomachean Ethics,* trans. Martin Ostwald (Indianapolis: Bobbs-Merrill, 1962), 1097a. Note the apparent tension in Aristotle between the life of moral virtue and the life of philosophical contemplation as the truly best life. Fortunately, the textual or philosophical exegesis needed to address this tension need not occupy us here.

3. Alasdair MacIntyre, *After Virtue* (Notre Dame, Ind.: University of Notre Dame Press, 1981), p.179.

4. Aristotle, *Nicomachean Ethics,* p.21, 1099a.

5. *Gorgias,* trans. W. C. Helmbold (Indianapolis: Bobbs-Merrill, 1952), 491e and 492a.

6. Ibid., 494a.

7. The deeper Platonic criticism is that pleasure itself is nonrational and cannot be known because it lacks objective structure or form. Unlike health and the products of craftsmen, such as architects or farmers, pleasure is purely subjective and so is without a techne. It admits of no independently existing principles by which to investigate or understand its nature.

8. See *The Apology,* trans. Harold Fowler (Cambridge: Harvard University Press, 1914), 38a.

9. It is not surprising that living happily is living rationally because rationality is viewed by the Greeks as the defining feature of human nature. Aristotle writes: "The proper function of man, then, consists in an activity of the soul in conformity with a rational principle," *Nicomachean Ethics,* p.17, 1097a.

10. Ibid., p.25, 1100b.

11. Ibid., 1157a.

12. Ibid., 1156b.

13. Ibid., 1156a and 1156b.

14. *The Republic of Plato,* trans. and ed. Allan Bloom (New York: Basic Books, 1968), 359d.

15. I am deeply indebted to Prof. Drew Leder for this observation, as well as for pointing out the power of other metaphorical images, such as the shadow.

16. Phil eventually comes to love Punxsutawney and to think of it as his home, just as Dorothy learns that there is "no place like home."

17. Socrates preys upon just this lack of self-awareness to humorous effect in various Platonic dialogues. The suggestion is that hedonists expose themselves to ridicule precisely because they have not examined themselves or the way of life they advocate. If all pleasures are good, Socrates points out to Callicles, then why not sit around (endlessly) scratching an itch? *Gorgias,* 494a.

18. This might be a reference to another Eastwood character, Bronco Billy. Covering the Groundhog Day celebration the next morning, Phil is shown on

the TV monitor asking whether Phil, the groundhog, "feels lucky." The phrase repeats a line from one of Eastwood's skein of films featuring the police detective Dirty Harry.

19. Edmund Pincoffs classifies humorousness as a temperamental kind of "meliorating" virtue, along with such virtues as cheerfulness and amiability, in *Quandaries and Virtues* (Lawrence: University Press of Kansas, 1986), pp.86–89.

20. Aristotle, *Nicomachean Ethics,* 1105.

21. Ibid., p.219, 1156b.

22. Ibid.

23. Compare Valmont with Claggart in Herman Melville's *Billy Budd.* In a crucial scene, Claggart talks with Billy during the ship's night watch. Claggart self-consciously voices his resistance to the attraction of Billy's good nature, saying that he will not be drawn into its power as Billy's shipmates have been.

3
The Work of Love in
The African Queen

Romantic Love and Virtue

Groundhog Day is filled with romantic interest, and the film ends with
Phil and Rita in love, planning a future together. But the film focuses on
Phil as an individual and his change from a life of indolence to one of
virtue. Rita is an auxiliary to Phil's moral growth, an inspirational model
of virtue, and therefore someone with whom Phil can aspire to a true
friendship. For a film that deals with a loving relationship as the medium
and force for virtuous development in both lovers, we turn to *The African
Queen* (1951).

John Huston's masterpiece is obviously a love story. What is not so obvious is the conception of love illustrated by the relationship between
Rose Sayer and Charlie Allnutt. Through its engrossing yarn, the film
weaves a rich portrait of the moral transformation that motivates romantic love. The conception of romantic love as romantic friendship, intro-
duced in *Groundhog Day*, is explored in depth in *The African Queen*. The
conception invigorates more conventional views of romantic love with an
Aristotelian understanding of virtuous friendship. Emphasis on virtue
adds the weight of moral purpose and direction to romantic love, even as
romantic love shapes the virtues according to the particular personalities
of the lovers.

The conception of romantic friendship does not simply borrow
Aristotle's account of virtuous friendship but modifies his understanding
to include the dialectical interplay between the friends. Aristotle thinks of

The African Queen: Charlie
and Rose team up to build
homemade torpedoes.

friends as loving the virtue they find already formed in one another. He
speaks of friends not as responsible for one another's continuing moral
growth but only as providing the occasion for observing or performing
virtuous acts. Within romantic friendship, however, virtue is dynamic and
dialectic. The virtues of the lovers develop, and they develop by means of
the lovers' interaction. Love is fueled by the appreciation the individuals
have for the moral improvement they experience in themselves. In romantic friendship, therefore, the growth in the virtues of the friends nourishes
the relationship, and in turn, the relationship nurtures their virtues.

As noted in discussing *Groundhog Day*, Aristotle also seems to imply that
what is actually loved in friendship is the array of virtues and that the person
is more the vehicle or bearer of the virtues than the object of affection per
se.[1] On Shirley Letwin's interpretation, "What each friend appreciates in
the other, however, is not the difference of a unique self; he values only what
he finds also in himself . . . [the virtues they have in common]."[2] In romantic friendship, an Aristotelian friendship of virtue becomes individualized
by the particular personalities of the lovers. The expression of virtue is
stamped with the distinguishing traits of the individuals. For example, one
person dismisses his kindness with gruff joking, whereas another individual
expresses her kindness so softly that it goes unnoticed. The virtues are so
entwined in the specific sinews of the lovers' personalities that they could
not be cherished apart from these unique individuals.

Groundhog Day and *The African Queen* especially personalize the virtues
by portraying their respective protagonists as humorous or fun loving, and
also as artful. Although less witty than Phil Connors, Charlie Allnutt has
a broad sense of humor and is spontaneous in his playfulness. In place of

Phil Connors generously bestowing the gifts of his artistry on other people, Charlie and Rose display a technical ingenuity and mechanical creativity that individualize their virtues of generosity and cooperativeness.

Reconceiving romantic love as romantic friendship builds virtuous transformation into the unfolding and flowering of romantic passion. It also binds together self-love and love for the other person as complementary consequences of one dialectical process. The perfecting of our moral character is at once the reason we love ourselves more and why we love the other individual. *The African Queen* bears out Robert Solomon's observation that romantic love is "the mutual creation of self-identity"—not just any identity, but a good one.[3] We experience the beloved making us a better person. But self-esteem can propel romantic love only because, as Solomon notes, "love embodies a reflective desire for self-improvement."[4] The self-improvement conception of love presupposes that we want to be good, perhaps as a concomitant of the natural human desire for happiness or well being.

The philosophical theme of the transformative power of love has been noticed by other interpreters of *The African Queen*. For example, Lesley Brill points out that the "relationship [between Charlie and Rose] will humanize and enlarge them both."[5] But he does not examine the view of love, embodied by the movie, that explains how love performs its moral work. Rather than accounting for the efficacy of love, Brill posits it, claiming that "the catalyst that effectuates [their] transformation is love."[6] In my interpretation, love is not so much like a chemical agent as it is an ongoing process of mutual development. Love denotes a relationship whose dialectical structure can actually explain the realization of the moral potential of its participants.

Lovers inspire one another to be better than they presently are and enable each other to see their potential for moral improvement. The beloved discovers and appreciates qualities in us that we were unaware, or only dimly aware, we possessed. This is an impetus for us to develop worthwhile qualities and a challenge to us to remedy character flaws. But the lover is also more directly edifying, evoking and developing new traits in us through interaction. The newness of these traits ranges from those just waiting to be summoned, such as a latent talent, to those requiring prolonged encouragement, such as the capacity for a challenging virtue.

Solomon's conception of romantic love as involving mutual positive self-creation invites completion by the Aristotelian ideal of virtuous friendship.[7] Moral virtue specifies what exactly is mutually created, providing loving interaction with a definite goal. Love is necessarily demanding, therefore, because the lovers must work for each other's moral progress. M. Scott Peck expresses the meliorative purpose of love as the will to extend oneself for the spiritual growth of someone—another person or oneself.[8] I see this as a generic, or root, concept of love. Particular loves, such as the love between parents and children or between romantic friends, are differentiated by the specifics of their defining relationships.

The root concept of love entails work—expending thought, emotion, and perceptual energies to help an individual develop spiritually or morally. Working for the spiritual growth of another person involves helping the person become more disciplined, attentive, realistic, and more capable of taking the risks necessary for his or her growth. Peck's conception is especially valuable in explaining why a loving relationship furthers the moral growth of the participants twice over. Not only do lovers benefit by receiving moral encouragement from one another, but they also become more virtuous as a result of extending themselves for the sake of the other person's growth. Love is work in that it calls into play hitherto untapped moral capacities and strengthens existing moral dispositions. Of the virtues discussed by Peck, the dialectical development of discipline and attentiveness are particularly conspicuous in *The African Queen*.

When we do the work of love for another person, we must postpone immediate gratifications, thereby becoming more disciplined ourselves. In *The African Queen*, Charlie and Rose have to defer meeting their own needs in order to reinforce the disciplined efforts of the other person. As Kierkegaard points out, self-constraint may also be needed to keep us from doing too much for the beloved or from imposing our ideas of moral progress on him or her.[9]

The effort to promote a loved one's virtue requires that individuals pay attention to who and what the other person actually is. Iris Murdoch puts the connection between love and attention this way: "Love . . . is an exercise of . . . really *looking*. The difficulty is to keep the attention fixed upon the real situation and to prevent it from returning surreptitiously to the self with consolations of self-pity, resentment, fantasy."[10]

Attentiveness is itself a virtue, but it includes discipline as an important component. Noticing what is actually going on, instead of projecting what we would like to see happen, requires discipline because what is really occurring may be difficult to sort out or painful to confront.

A still more pervasive positive effect of performing the labors of love is that we are enlarged through caring about the character of our beloved.

Attentiveness seems to be part of, or a condition for, what Solomon sees as the expansion of selfhood: "Love may be a matter of self, but what defines the self in love is first of all *caring* for another person. Love is an expansion of self to include—and even to favor—the other."[11] We grow because our perspective and sympathies open up through caring about the other person's interests. As we will shortly see, in putting each another's needs ahead of their own, Rose and Charlie become more expansive as people—more free with themselves and more open to possibilities than they had been.

In presenting romantic love as combined with virtuous friendship, *The African Queen* obviously departs from popular perspectives of romantic love pervasive in American culture even now. If the notion of romantic friendship seems overly moralistic, the more conventional conceptions of romantic love are perhaps overly imbued with elements of courtly love, courting, and traditional gender roles. These conventional notions of love are descended from the romanticism of the nineteenth century, which was, in turn, shaped by medieval courtly love.[12]

Popular portrayals of romantic love imply that the perception of the beloved formed in courtship persists into the long-term relationship of the couple and that the perception continues to be defined by traditional conceptions of masculinity and femininity. The idea of the love object, nurtured during dating, resembles the knight's vision of his lady fair, formed from a distance and glorified by her finery, as well as by the knight's imagination. In these popular renderings, success in the relationship depends largely on how well the couple fulfill each other's original, idealized images of one another—images formed within the cultural outlines of gender expectations first fulfilled during courtship.

Conventional understandings of romantic love do not emphasize moral growth. The beloved is perceived as a relatively finished object, and the hope is that we have fathomed its depths and astutely assessed its merits. From the perspective of love as a romantic friendship, however, the individuals and their relationship are understood to be a work in progress, an evolving moral process. In fact, it is just because this evolution has already begun that people fall in love.

By infusing romantic love with a virtuous friendship, *The African Queen* clarifies the nebulous and murky notion of falling in love. When we fall in love, we are thrilled with the shining vision of ourselves as ennobled by the beloved. Solomon's theory agrees with popular songs and stories in depicting falling in love as a sudden revelation. Imagining the fine things they are capable of with the beloved at their side, lovers experience "a rapid conceptual transformation of the self."[13] Flooded with the imagined story of what their new lives can be, a "romance" in the original sense of the term, they are exhilarated.

However, the conception Solomon shares with popular culture may be misleading. *The African Queen* suggests that the moment of falling in love should not be viewed as an isolated incident. Instead, the epiphany should be understood as the (provisional) climax of a process during which the pair have overcome conflicts and resolved differences between them. When we finally come to see ourselves ennobled by the other person, it is because we have been undergoing moral change, mostly imperceptible and usually unsought, at the hands of our beloved. The process of falling in love occurs while the potential lovers gradually bring out the best in one another. The moment of schmaltzy violin music is the culmination of an arduous, dialectical movement of self-development and hard-won harmony with the other person.

If the revelatory moment is the birth, or discovery, of what has been quietly gestating, then virtuous friendship is woven into the fabric of romantic love all along. The mutual moral edification does not occur only after the pair have fallen in love but is the gravitational force responsible for their fall. To speak of ascending in love might be more apt, since the lovers experience themselves as morally elevated in their romantic transports. However, Peck explains the transporting experience in a way that does jibe with the metaphor of tumbling downward. He says that falling in love is a sudden collapse of ego boundaries, which yields a merging of identities. "The explosive pouring out of oneself into the beloved . . . is experienced by most of us as ecstatic."[14]

The African Queen suggests that the work of love, which has been building up to the collapse of ego boundaries, escapes the notice of the incipient lovers. They have been promoting one another's virtuous transformation, but unawares. After they fall in love, the mutual moral encouragement is undertaken with awareness, passion, and care for one another. The difference is similar to Aristotle's distinction between individuals who merely do virtuous things and the actions of truly virtuous people.

To act virtuously, as virtuous people do, individuals must know what they are doing, perform the act from a stable (virtuous) disposition, and choose the virtuous thing for its own sake.[15] Clearly, we can do kind or courageous or just things without meeting these conditions. In a similar fashion, only after falling in love do Charlie and Rose perform the work of love knowing what they are doing, from a caring disposition, and simply for the sake of the beloved. Before their emotional epiphany, they promote one another's virtue without the awareness or motivation characteristic of romantic friendship. They were moving toward the time when, in love, their mutual moral melioration would be undertaken with purpose and care.

The film also locates physical attraction as the effect rather than the cause of love. C. S. Lewis comments on sexual desire in particular: "Without Eros [romantic love] sexual desire, like every other desire, is a fact about ourselves. Within Eros it is rather about the Beloved."[16] Our sexual desire is aroused because we love this particular individual, rather than our desire leading us to someone who can satisfy it. Because sexuality is tangential to our theme, and the film, I cannot give it the attention warranted by a comprehensive analysis of romantic love. I only note in passing that the virtues enter into sexual interaction much as they figure in other areas of lovers' lives. We can, and do, exhibit our virtues (and vices) in lovemaking: being generous in giving pleasure (or selfish in only taking it); being considerate of our partner's needs or wishes (or callous in ignoring them); being patient (or impatient) with our lover's responses to us. As with other interaction, we can foster or inhibit our lover's moral development by our sexual behavior.

The African Queen proceeds to explore how love develops our virtues through cooperative work. The work of love is mostly done at work: the everyday contexts of joint venture such as tackling domestic chores, resolving disagreements, making decisions, and overcoming serious problems. The film suggests that the power of love to transform us morally occurs most unobtrusively, yet most surely, when we toil with our beloved. Charlie and Rose help one another develop their respective virtues within the intimacy and passion of romantic love. But the context of their romance is labor, in all its mental, emotional, and physical incarnations. *The African Queen* illustrates the moral work of love by depicting the lovers at work.

Two Different Worlds

To appreciate how Rose (Katharine Hepburn) and Charlie (Humphrey Bogart) transform one another, we must begin with what they are like before their moral improvement. The beginning of *The African Queen* presents two individuals whose contrasts go beyond their visible dissimilarities. The first shots of Rose and Charlie set the scene for their further opposition. Rose is doggedly playing the organ and singing hymns for the congregation in her brother's missionary church in German East Africa, in 1914. Charlie is approaching the mission, regally reclining aboard his boat, the African Queen, smiling with the pleasures of gin and cigars.

When Charlie approaches the church and flicks his cigar butt on the ground, the film gives an antagonistic edge to the contrast between Charlie and Rose. The natives scramble for the stogie, abandoning their uninspired, unintelligible church singing. The failure of Rose and her brother, Samuel (Robert Morley), to create musical or spiritual harmony among the native population is revealed by the ease with which Charlie's discarded cigar attracts the congregation to earthly delights.[17]

War between Britain and Germany soon throws Charlie and Rose together. Rose loses her home and her brother when German troops destroy the compound of the (British) ministry and rough Samuel up. Charlie returns to the mission to find that Samuel has died and that Rose needs rescuing. But what Charlie thinks will be a brief jaunt on his boat turns into a long journey down river and down into his most basic desires and emotions. The fun of the film is seeing how the initial conflicts naturally arising from such a mismatched pair as Charlie and Rose are replaced by mutual affection and exemplary cooperation. What launches the couple's voyage is Rose's proposal to take the African Queen downstream to the lake patrolled by the German ship, the Louisa. Once there, they are to knock the Louisa out of commission, thereby enabling British troops easy access to the interior of Africa.

Before the improbable pair can fulfill Rose's patriotic plan, however, they must overcome daunting obstacles: German-led forces at Fort Shona; river danger and boat damage; leeches and black flies; and finally, the African Queen becoming bogged down. In saga-like fashion, Rose and Charlie have to negotiate numerous perils and hardships before being in position to reach for the ultimate prize. Of course, the prize they unexpectedly come away with is love for one another and the moral growth that is a concomitant of that love. Rose and Charlie foster in each other moral virtues that they originally lacked and that make them more lovable. Moreover, the love they give and receive are the soil and sunshine in which these virtues are cultivated. Before the scruffy jack-of-all-trades casts off with the starchy missionary, the movie deftly conveys their disparate natures.

Handing the minister his mail, Charlie apologizes for being late, noting that he has been kept in the city by "one thing and another, you know how it is." Charlie implies a sexual dalliance when he adds, "Maybe you don't [know how it is]." Charlie's identification as a man of the flesh is rounded out with the serving of tea and the addition of food to Charlie's appetite for booze, smoke, and women. His appetite is given voice in the repeated rumbles and groans of his stomach, as he must put up with the deliberate-ness with which Rose serves the afternoon repast. After trying to ignore the humorously crescendoing importunings of his body, Charlie comments, "Just listen to this stomach of mine. Way it sounds, you'd think I had a hyena inside me. Ha, ha, ha." He then accepts more bread and butter to appease the voracious little beast within.

Charlie attempts to inquire as to why a man's stomach should act like this, but Rose deflects the conversation to polite talk of tea and cakes. Cloaked in the comic conflict between the protagonists, the film subtly introduces Rose's aversion to the body—its needs and vagaries, and also its charms. Accepting the fact that his stomach insists on making its operations heard, Charlie smiles and says: "Not a thing I can do about it." In yielding to his inability to control his organic functioning, Charlie opposes Rose's insistence on rejecting our corporeality. She denies or avoids it by pressing on with the etiquette of tea. Rose's inability or unwillingness to enjoy her body, and the sensory experience it affords, characterizes her entire outlook on life and defines her vice.

The contrast between Charlie and Rose could be cast in terms of the conflict between the natural and the conventional, as James Fultz does: "The [tea] scene sets whatever is natural and vital and unseemly because spontaneous . . . against whatever is artificial and merely conventional and essentially dead."[18] Although the scene lends itself to this interpretation, I think it indicates something more, and a bit less, than the clash between the natural (as good or "alive") and the artificial (as bad or "lifeless").

The tea episode indicates something less in that the film proceeds to illustrate that the natural is not always good or life-giving and that conventions are not necessarily bad or deadening. The episode points to something more in that instead of establishing a clear dichotomy between good and bad, it raises questions about human nature and virtue with which all people must grapple. Charlie and Rose illustrate the necessity of struggling with these questions and how romantic friendship facilitates this struggle.

For example, Charlie's claim that there is not a thing he can do about his stomach's grumblings points in two directions. The assertion rightly calls attention to the physical dimensions of our humanity, which we must learn to accept because they are undeniably part of us, for good or ill. In these opening scenes, the body is deployed metonymically to represent essential human nature. We will come to see human needs other than the physical, such as the need for conversation, as also inescapable because embedded in our natures. Notice, by the way, that conversation includes the conventions of language and presupposes the social conventions that make good conversation possible.

The scene of the stomach-at-tea also reminds us that we can change some important aspects of ourselves. In saying that there is not a thing he can do about his stomach's noisy demands, Charlie suggests that there is nothing he can do about himself. We soon realize that Charlie falsely, and self-servingly, believes many things are beyond his control. However, in asking why a man's stomach should act this way, Charlie obliquely and tentatively initiates an inquiry into human nature. The suggestion of such an inquiry may foreshadow Charlie's self-questioning, a modest version of the Socratic self-reflection needed to become more virtuous (noted in discussing *Groundhog Day*). In this one little scene, the film's major oppositions are announced: the opposition between the moral personalities of Charlie and Rose; the opposition between what we can and cannot change in general—and the malleable and intractable aspects of human nature in particular; and the opposition between complacency about ourselves and willingness to change.

The isolation of the religious brother and sister from the physical world, their figurative disembodiment, is evidenced in their ignorance of the war between Germany and England. Charlie is of this world. He has strong bodily needs and pleasures, knowledge of politics and geography (he is the bringer of news), and he operates his useful, little boat. Charlie is also a mechanic or handyman, someone whose work is to make physical things work.

Charlie's news of the war provides a verbal transition to the military conflict in Africa. Over the missionary siblings' prayers for British victory, we hear native drums growing louder. The drums herald the on-screen arrival of the German troops, who proceed to herd the African natives and raze their homes in the church settlement. Fire and drum convey the destruction of the missionary enclave Rose shares with her brother, but they are also a less obvious sign of the end of life as Charlie has known it. Because Charlie is not in this scene, the impact of the war on him is temporarily muted.

The fact that the war shatters the subcultures Rose and Charlie inhabit is crucial to the film's vision of love. The physical, psychological, and social differences between the two protagonists could not be bridged without catastrophic disruption of their lives. At least Romeo and Juliet shared a common culture and way of life, for all the strife between their families. Rose and Charlie could not begin to find each other within the old social order. Isolated by the death of her brother and the eviction of the natives, Rose has no choice but to accompany Charlie. *The African Queen* is realistic in situating the possibility of the couple's love in a boat after they have been torn from their familiar ways and flung together.

One Small Boat

The story occurs in three settings: the village with the church mission, the river, and the lake. Transitions between the settings reposition Charlie and Rose, first, to flee the village and begin their river expedition, then, to give their adventure closure on the lake. Most of the story occurs on the river, and there are important transitions on the river journey, dividing it as well. Because the transitions on the river involve major changes in Charlie, Rose, and their relationship, they may be thought of as transformations or transformative transitions.

The burning of the village inaugurates Rose's transition from her insulated life of otherworldliness to a voyage of moral growth. The couple touch land again only for the sake of the African Queen, in order to continue their journey. They come ashore to repair the African Queen, and they walk on the river bottom to pull the boat through uncooperative waters. Water is fluid, a medium of movement, whereas earth is solid, promising stasis. The first transition, then, uproots Rose and Charlie from their earthbound routines, casting them off into a moving medium of personal reformation.[19]

Because Charlie travels by boat, it may seem odd to claim that he is as earthbound as Rose, but Charlie's aquatic movement is equally bound to, and by, the earth. Earth literally bounds Charlie's existence in that he ferries himself, with goods and news, back and forth, from one piece of land to another. Charlie takes no excursions in his boat. More figuratively, Charlie's life is bounded by his routines of work and carnal enjoyments. For all the appearance of freedom and movement in Charlie's life, it is as unchanging as Rose's stolid existence.

From the time Charlie returns to the village to see how the missionaries have fared, Rose and Charlie begin moving away from their former lives and selves. Ensuing pauses in the narrative punctuate the downstream course of the boat and the movement of Charlie and Rose into each other's lives. The opening shot of the film also cues us that movement is essential to the story that is to follow. The camera tracks the trees canopying the river, ostensibly providing a heavenward view from aboard the lazily moving African Queen. Rose and Charlie will discover and recreate each other during their journey toward a new life in which they are mated. But first, their glaring differences in character must somehow be softened and penetrate into one another.

The cinematic alignment of Charlie with human corporeality is reinforced by his concern for the decomposition and burial of the body of Rose's dead brother. Even as the missionary siblings had tried to save the souls of the natives, Charlie returns to the village to save Samuel's corpse from putrefaction and to save Rose from isolation and danger. Once aboard the African Queen, Charlie merrily notes that they have all the (creature) comforts of home, including two thousand cigarettes and two cases of gin. Rose is committed to ideals, such as God and country, and they will prevail over Charlie's protestations on behalf of physical ease and safety.

Charlie and Rose discuss the German military position and possible British strategies. Rose hits on the idea of going down the river and ramming the African Queen into the German gunboat, the Louisa, which patrols the large inland lake. If they are successful in blowing up the Louisa, British troops would have a relatively easy path into German East Africa from the Congo. Charlie protests that they cannot possibly make it down the river because it is too wild and it is also guarded by the Germans at Fort Shona. Rose admonishes him, saying, "How do you know, you've never tried!" Charlie's hyperbolic retort, "I haven't tried shooting myself in the head either," is meant to make plain how some actions are simply self-destructive. Charlie implies that he can tell the difference between such futility and trying something risky that holds some hope of success. The rest of the story is about trying what seems practically impossible. However, it is easy to overlook a casual exchange that occurs moments earlier.

To the strains of light-hearted music, we see Rose and Charlie chugging down the river toward what Charlie thinks will be a safe haven in which to wait out the war. When he asks Rose to steer the boat, she begs off, saying she does not know how. Ever so lightly, the movie hints at Rose's unwillingness to try to do something physical that seems too difficult. Rose's trepidation provides a lower-key parallel to Charlie's more blatant fear of descending the river. Charlie keeps encouraging Rose until she nervously takes the tiller. He gently helps her try.

Once the decision to go downriver has been made and the couple are under way, Charlie resumes his lessons in navigation. He teaches Rose to steer and how to read the river for shallows and snags. Charlie also explains to Rose that they need steam power even though going downstream. Unless they move faster than the current, they cannot control the boat. The theme of what we can and cannot control resurfaces. The boat is in their control, and the river is not, but knowledge of the river may enable the couple to manage what is within their control successfully. Rose goads Charlie to try something difficult, for the sake of his country's cause. She is moving him to take moral principles seriously and to place less importance on his bodily pleasures. At the same time, Charlie is teaching Rose how to maneuver in the physical world. She is learning to use her body and eventually to enjoy it. Each is leading the other toward him- or herself, toward the dimension of human life that they enjoy and in which they are at home. Love begins in encouraging the other person to see him- or herself as capable of positive change.

The discussion Charlie and Rose have concerning the river voyage also contains a symbolic reference to names. The river is called the Ulanga until the strong rapids, after which its name is the Bora. Charlie points this out in hopes of dissuading Rose, to show that people thought there were two rivers, so severe a demarcation are the rapids. But for Charlie and Rose, the large rapids will be a transition of transformation, delineating when they fall in love. The change in names for the river will signify their magnificent change, expressed in the new terms of endearment they will have for one another.

Aboard the boat, Charlie scurries to the boiler and administers a series of quick, little kicks. He explains that one of his native mates dropped a screwdriver in the boiler, and he has to kick it to avoid an explosive clogging. When Rose suggests removing the screwdriver, Charlie says he kind of likes kicking the boiler. Referring to the African Queen, he says, "She's all I've got." The marital implications of this phrase resonate through the story's finale. The boat is like Charlie's wife, about whom he often speaks with affection and admiration, even to the effect that the Germans would "love to get their hands on her." Kicking the boiler is a demonstration of Charlie's fondness, a way for him to "stay in touch" with the life force of his vessel.

The wrecking of the African Queen at the end of the film can be viewed as making way for Rose as Charlie's partner for the journey he will take into his new life. Rose has already replaced his native shipmates, who have been frightened off by the drum messages of German hostility. Corresponding to the initial destruction of Rose's home and family, the climactic demolition of the African Queen brings to an end Charlie's miniature kingdom. With the death of his beloved Queen, Charlie is symbolically released to the human companionship of a wife.

Charlie and Rose get to know one another by talking about what their lives were like before they came to Africa. Charlie initiates the exchange of histories, a hint of his need for conversation and sociability, which soon proves pivotal to the plot. Rose recalls the peace and quiet of Sundays in England, while Charlie remembers lively Saturday nights, "rubbing elbows" amidst a crowd of jostling, noisy revelers. Yet each of them is amenable to the tastes of the other person. Charlie is quite happy to wait the war out in a calm backwater, and Rose is soon to enjoy an exciting, noisy experience of her own.

After Charlie navigates down the first, smaller rapids, he asks Rose how she liked it. His hopes of scaring her out of continuing the river journey are soon dashed, however, as she replies, "Kind of a dream." Enrapt and patting her face, Rose elaborates: "I never dreamed . . . I never dreamed any mere physical experience could be so stimulating." The rapid descent, the cool water spray, and the danger have in fact awakened Rose from a dreamy life of quiet, sermonized Sundays. Her senses are coming alive.

The exhilaration of Rose's river run alludes to her previous lack of sensuous receptivity. The fact that Rose repeats the phrase "never dreamed" may also speak to her lack of imagination. Imagination integrates mind with body, as intellect combines past sense experiences or extrapolates from past experience to future possibilities. Rose's imagination has lain dormant partly because her senses have not been supplying it with material with which to work. More broadly, Rose has "never dreamed" of what she has the potential to become. Rose will come to entertain a new image of herself, stimulated by loving interaction with Charlie.

Receptivity to what is going on around us, especially sensitivity to the circumstances and needs of other people, is necessary to various moral virtues. Had Rose and her brother been more aware of the interests and needs of the African natives to whom they thought to minister, for instance, their mission might have contributed more to the lives of the natives. Recall the early scene at which the missionary brother and sister entertain Charlie, and his stomach, at tea. James Fultz construes the composition of the camera shot as representing the source of Rose's lack of openness in the conventions of middle-class, religious life. "The tight framing of the three at the tea table, and the perfect balance in their placement, suggest the bourgeois rigidity and closedness of brother and sister."[20]

Since the exciting sensations of the rapids are predominantly tactile and kinesthetic, we might conjecture that Rose has been "out of touch"—with other people and with her own physical nature. She has been closed off from other individuals and from her self, in a way Charlie, pleased to "rub elbows" with other people and to kick the African Queen's boiler, is not. The river and Charlie are opening Rose to physical and interpersonal possibilities of which she has not dreamt. The quickening of Rose's senses also suggests that she is emerging from a prior dullness of personality, a lack of vivacity or joy. We are reminded of the dull, plodding way Rose played the organ and sang hymns for her brother's congregation. Rose may be starting to develop the virtue of joyfulness or vitality. It is a virtue that can promote other virtues, such as hopefulness and perseverance, both of which Rose will need as the story unfolds.

That evening, Charlie gets drunk and reneges on his agreement to go down the river to sink the German ship, the Louisa. When he denies that he had ever agreed to the expedition, Rose accuses him of being a liar and a coward. Charlie self-pityingly replies that Rose is not a lady, presumably for speaking so harshly to him. He then lashes out, calling her a "crazy, psalm-singing, skinny, old maid." Only Rose's chin quivers as she absorbs this stinging rebuke, but it probably cuts deep, in that Charlie's outburst echoes the earlier derision of Rose's womanhood by her brother.

As Samuel lay dying, he spoke deliriously of Rose not being "comely among the maidens," but still fit to serve the Lord. At the time, Rose's face registered an unhappy sentiment—a mixture of injury, resentment, disappointment, and resignation.[21] The implication is that in giving up on the hope of realizing her female nature in conjugal love, Rose has retreated from her body altogether. She represses her womanhood, denying her body and the pleasures it can provide. The film thereby points to gender and sensuality as other facets of our human nature we cannot overcome without sacrificing additional valuable features of our humanity.

Come morning, Charlie awakens to the sight of Rose dumping out his gin. He makes no effort to stop her but only moans, "Oh, have pity, Miss." Charlie's anger of the night before is replaced by meekness, and his attempts to placate Rose for his drunken tirade. He shaves and remarks how good it is to have a lady aboard to set a man a good example. Charlie wants Rose to see how he is quite literally cleaning up his act, but she just ignores his palaver. He keeps praising her in hopes of ending her coolness toward him. Although Charlie is talking simply to get back in Rose's good graces, he speaks more truly than he realizes.

Commenting on how good he will look when rid of his stubble, Charlie tells Rose that she will hardly recognize him. Little does he know that he will be changed, in nonphysical ways, almost beyond self-recognition. The shaving is a cinematic figure of the transformation that is soon to come, for Rose does indeed set Charlie an example. Her ideals and expectations of him give Charlie something to strive for and live up to. He will come to see a brighter image of himself in Rose's gaze. As Charlie's beloved, Rose will be a mirror to his soul. The reflection Charlie now sees of his smooth, clean visage in the shaving mirror foretells the more virtuous vision of himself he will come to honor, one to which Charlie would never have "dreamed" he could aspire.

But for now, Charlie's efforts at thawing Rose are getting him nowhere. He tries to excuse himself for overindulging the previous night, claiming that "it's only human nature." Rose loftily delivers her riposte: "Nature, Mr. Allnutt, is what we're put in this world to rise above." Her high-minded admonition inverts Charlie's smiling resignation at tea over his stomach's rumbling, about which, he asserted, there was nothing he could do. Charlie and Rose each have half the human story right. The work of their love will be to teach their half of it to the other, making each a more complete person.

There are some things we cannot do anything about and should not try to change. Genuine human needs, like Charlie's need for human conversation and friendliness, cannot be denied successfully. People also need humor and beauty. After Rose and Charlie fall in love, Charlie clowns around to amuse Rose, and the moonstruck couple admire the loveliness of flowers along the riverbank. To try to overcome or suppress these human needs is self-destructive, humiliating the spirit along with the flesh. On the other hand, Rose correctly argues that we must try to overcome corrosive aspects of our nature. The temptation to overindulge our appetites or to break faith with another person when it suits us is a weakness that should be resisted. What we see in the evolving relationship between Charlie and Rose is how romantic love helps us sort out this crucial difference between fulfilling our humanity and resisting our baser natures.

Unlike many of the more turbulent turning points, the scene of Charlie trying to reestablish civility with Rose marks a subtle, but critical, transition in their relationship. Charlie and Rose communicate their needs and their philosophies. Charlie relents from devoting himself to bodily appetite and safety. He apologizes for his drunken behavior but pleads for social intercourse, saying, "Fair is fair, you need to say something." Rose explains that what is angering her is his going back on his word to travel downriver in order to incapacitate the Louisa. Frustrated, Charlie yells that he is taking his promise back, but it is so much bluster, as he immediately accedes to her wishes.

Charlie's need for conversation and companionship enables Rose to blackmail him emotionally. The film suggests that this is a part of human nature above which we cannot rise. We need friendship to develop our character and to be happy. Rose has these needs as much as Charlie does. We infer that the deprivation of the warmth and intercourse of romantic friendship that Rose suffers have begun to wither her.

On the other hand, Charlie's reneging on his promise is what provokes Rose's blackmail, and this indicates another human need. We need to be able to trust one another. Human community requires adhering to moral standards of speech, such as keeping our promises—a theme we will find more fully developed in the film *Rob Roy*. If you wish me to speak with you, Rose is implying, you must speak truly and not go back on your word. Although Charlie's need for sociability is one that cannot be denied, Rose is teaching him that moral rules govern language use, at least where she is concerned.

Ascending into Love

As they wend their way downriver to face Fort Shona and the more serious rapids, Rose and Charlie are approaching the film's defining moment—when they fall in love. No sooner do they manage to squeak by the rifle fire from the fort than they must face the rapids. The quickening cinematic pace of the storytelling appears to accelerate the pair's emotional involvement. Hurtling down the rapids, Charlie and Rose work as a team. They man the tiller together, then Rose takes over as Charlie keeps the boiler working. He then dashes over to help her steer. In a rush, the ordeal is done, and they both start exclaiming about their victories over human enemy and natural peril.

Yelling and smiling, Charlie embraces Rose as they merrily twirl. Charlie takes off Rose's hat and throws it in the air, as if to bare her to nature, and to bare a concealed part of her nature so that it can take flight. Rose will go hatless throughout the rest of the story. When Charlie plants a kiss on her lips, Rose returns it. They quickly sober. The couple look in each other's eyes with a dawning apprehension of what is happening to them. Each realizes that they share a new appreciation for and attraction to the other.

Charlie and Rose become self-conscious, aware of themselves as objects of romantic love and sexual attraction. They also perceive the mutuality of their awareness. Following Sartre, Thomas Nagel calls this process "reflexive mutual recognition" and claims that "the proliferation of levels of mutual awareness" accounts for the complexity of which human relationships alone are capable.[22] The film depicts Charlie and Rose silenced by the recognition of each other's perception of mutual awareness. In their shy looks and bashful turning away from one another, these levels of self-reflexivity are swiftly, cinematically telescoped.

The film portrays falling in love happening in a single revelatory moment of mutual recognition. Although this provides dramatic punch, it is liable to obscure how the scene of amorous disclosure and discovery actually resolves a choppy, complex interaction during which Charlie and Rose have been unreflectively promoting one another's virtue. The story of the couple's journey implies that individuals fall in love when their shared experiences have built up to it. Of course, in ordinary life, there well may not be a definitive instant of falling in love, and it might not be mutual either. *The African Queen* plays upon our idealized notion of falling in love as an instantaneous melting into one another. But the film tempers this popular view by showing how Charlie and Rose began the work of fostering one another's moral growth before their "collapse of ego boundaries."

Recall how Rose has elicited Charlie's sense of honor and patriotism and how she forces him to be a man of his word. Charlie, in turn, has helped enliven Rose's sense of embodiment, loosening the rigidity and fears that bind her. Each of the lovers has been bringing the other person closer to his or her own habitual dimension of humanity. The result is that Rose has become less prissy and reserved and Charlie has broken from his habit of putting his appetites first—enabling him to meet nautical and military challenge with courage.

When Charlie and Rose fall in love, or recognize that they are in love, they see themselves as ennobled by one another. Each enables the other person to see her- or himself developing into a finer individual. In Charlie's warm regard, Rose sees herself as a physical, sensuous woman—competent to handle a boat or a man. Rose provides Charlie with a reflection of himself as a valiant soldier fighting in a just war. The fresh visage of Charlie, which Rose had prompted him to shave into view, was a harbinger of the revised portrait of his inner self her love would help craft. Imagining the wonderful things possible with this new person, the lovers "weave two futures together and thereby form a union of two selves."23 Rose and Charlie are as flushed with the prospect of what their lives can be together as they are with their triumphs over Fort Shona and the rapids. They view each other as someone with whom they can fully realize their new and improved selves. They are imagining the narrative of a "rosy" future together, a "romance."

During their kiss, the music modulates from the up-tempo, brassy, triumphant strains that had accompanied their celebration to a lyrical passage, thick with strings. Charlie and Rose are in tune with one another, yet they both look disturbed, perhaps by the sense that something strange is upon them. A wonderful and slightly fearful force has been loosed. When Charlie and Rose look away from each other and into themselves, they are clearly wondering about their recently revealed feelings of affection and attraction. But the couple may also be noticing other changes in themselves as well. Their mutual regard implies that Charlie and Rose are really seeing each other for the first time. The inner worth each perceives in the other person is accompanied by a change in how they see each other physically.

When Charlie previously described Rose as a "skinny old maid," he had been drunk. His eyes and mind were clouded by booze, an occasion that stands for the pervasive distortions of a life spent in self-indulgence. Charlie's perception of Rose, himself, and the world had been blurry because of his comfortable habits of carnal indulgence. The first throes of love are a clarifying experience, and as love grows, so does the clarity of the lovers' vision of one another and the world.

Rose is wet with the river whose natural energy appears to have quickened her own physical and emotional nature. It echoes the earlier scene in which Charlie and Rose bathed in the river at the same time. Charlie had preserved propriety by suggesting that they wash up at opposite ends of the boat and that they not look at each other. Again bathed by the river, the two of them now look at each another. We see the physical changes Rose and Charlie enjoy in each other. Rose's priggish manner and Charlie's loutish demeanor have been replaced by an outward softening that appears to begin with an inner warmth. Rose and Charlie are lit from within and glow.

Gone is the dried out, censorious lady of reserve. Instead, Charlie sees a bonnetless, physically attractive woman, sparkling with water and exuberance. Eugene Archer observes that as a result of deliberate modification in camera angles and shots, Rose appears "soft and supple," metamorphosing from her previous persona, in which she was "seemingly composed entirely of angular planes [all knees, elbows, and cheekbones]."[24] As if revitalized by the water and sunned by Charlie's love, "Rose blooms."[25]

Charlie has been prepared for this moment by Rose's strength and pluck in handling the tiller during the roller-coaster ride down the rapids. Rose has been similarly readied for seeing Charlie in a new light by the bravery he exhibits in fixing the boiler hose while under fire from Fort Shona. While shooting the rapids, Charlie also came to Rose's aid by swiftly pulling off a wet tarp that impeded her steering the boat. Charlie's celebratory removal of Rose's hat is thus immediately presaged in his uncovering Rose from the confines of the tarp. Both acts free her from constraints on her physical nature.

The smitten couple carry on, in a haze of euphoria. Rose quietly, hesitantly, asks whether her handling of the boat was all right. Turning away with a shy, knowing expression, Charlie replies, "Yes, Miss. It was better than all right, Miss." He then changes the subject to fuel. The dreamy pair tend to the boat, swooning with the delight of being near one another. Rose works the bilge pump and Charlie helps her from behind, nuzzling her and saying she should not wear herself out. Catching himself mooning, Charlie steps away, as Rose pumps absentmindedly, following Charlie with her starry-eyed gaze. During this romantic interlude, violins play a sweet, pastoral melody and talk turns to the beauty of flowers they have never seen before.[26] As if inadvertently, Charlie casually rests his hand on Rose's shoulder. Rose seems breathless, atremble. She puts her hand on top of Charlie's, without looking at him. As Charlie leans toward her, Rose slowly inclines her head, eyes still averted, and they embrace and kiss.

From now on, Charlie and Rose will be able to name their relationship and feelings for one another. Just as the river changes names from the Ulanga to the Bora, they will now speak to each other in terms of endearment. The journey down the river has taken them away from their old lives, in which "Miss" and "Mr. Allnutt" interacted. Now they will be Charlie (or dear) and Rosie (or Rosie old girl). The couple will also realize how and why they are helping one another and take joy in caring more about the other person than about themselves. The self-consciousness entrained by the epiphany of love will inform their mutual moral edification, where before the two of them promoted one another's virtues less purposefully because less knowingly.

The next morning, Charlie talks of returning to this beautiful spot after they wreck the Louisa. When Rose asks whether he thinks they can do it, Charlie replies: "Do it? Of course we can do it! Nothing a man can't do if he believes in himself." Rose has helped Charlie believe in himself through her expectations and faith in him. He is developing the virtues of self-respect and self-confidence. Rose's love and support clearly fortify Charlie to see himself able to accomplish what he once thought impossible. Reassured, Rose says, "Thank heaven for your strength"—a far cry from her previous scolding of Charlie for cowardice!

From the earliest scenes, Charlie has been making little jokes, often with animal references. He speaks of his stomach as if it were a hyena when it grumbles; he sarcastically points to crocodiles getting ready for their supper (of Charlie and Rose); and he cautions against hitting hippopotami, saying there is only room for two in the boat! Having fallen in love, however, Charlie's humor becomes even broader and less restrained. He shows off for Rose, and she howls with girlish glee as Charlie mimics first the hippos and then the monkeys.

It is human nature to laugh and to share laughter with those we love. The human ability to imitate other animals may also speak to our protean nature—to adapt, to express, even to overcome our own weakness. Although not a moral excellence, a sense of humor, whether active or receptive, is certainly a social virtue. It is one that can also augment moral virtues, such as courage, by enabling us to do the difficult thing. Laughing to relieve tension, or to put danger in perspective, helps us persevere through hardship. Humor can also relax us enough so that we can use our ingenuity to solve thorny problems.[27] The film shows how romantic love inspires us to flights of fancy and silliness, as well as to feats of courage. Moreover, Rose's giggling is further evidence of her feeling at home in her body; she quakes and shakes with childish delight at Charlie's antics.

Love at Work

Love is about sharing: sharing food and dreams, humor and hardships, bodies and dangers. In the sharing, lovers can help each other develop as moral individuals. They bring out the best in each other, functioning as critic, booster, helpmeet, or audience—as Rose is for Charlie's animal impersonations. But the couple's amorous, humorous respite is short-lived, as the African Queen suddenly comes upon an unanticipated, violent waterfall. The lovers survive, barely, and the serious damage to the boat bears out Charlie's misgivings about the voyage. Charlie is skeptical of Rose's optimistic suggestion that they mend the twisted propeller shaft. Rose persists, speculating that perhaps the shaft can be worked on without taking the boat out of the water. She tells how she once saw a native work with metal on stone, over a charcoal fire. While Charlie mulls the idea, Rose coaxes him, lightly and brightly, saying, "Why don't you try it?"

Charlie explains how a straightened shaft will soon become twisted as a result of the lack of balance between the propeller blades. Unperturbed, Rose calmly states that they will have to make a new blade and weld it to the propeller. Rose's solicitous demeanor in discussing their options departs markedly from her previous imperious manner in demanding that they go downriver to attack the Louisa. The durable flintiness of her character has been alloyed with a softer, more precious quality. In response to Rose's gentle promptings, Charlie chuckles at her hopefulness and rich supply of ideas, instead of railing about the craziness of her suggestions, as he had earlier.[28]

Over Charlie's protest, Rose joins him under the boat to wrench off the propeller and then works the bellows for the improvised smithy. She pumps air for her lover to repair their makeshift mobile home, where once she pumped air to play her brother's staid church organ. Using her body to fix something physical replaces Rose's former spiritual work. Moreover, she and Charlie are successful in restoring the boat to meet their physical needs and accomplish their higher, military-political goal. In contrast, Rose and her brother were not able to minister to the spiritual needs of the natives. Dirty and toiling away, Rose is Charlie's friend and helpmeet. Helping him repair the shaft and replace the propeller blade, Rose is also helping him develop such virtues as discipline, industry, and cooperation. Instead of satisfying his bodily appetites, Charlie is pushing his body to extremes in straining to achieve a selfless goal. Using the ingenuity of their minds and the sweat of their brows, the couple finally secure the repaired parts under water, a model of teamwork.

The lovers make explicit their mutual esteem and their appreciation for the help each provides in the other's growth. Lying together cozily in the stern of the boat, steering and talking, Charlie asks Rose whether she is proud of herself.[29] Instead of dwelling on her cleverness in getting the African Queen shipshape, she focuses on Charlie. She says, "I don't think there's another man alive who could have done it." Charlie points out that his triumph is inseparable from hers: "Right you are, Rosie. 'Cause no other man alive's got you!"

Charlie proceeds to describe Rose's navigating over the falls as heroic—"Head up, chin out, hair blowin' in the wind." Basking and blushing in his praise, Rose laughs at the thought of being a heroine and tells Charlie that he has lost his mind. Their joint labor in fixing the boat is the mundane complement to their dramatic work together in maneuvering by the fort, down the rapids, and over the falls. What sets this movie apart from so many romantic adventure films is that the lovers help each other do difficult things together and develop morally as a result. Moreover, they prevail not only in spectacular straits, as couples typically do in adventure fictions, but also in more ordinary, workaday difficulties.

The cooperative effort in repairing the African Queen is the second episode of quiet transformation. It parallels the earlier conversation about human nature and truthfulness, which results in Charlie sincerely acquiescing to the voyage. These transformative transitions flank the more thrilling, dangerous escapades that culminate in the drama of their falling in love. Falling in love is not itself a moral transformation; however, it caps off the moral work of love that has been quietly unfolding and brings to the lovers' awareness how it will continue. As the couple work together, they purposely devote themselves to the welfare of one another.

Although many of the virtues Charlie and Rose develop are complementary, they both become more attentive, considerate, and appreciative. Charlie and Rose worry about each other and appreciate what the other person does. They are ennobled by caring about one another and by the interest they take in each other's well-being. Shulamith Firestone describes the enrichment, brought about by love, as resulting from "each enlarging himself through the other: instead of being one, locked in the cell of himself with only his own experience and view, he could participate in the existence of another."[30] As we shall see, in what Rose calls their "first fight," each is more concerned for the beloved's safety than for his or her own welfare.

Again in contrast to the high-voltage exploits upstream, the couple must now contend with the nagging, debilitating obstacles of black flies and slackened current. Under attack by black flies, Charlie first covers Rose to protect her and then gets the boat away from shore. We are reminded how, going down the rapids, Charlie freed Rose from a wet tarp that was an impediment at the time. In uncovering and covering Rose, Charlie is alternately freeing her body to act or protecting it from harm.

The river soon breaks up into several, sluggish channels, one of which must be chosen. The two of them continue to act in concert, as they deliberate and decide together on which uninviting route to take. Rose steers and Charlie gives navigational direction. No matter how tired and dispirited they are, their cooperation is unflagging.

Their fears over waning progress are confirmed, and the African Queen is soon bogged down. Charlie gets into the water and pulls the boat while Rose poles them along. After pulling leeches off Charlie, Rose also slogs through the water, hacking away reeds to clear a navigable path. Exhausted, the two of them face the fact that they are aground. The earth, from which they were freed to embark on their journey, seems to have reclaimed them and cut short their new, shared life. That night, as Charlie shivers with cold or fever, Rose tells him, "You're the bravest man that ever lived." She will not let him deride himself as "a poor specimen of a man" but bucks him up to maintain his self-respect. As if sensing that Rose could blame herself for the slow death that awaits them, Charlie tells her that he is not sorry he came.

Closure and New Beginning

During the night, rains lift the African Queen out of the mud, and the couple realize they are but yards from the lake. Charlie and Rose work together in outfitting the African Queen with the homemade torpedoes Charlie has fabricated, discussing tactics for blowing up the Louisa. They quarrel over who should stay on shore, each worrying about the other's endangerment. The virtue of care has evolved especially quickly for Charlie, whose sensuous self-indulgence had been his defining characteristic. Loving interaction with Rose has led him to put his country's welfare, and Rose's safety, above his own.

We should appreciate the irony and insight contained in Rose's remark that they are having their "first fight." Of course, they fought from the beginning of their trip, but this is the first battle for the lovers "Charlie dear" and "Rosie." In calling this their first fight, Rose intimates that events are to be reckoned from when the two of them fell in love, at which time a new era began. To Rose's accusation that Charlie has lied about needing her help and losing his heart to her, Charlie capitulates, reaffirming their roles: "It'll be you at the tiller and me at the engine. Just like it was from the start."

Up until this point in the story, water has been the medium of the couple's geographical and moral progress. Not only has the river taken

Charlie and Rose from their respectively landlocked, loveless lives, but the rains freed the African Queen, and the two of them, from an earthbound death. However, as the couple head the African Queen out toward the gunboat, water betrays them. A rough storm comes up and sinks them. Charlie and Rose are taken on board the Louisa and correctly accused of being enemies of the Germans.

As Charlie and Rose are interrogated by the Germans, we are reminded of how perceiving the love another person has for us can encourage us to see our moral potential and consequently act to realize it. Brimming with pride for Charlie, Rose urges him to tell their German captors how he created the detonation device for the makeshift torpedoes that were to have been the undoing of the Louisa. She beams as he explains the mechanism of his explosive contraption. Before they are to be hanged, Charlie asks if the German captain of the ship (Peter Bull) can, and will, marry them. The officer agrees, although he finds it foolish of them to want to be married with their death impending. The story supports a contrary view.

Because the couple will be married for so short a time, the marriage is even more important as a symbol of their lives together. A momentary marriage can have only symbolic meaning. We should not underestimate the importance of marriage, in general, but especially for the social period in which the film was made. Marriage is a public announcement of the radical change in the social and political status of the partners. Contemporary audiences may find the marriage to be melodramatic excess or a "sop to popular sentiment."[31] However, the official recognition of their union symbolically conjures an implicit, absent public before whom Charlie and Rose make a lifelong commitment. They are declaring their wish to be understood as husband and wife, however short their time together. The fact that the ceremony is hastily improvised, aboard a foreign vessel, harmonizes with the improvisational quality of their shared adventure and the course their relationship has taken.

We might also note that the German military is responsible for throwing Rose and Charlie together in the first place, and now it officiates at their formal union at story's end. Foreign military power destroys the comfortable, if stagnant, pattern of their lives, but then its official authority puts a public imprimatur on their hard-earned love. The film shows that what we cannot control (or "rise above") involves both natural and human forces, including aspects of our own human natures. Successful living requires adapting to those forces, even using them to our advantage. The virtues are character traits that first enable us to recognize the things we cannot control and then help us respond to them constructively. As Charlie might say, we avoid crocodiles but request that the German military perform a wedding.

The African Queen transports Charlie and Rose, and it is home to their romantic transports. The Queen has been the vehicle of the couple's mutual transformation, but she yields to the stately Louisa as the stage of their marriage. As if to protest her displacement, by the Louisa as nautical vessel and by Rose as Charlie's companion, the African Queen shows up like a late wedding guest. The Queen's sunken hull rams the Louisa with its handcrafted torpedoes and delivers an explosive blow, thereby saving Charlie and Rose from a hanging and setting them free. The couple are now in and of the water, immersed in the cinematically figured medium of transformation.

For the second time, Rose yells, "We did it!" The first time this phrase signified the pair's twin triumphs over Fort Shona and the rapids. Now, Charlie and Rose have belatedly carried out their military mission and saved themselves in the bargain. The "we did it" can also be taken to refer to their mutual self-transformation. Charlie and Rose have helped recreate one another into stronger, more virtuous individuals.

The mutual transformation is the work of love, and *The African Queen* portrays work, tedious as well as exciting work, as the mundane context in which love performs its elevated, moral office. Navigating the gauntlet, repairing the African Queen, persevering through torpor, and destroying the German gunboat were the work during which Charlie and Rose nurtured one another's finer sensibilities and capacities for moral excellence. They have become more attentive and caring and more confident in their own abilities. They have come to love and value themselves as a result of the uplifting efforts of their helpmeets.

Smiling and doing a supine dog paddle, Charlie reprises his earlier drunken, silly song, and Rose chimes in. The picture of Rose making her way through the water, singing a little ditty with her husband, is a far cry from the opening scenes of Rose accompanying her brother in church. She is no longer perspiring, plodding through religious hymns in an attempt to reach uncomprehending, unresponsive natives. Charlie has helped Rose learn to trust and enjoy her body and the wonderful experiences it can provide. For his part, Charlie's song is sober now, and the pair are in the water because Charlie agreed to sacrifice his African Queen for patriotic ends. A synthesis of their moral virtues has made each of them more complete as a person. The closing shot of the couple moving through the water, and out of the camera frame, is an image that suggests that marriage should continue the work of love in mutual virtuous development.

Notes

1. The notion of the individual as embodying virtue, which is the true object of love, is echoed in Immanuel Kant's description of humanity, rational nature, or morality as the actual object of respect. Individuals instantiate humanity or rational nature. *Foundations of a Metaphysics of Morals*, trans. Lewis White (New York: Bobbs-Merrill, 1959), for example, Sections 429–431, 435–436.

2. Shirley Letwin, "Romantic Love and Christianity," *Philosophy* 52 (1977): 131–145, 134. Letwin goes on to note that for Aristotle, people are incapable of rationally perceiving the genuine individuality of one another. Reason can grasp only universals, or forms, as with rationality itself, which is the form of the human species (p.135).

3. Robert Solomon, *About Love* (New York: Simon and Schuster, 1988), p.203.

4. Ibid., p.206.

5. Lesley Brill, *John Huston's Filmmaking* (Cambridge: Cambridge University Press, 1997), p.57.

6. Ibid., p.61.

7. Aristotelian friendship is between equals, and Solomon's emphasis on mutuality accords with this. The film portrays Charlie and Rose as roughly on a par, their differences as complementary, rather than invidiously distinguishing between the two of them. Commenting on cinematic departures from C. S. Forester's novel, James Fultz notes that instead of Rose being Charlie's superior, the film protagonists "seem more nearly equal as partners," in "A Classic Case of Collaboration . . . *The African Queen*," *Literature/Film Quarterly* 10, no. 1 (1982): 13–24, 21. The film's reconceptualization of the literary work makes it amenable to an interpretation that stresses the romantic friendship between the main characters.

8. M. Scott Peck, *The Road Less Travelled* (New York: Simon and Schuster, 1978), p.81.

9. Soren Kierkegaard, *Works of Love*, trans. Howard Hong and Edna Hong (New York: Harper and Row, 1962), p.206.

10. Iris Murdoch, *The Sovereignty of Good* (New York: Shocken Books, 1971), p.91.

11. Solomon, *About Love*, p.256.

12. The origins of romantic love in courtly love are explicated by Irving Singer in *The Nature of Love*, vol. 2 (Chicago: University of Chicago Press, 1984–1987).

13. Solomon, *About Love*, p.148.

14. Peck, *Road Less Travelled*, p.87.

15. Aristotle, *Nicomachean Ethics,* trans. Martin Ostwald (Indianapolis: Bobbs-Merrill, 1962), 1105b.

16. C. S. Lewis, *The Four Loves* (New York: Harcourt, Brace, Jovanovich, 1960), p.136.

17. Lesley Brill believes that the natives scrambling for Charlie's discarded cigar "embodies a theme that will run through the film, the clash of spiritual and carnal needs," *John Huston's Filmmaking,* p.58. My interpretation of the film sets the opposition between the carnal and spiritual within the larger question concerning which aspects of human nature, including the bodily aspects, should be pursued and which should be overcome. I proceed to the film's exploration of romantic friendship as a context for responding to this fundamental question, which, appropriately enough, is never answered once and for all.

18. Fultz, "A Classic Case of Collaboration," p.16.

19. Where I concentrate on the contrast between water and earth, Brill insightfully examines the connections between water and fire. For example, he notes that "the mixture of water and fire is associated with overcoming obstacles [e.g., the steam powering the African Queen]. Separately, they tend to be destructive or dangerous, as in the burning of the village and the violence of the rapids," *John Huston's Filmmaking,* p.70. Brill proceeds to give other instances that bear out his thematic nugget. However, he does not relate the water and fire imagery to the relationship or to the moral development of Charlie and Rose. The imagery might be taken to suggest how void of constructive possibilities Charlie and Rose are when isolated from each other, but how creative they are when working together—as when they work the fiery forge to return the African Queen to the water.

20. Fultz, "A Classic Case of Collaboration," p.17.

21. Interpreting the film as a farce, Eugene Archer views Rose's quavering, "Chaplinesque," reaction as "the funniest death scene ever filmed," in "John Huston: The Hemingway Tradition in American Film," *Film Culture* 19 (1959): 66–101, 90. I am not sure what inclusion in the genre of farce entails, but if it entails a loss of poignancy for this scene, then I resist classifying *The African Queen* as farce. I am more sympathetic with Brill's classification of the film as a "comic romance," taking romance to signify lively adventure, but not necessarily involving love.

22. Thomas Nagel, "Sexual Perversion," in *Moral Problems,* 1st ed., ed. James Rachels (New York: Harper and Row, 1971), p.77.

23. Solomon, *About Love,* p.165.

24. Archer, "John Huston: The Hemingway Tradition," p.90.

25. Brill, *John Huston's Filmmaking,* p.59.

26. Richard Jameson comments on the Edenic aspect of this scene, noting that the flowers are "those . . . that maybe no one had ever seen until Charlie and Rose became lovers," in "John Huston," (reprinted from *Film Comment,* May 1980), in

Perspectives on John Huston, ed. Stephen Cooper (New York: G. K. Hall, 1994), pp.37–88, p.65. Jameson also notes a biblical allusion to the Great Flood. The rains that lift the African Queen from the weedy delta also sweep downriver "half the species in Creation" (p.65).

27. In discussing *Groundhog Day,* we saw how Phil Connors used humor as an auxiliary to such moral virtues as kindness and friendliness. When we examine the film *Parenthood,* in the next chapter, we will see how humor and playfulness enter more deeply into the moral virtues.

28. Aware that Katharine Hepburn is Rose, we might notice how Rose's change from a scalding critic to a helping partner is reminiscent of a speech in *The Philadelphia Story* (1940). In that speech, Dexter (Cary Grant) tells Tracy (Hepburn) that she should have been less of a "scold" and more of a "helpmeet" during their (now defunct) marriage. Similarly, when a drunken Charlie calls Rose a "skinny old maid," we may remember Spencer Tracy's character telling a companion, in *Pat and Mike* (1952), that there isn't much meat on her (Hepburn's character), but that what's there is "choice." Unlike many, often illuminating, film analyses, mine do not explore the relationship between actor and character or how knowing an actor's stardom or previous films can affect an audience's current experience. However, having called attention to the parallels between Hepburn in *The African Queen* and in her other roles, I might add that the parallels highlight two important aspects of the transformative power of love: appearance and inter-action. Charlie sees a "choice" svelteness in place of a skinny old maid, and Rose's scolding has given way to supportive encouragement.

29. Notice how the image of the couple relaxing in the rear of the boat has re-placed the opening shot of a reclining Charlie, alone (except for a native servant) and delighting in bodily pleasures.

30. Shulamith Firestone, "Love in a Sexist Society" (reprinted from Firestone's *The Dialectic of Sex*), in *Eros, Agape, and Philia,* ed. Alan Soble (New York: Paragon House, 1989), pp.29–39, p.30.

31. Fultz, "A Classic Case of Collaboration," p.19. Obviously, I think that Fultz errs in seeing the marriage, added to the published script, as a narrative lia-bility. Fultz can find no redeeming thematic value in this scene or in other con-cluding "wildly implausible" plot twists, such as the fluke destruction of the Louisa. Bosley Crowther, among other reviewers, concurs with Fultz's assessment of the story's climax (*New York Times,* February 21, 1952).

4

The Virtues of
Parenthood

Central Virtues

Expanding our context for the development and exercise of the virtues, we move from the dyadic interaction found in the romantic friendship of *African Queen* to the larger context of family. In Ron Howard's film *Parenthood* (1989), we examine the dialectic interplay between parents and children, as the process of child-rearing affects the virtues and vices of both. Keeping with the title of the film, my emphasis is on how child-rearing affects the moral character of parents. I am drawn in this direction because the impact of parents on their children has been so much studied, and it is more obvious than the influence of child-rearing on parental virtue and vice. When I do examine the virtues and vices of the children in the film, it is with an eye to what these moral strengths and flaws reveal about the parents who fostered them.

Being a parent is not necessary for developing the virtues that I find illustrated in *Parenthood,* although some of the vices may be unique to parenthood. However, the responsibilities, demands, and opportunities afforded by raising children, especially in the nuclear family typical in contemporary Western societies, all but guarantee that parents will develop some version of the relevant virtues—or their correlative vices. The experiences and relationships are extreme, like warfare or cutting-edge science, and as such create a crucible that is bound to modify the character of those involved. The virtues are constitutive of good parents, and the corresponding vices make parents deficient in rearing their children.

Parenthood: Garry phones his father as Helen watches with a sinking heart.

Within its humorous incidents and dialogue, *Parenthood* manages to cover a great deal of moral ground. In fact, a sense of humor itself seems to be one of the virtues the film finds entwined in the best rearing of children.

Child-rearing involves a tension between protecting children and fostering their growth and independence from us. Cushioning the blows our children are bound to receive must be complemented by helping to prepare them to meet the world on its own terms. Complicating the work of raising children is the fact that not only do the children change but the world changes as well. Consequently, parents cannot always rely on what has worked in the past as they respond to their children's growth. Parents must adapt to great changes—in their children, the world, and in their children's relationship to the world.

The complex virtue that enables parents to deal successfully with their children in a changing, sometimes threatening, world is a kind of interpersonal adaptability. *Parenthood* shows why social adaptability is valuable throughout the radical alterations that occur during the parent-child relationship and into the child's adulthood. It is the central moral virtue of the film. Most of the other virtues of parenthood enter into social adaptability or contribute to its full realization. For example, the story illustrates how the moral virtues of attentiveness and humility are essential to social adaptability. In its overall tone and through its characters, *Parenthood* also recommends the nonmoral virtues of cheerfulness and playfulness as auxiliary to parental adaptability. Because adaptability is so pivotal to the film's vision of virtue, I usually discuss the other virtues and vices of the characters in relation to this cardinal excellence of parenthood.

Social relationships, and life in general, require the ability and willingness to adapt to change. Without this flexibility, we cannot flourish. The adaptability demanded of a parent, however, is more strenuous, if not singular. It is the disposition to modify our attitudes, perceptions, and behavior in response to the gradually developing autonomy of a being dependent on us for its existence. Parental adaptability implies a readiness to be self-abrogating: to work for the very autonomy that will render parents less needed and present in their children's lives. As children develop, parents must alter their perspective on how they view themselves, their children, and their relationships with the children.

Other arenas of social adaptability include the capacity to work constructively with those very different from us; the ability to persevere in an important relationship despite serious obstacles such as separation or tragedy; and the disposition to make new friends or get along with neighbors. Rearing a family is privileged with regard to this social adaptability for several reasons. For one thing, no other relationship demands the degree of adaptation to change in the other person, as well as to change in the nature of the relationship itself. Consider the extremes of caring for a helpless baby, on the one hand, and respectfully listening to financial advice from a knowledgeable forty-year-old, on the other.

Interpersonal adaptability includes the ability of parents to see what may be positive in a situation and make the most of it. It goes beyond passive tolerance or gritty endurance (both of which may also be virtues) by requiring social effort, sometimes creative effort. The personalities, needs, and interests of family members dictate what specific accommodations interpersonal adaptability asks of us. It may call for us to make allowances for our child's lack of scholastic interest or for us to be supportive of a child's newfound talent. We have to modify our expectations and behavior to meet the needs of others. We must also increasingly give up control of our children and teach them to take intelligent risks.

Accommodating the needs and interests of family members has a complement that is self-oriented: the ability to develop ourselves within, and by means of, our family relationships. We must look for ways of realizing our own interests and talents within the specific shape our family takes. Ideally, the two dimensions of interpersonal adaptability, accommodation and self-realization, are mutually enhancing, so that we are able to grow in the course of accommodating the needs of others. Not surprisingly, this virtue is more likely to be encouraged in any particular family member to the extent that it is displayed by others.

Interpersonal adaptability is a virtue of orientation, orienting us toward other people and orienting us toward ourselves in relation to them. It thereby functions nonepisodically, as a prevailing attitude, discriminating what we see and emphasize, what we appreciate and are moved to respond to. In this respect, interpersonal adaptability is akin to virtues like generosity or piety—directing our typical ways of perceiving, thinking, feeling, and acting.

Parents fail to adapt socially to their children when they try to mold children to meet their own needs. The vice of vicarious projection, popularized in the stage mother and the sports-crazy father, seems one to which parents are especially vulnerable. Because parents invest so much time, energy, and emotion in raising their children, it is natural that they have a vested interest in who or what the child becomes. Aristotle captures parental investment in children by likening children to the products of craftsmen. He further expresses parental identification with children in describing children as part of their parents.[1] Vicarious projection necessarily involves a concomitant failure of parents to realize the virtue of attentiveness. When we project our hopes or plans onto our progeny, we necessarily fail to notice the children's own makeup. We cannot adapt to how our children are changing, or failing to change, if we are wrapped up in our vision of what we want for them.

In *Parenthood*, Nathan is the most blatant example of a parent in the grip of vicarious projection. His own academic failure impels him to try to mold his preschool daughter, Patty, into a genius. As a result, it never occurs to Nathan that Patty may have interests or desires of her own, and he is unable to see how his systematic education is depriving her of opportunities for healthy development. Dedicated to his vision of what Patty should become, Nathan can only see how much progress Patty is making or where she is lagging.

Another alternative to interpersonal adaptability is the vice of unreflective acceptance. Affirmation of children may be so zealous that parents deceive themselves about their offspring's shortcomings or about the truly onerous nature of parental duties. People with this vice are often incapable of acknowledging their own needs or choices. They defer too readily to their children, submerging their identities within the family and its requirements. Parents who are uncritically accepting of their children demand too little for themselves apart from their role in their children's lives. Although he is far from being uncritically accepting of his daughter, Nathan exhibits a variant of this defect in that, apart from being Patty's mentor, he seems to have no life of his own.

At the opposite extreme is the rejection or denial of family. Either because of difficulties in dealing with our children or because of our self-conception, we repudiate our relationship with them. Such repudiation may serve the parents' need to see themselves as free of relationships or parental duties, or it could be the response to failure as a parent. A good example of someone who rejects a family relationship, although not a child, is Pip, in Dickens's *Great Expectations*. Pip disavows Joe, his loving brother-in-law, because of his own ambitions and misplaced shame.[2]

In *Parenthood*, Garry's absentee father has so distanced himself from Garry that he doesn't even recognize his voice on the telephone. In both rejecting the family and submerging oneself within it, the individual is unrealistic about the relationship between him- or herself and the family. In contrast to the vices of parenthood, the virtues have at their core realistic perception.

The moral space between vicarious projection and unreflective acceptance can be occupied by another disposition besides the virtue of interpersonal adaptability—grudging acceptance. Grudging acceptance is not so much opposed to the virtue, the way a genuine vice is, as it is an attenuated or truncated variation on interpersonal adaptability. In grudging acceptance, we bemoan our fate but don't disown our responsibilities. We passively accept our children as burdens (as well they may be), and merely as burdens (which we need not let happen). We unenthusiastically go to the family gathering and suffer the faults of our offspring or other family members. For most of the film, Frank seems to take this attitude toward his mother-in-law (Grandma) and his son Gil. Grudging acceptance also characterizes Larry's attitude toward his own son, Cool, although Larry can also be construed as rejecting Cool, most decisively at the conclusion of the story. In grudging acceptance, it's as if the individual dimly recognizes the value of interpersonal adaptability but resists the wholehearted effort it requires.

In order to adapt to our children as they grow, and grow out of our care, we must pay attention to who and what they are independent of ourselves. This is the virtue of realistic attentiveness, to which I have alluded. Attentiveness is the disposition to pay attention to other people out of concern for their well-being, as in, "He is very attentive to her needs." Attentiveness is disinterested, not infected with desire or the imposition of one's own needs. When we are attentive, we are realistic, noticing what is actually going on. Speaking of undemanding love, George Nakhnikian describes the realism of which I speak as "being disposed to accept [the other person] as he is, not as we imagine him to be or as we would wish him to be."[3]

The virtue of attentiveness incorporates our ability to register what other people are doing on their own terms instead of filtered by our interests. Where children are concerned, it may take effort for parents not to impose their interpretation, or fantasy, on what they perceive their children to be doing. Attentiveness means taking up the child's behavior and speech from his or her point of view, and this is sometimes painful, as when a child is having problems or makes a decision of which parents disapprove.[4]

No parent is perfect or sees his or her children without prejudice, but to the extent that we see children in a distorted way, to that *extent* we are guilty of inattentiveness. We are attending more to our own needs or wishes for our offspring. The failure to see realistically results from some degree of lack of concern for the child, as we are truly more concerned with ourselves. As noted earlier, vicarious projection entails inattention. Focused on their own goals for their children, parents cannot see who or what their children are. Vicariously projecting parents are incapable of acknowledging what their children wish for themselves, where their talents may actually lie, or what they truly value. Parental visions of what their children should become inevitably obscure the reality of who they are.[5]

Failure in attentiveness can also simply be neglect, the counterpart (for attention) to rejection (with regard to adaptation). Parents are neglectful for a variety of reasons, ranging from self-absorption to some deeper need to deny the place of children, or family, in their lives. *Parenthood* begins with Gil's fabricated memory of his father's neglect. The impact of Frank's neglect of Gil has ramifications for Gil's self-conscious decisions with regard to his own parenthood. In its portrayal of Gil, the film suggests that parents who felt neglected as children may compensate by becoming hyper-responsible for the well-being of their own children.

Interpersonal adaptability also presupposes the moral virtue of humility, particularly as it is shaped by parental responsibilities. As Sara Ruddick describes it, "Humility is a metaphysical attitude one takes toward a world beyond one's control."[6] Less grandly interpreted, humble individuals take an accurate view of the world beyond their control in that they keep their own abilities in proper perspective. On Norvin Richards's analysis, individuals who are humble have a sense of themselves that is accurate and firm enough to "resist temptations to overestimate" themselves or their accomplishments.[7]

Humility is essential to raising children because parents must deal with the fact that they cannot protect their children from all harm. In addition, parents must accept their ever-diminishing control over children who are becoming increasingly self-governing and involved in a world outside the home. Balancing parental acceptance of a limited role in their children's fortunes is parental awareness of the opportunities that exist for helping their children. To adapt to their children's natures and their circumstances, parents need to acknowledge what they cannot control and then act within those recognized constraints.

Parents who assume too much credit for their children's successes or failures are guilty of lacking humility, even though they may not lack love or compassion. The arrogance that most dramatizes lack of parental humility is flamboyantly reflected in Nathan, who tries to engineer his child's life.[8] However less arrogantly, Gil feels excessive responsibility for his children's welfare, and this also bespeaks a lack of proper appreciation for his role in his offspring's lives. Gil's hyper-responsibility for his son's happiness masks, but nevertheless manifests, a lack of humility in that Gil falsely believes that he can make Kevin happy. Helen, on the other hand, struggles with the conflict between trying to protect her teenage daughter, Julie, and accepting the limits of her control over Julie's life. Only when Helen is able to realize parental humility is she able to plumb her considerable resources for interpersonal adaptability and actually help Julie.

Auxiliary Virtues

Interpersonal adaptability, attentiveness, and humility are the moral virtues of parenthood central to the film. But *Parenthood* also does a good job of showing how an array of auxiliary, nonmoral virtues supports these central virtues. Auxiliary virtues, such as amiability, are character traits that often facilitate acting on moral virtues or make acting on these virtues more efficacious.[9] The auxiliary virtues endorsed by *Parenthood* cluster around a lighthearted enjoyment of life, especially its vicissitudes.

The nonmoral virtue most closely connected to interpersonal adaptability is cheerfulness. Within the context of child-rearing, Sara Ruddick specifies it as resilient cheerfulness, a "matter-of-fact willingness to continue, . . . to welcome life despite its conditions."[10] For parents, paramount among life's conditions are the dangers that seem poised to strike their children from every direction, as well as the inevitable disappointments children must suffer. People who possess resilient cheerfulness are realistic about the difficul-

ties their children face. Ruddick cites Spinoza's observation that cheerfulness "increases and assists the power of action."[11] We need clear-sighted
cheerfulness in order to summon up the strength to act on behalf of our
children, within the limited abilities and circumstances kept in perspective
by our humility, of course. *Parenthood* suggests that cheerfulness is practically indispensable if parents are to adapt to the often disconcerting changes
in their children and to those changes left in their children's wake.

Ruddick refers to the vice that corresponds to resilient cheerfulness as
"cheery denial." In the face of the threats to our children's growth and
happiness, denying that they must face them is a natural way to maintain
one's good cheer. In *Parenthood*, Frank is forced to confront the cheery denial he chronically assumes with regard to Larry, his youngest child. The
film holds out the possibility that Frank is capable of developing genuine
cheerfulness, which does not blink the truth, only because Frank achieves
a measure of self-awareness. At the opposite pole from resilient cheerfulness is the defeat of despondency or helpless resignation. We may finally
be crushed by the ugliness and violence that beset our children and perhaps our own inability to shield them from disaster. As a comedy,
Parenthood does not dwell on this giving up, but we catch glimpses of it in
Gil and his sister Helen, when they are weighed down by the obvious un-
happiness of their children.

Although cheerfulness is not necessary for interpersonal adaptability, it
supports and augments the ability of parents to adjust successfully to
change in their children's needs, interests, and autonomy. As the passage
from Spinoza indicates, resilient cheerfulness provides energy and hopefulness, without which parents are unlikely to be able to summon the effort to respond effectively to their children and their children's predicaments. Cheerfulness shares with the three moral virtues a realistic stance.
They all resist the pressures, endemic to parenthood, to gloss over un-
pleasant aspects of children's lives or to distort the actual role parents play
in their children's lives. Because social adaptability and cheerfulness are
action-oriented, enabling parents to improve their situation, they also foster a realistic perspective by making reality more palatable.

Closely aligned with cheerfulness as an auxiliary, nonmoral virtue is
playfulness and the humor that is one of its genial manifestations.
Parenthood shows how playfulness works with resilient cheerfulness and
social adaptability in decisive moments of parent-child interaction. For
example, Helen's son Garry tells her he wants to go live with his father
because it's become too crowded in Helen's home. Helen's feelings are

hurt, but she rebounds, kidding that there is now more room since Julie and Tod cut their hair. The film repeatedly illustrates how playfulness buttresses a balanced perspective on the ups and downs of rearing children, and subsequently dealing with children as they become adults. *Parenthood* intimates that playfulness and humor, which color the film as a whole, can lighten the burdens and deepen the joys of parenthood itself.

In most films, humor points to something else, of greater thematic importance. Recall that *Groundhog Day* employs the comic device of repetition to convey the futility of Phil Connors's manipulative designs and thereby drive home its morally charged view of the good life.[12] In contrast, *Parenthood* gives humor and, more broadly, playfulness a larger part to play in the development and exercise of moral virtue. Humor and playfulness are not merely vehicles for expressing virtues but actually support these virtues, entering practically into their modus operandi. *Parenthood* is suffused with comedy, both by the characters, in their jokes and jibes, and by the film's own organization, timing, and shot selections. The film rewards the parents, such as Helen, whose humor enables their moral virtues to flourish, and it punishes parents, such as Nathan, who are so lacking in frivolity as to demean its value.

Family Problems

Parenthood presents three generations of the Buckman family: Frank and his wife, their four children (Gil, Helen, Susan, and Larry), and the children of those four siblings. Happily on the periphery of the various goings-on is Grandma, Frank's mother-in-law. The film cuts back and forth between and among the families of the siblings and their father. The siblings are having problems with their nuclear families, and the story is about how these problems are more or less resolved. Gil (Steve Martin) and his wife, Karen (Mary Steenburgen), have three children, the oldest of which is excessively tense and worried. Kevin's problems in school add to Gil's stress at work, where he wants to be promoted but is unwilling to sacrifice time with his family to do so. Helen (Dianne Wiest) is divorced, raising two kids on her own. Helen's daughter, Julie (Martha Plimpton), marries her boyfriend, Tod (Keanu Reeves), after becoming pregnant. At the same time, Helen futilely reaches out to her withdrawn and apparently disturbed son, Garry (Leaf Phoenix).

Susan (Harley Kozak) is married to Nathan (Rick Moranis), whose regimented rearing of their preschool daughter, Patty, is designed to insure that she develops into a genius. The youngest sibling, Larry (Tom Hulce), is a ne'er-do-well who pops in on the extended family's Thanksgiving with his illegitimate son, Cool. Larry's gambling debts put his life at immediate risk, but his more chronic problem of irresponsibility is the product of being indulged by his father, Frank (Jason Robards). Thus, to the difficulties each of the Buckman siblings is going through, *Parenthood* adds the fatherhood struggles of Frank with Larry.

Although the four siblings interact on and off, they resolve their difficulties pretty much on their own, as does Frank. Gil becomes less neurotic in his concern for Kevin, and Helen has the newlyweds, Julie and Tod, live in her home, where Tod lifts Garry out of his adolescent funk. Nathan learns to let Patty have a childhood, replete with fun and silliness. And Frank discovers how to offer help to Larry without encouraging Larry's shiftless dependence. Realistically punctuating its conclusion, *Parenthood* depicts an unreformed Larry, incapable of either fatherhood or taking his father's wisely proffered help.

The film begins with a daydream fantasy. Sitting at a baseball game with his family, the adult Gil is creatively reconstructing his annual childhood day at the ballpark, during which his father typically left him in the care of an usher while attending to his own business. The young Gil tells the fantasy usher that his father, Frank, learned that children were a burden, a "prison rather than a playground," as a result of Frank's own father's attitude toward him. So Gil has a theory as to why his father neglects him, but the theory doesn't ease his pain. The bereft experience of the erstwhile child-version of Gil explains why he is so determined to be a good father and help his children grow up to be self-confident, happy people.

The opening scene not only combines humor with imagination, two motifs of the film, but it presents a parent who is self-conscious about his parenthood. Within the daydream, the young Gil tells the usher that he is merely an "amalgam" of all the ushers with whom his father has left him. Gil's fantasizing about his childhood will be paralleled by his fantasizing about the adulthood of Kevin, his oldest and troubled child. Thus, even though the object of the opening fantasy is a past event of childhood, or the coalescing of a class of past such events, its significance for Gil is as a parent, with import for the future of his own children. The baseball context will also be replayed in Gil's son's life. Kevin will play ball, not very playfully, and Gil will be taking an active, coaching role, unlike his hands-off father.

Gil's fantastic recollection also serves notice that Gil is an imaginative, playful person but one who worries and whose playfulness doesn't really help him cope with the stresses of parenthood. This is subtly conveyed to Kevin, who is tense, nervous, and full of self-doubt. When the principal of Kevin's school later recommends to Gil and Karen that Kevin attend a special school for his emotional problems, Gil denies that his son's problems are all that serious. But he then quickly shifts gears, blaming Karen for Kevin's crying and inability to finish his work.

Gil alternates between cheery denial of Kevin's problems and hyper-responsibility for them. As Gil's story unfolds, *Parenthood* suggests that his excessive responsibility may explain the cheery denial. When parents feel inordinately responsible for their children's well-being and difficulties, they naturally seek to minimize the difficulties in order to relieve their own doubt and anxiety. In taking a disproportionate amount of responsibility for Kevin's psychological stress, Gil also implicitly betrays a lack of humility.

The film proceeds by cutting from one parent, and his or her nuclear family, to another. The first few sequences take us from Gil to Helen and then from Susan/Nathan to Frank and Larry. Easily lost in this regular, panning-like movement is Grandma, who also makes the rounds from one of her grandchildren's family to another as available space for her requires. Because *Parenthood* has many main characters embroiled in their own familial subplots, I will canvas them briefly, thereby imitating the film's cinematic introduction of the protagonists and their problems to the viewing audience.

Talk about Kevin's problems provides a transition to Helen's son, Garry, and his disturbed behavior. Helen is divorced, with custody of Garry and his older sister, Julie. Garry is entering puberty a withdrawn, taciturn, apparently unhappy boy to whom Helen constantly reaches out. She gamely, chirpily, tries to engage Garry in conversation, but he is distant, unwilling to say where he is going or what he is carrying in his ever-present brown paper sack. Helen's relationship with Julie is more engaged but also more volatile. Her plans for Julie to go to college are compromised by Julie's romance with Tod. In her dealings with Tod, Helen exhibits the virtue of interpersonal adaptability. Because she is able to adapt to Julie's involvement with Tod, moreover, Helen is able to strengthen her relationships with both of her own children.

But it takes Helen awhile to adjust to Julie's commitment to Tod. To the film's credit, we watch Helen struggle, become frustrated, and flounder before responding to her children's needs and interests with flexibility and creativity. Even before her successful social adaptation, however, Helen displays the humor and cheerful resilience that so often augments interpersonal adaptability. When there is a mix-up in photo packets, Helen winds up perusing sexual pictures of Julie and Tod. Holding the pictures, Helen smiles at Julie entering the house, saying, "I, I, I, I think this one is my favorite." To Julie's reply that the photo session was just for fun, Helen quips, "I'm glad it's not a job." Her one-liners continue, as she exclaims, "Uh, whooo, here's something for my wallet."

When Helen berates Julie for having sex in her house, Julie humorously and contemptuously derides Helen's lack of a sex life, pushing Helen into losing her temper. Kicking the door Julie has slammed behind her, Helen yells, "I would just like a little respect. You know why I'm having sex with machinery [a vibrator, accidentally discovered during the family's Thanksgiving]? Because your father left to have a party, and I stayed to raise two kids, and I have no life. Goddamn it." Helen is upset with Julie's disregard for her feelings and also is facing the weight of being a lone parent. But she is realistic—missing male companionship, distraught that Julie is throwing away college and a productive future, and upset with her son's reclusive behavior.

Julie tells Helen that she is leaving home, and Helen threatens her with exile: "If you walk out of this house against my wishes, don't you ever think about coming back here." Helen immediately recants, pursuing Julie outdoors, telling her that she is always here if Julie needs her. These opening scenes of Helen and her children suggest that Helen is weak, needy, overwhelmed, and inconsistent. She seems the least likely to emerge as the parent most imbued with the virtues needed to cope successfully with her children. However, Helen's genuine attentiveness and humility promote her social adaptability. She is realistic about her problems and her children, and she is able to recover her good humor, never succumbing to the cheery denial or fantasy that besets other members of her extended family.

The film next introduces the tidy family of Nathan, Susan, and Patty. Nathan, who has taken charge of educating Patty in the hopes of helping her achieve brilliance, tells Susan that he sometimes feels they want Patty's brilliance more than she does. Having just heard Susan explain to Helen that Patty has not been making enough effort in such subjects as math and French, we are not prepared for the camera cut to an adorable little four-year-old. Our laughter at the sight gag is tempered by the straits in which Patty's parents have put her. Nathan arranges Patty's life for her, meticulously structuring her experience so as to maximize her growth in language skills, science, mathematics, even the martial arts. He is the parent-as-teacher taken to ludicrous extremes for both comic and edifying effect. When Nathan leaves the room with Susan, for example, he tells Patty that he and mommy will be back in two minutes. He then asks, "How many seconds is that?"

Unlike the audience, Nathan is oblivious to the way his tutelage is depriving Patty of a childhood. Whereas Gil's vigilance over his children is often exhibited in a manic playfulness, Nathan's vigilance produces stifling seriousness. Nathan's seriousness about Patty's development is mirrored in her inability to have fun and her general lack of playfulness. For example, at Kevin's birthday party, Patty can't understand why Kevin's little brother, Justin, spins around until he collapses. Playing at something with no educational goal eludes her, as if an esoteric mystery.

Nathan's vicarious projection leaves no room for him to be attentive to Patty's own interests or needs. In addition to lacking in attentiveness, Nathan is devoid of humility. He mistakenly sees his influence as the only one needed for Patty's growth. Although the film begins with Susan's complicity in Nathan's regimen for Patty, Susan soon sees its deleterious consequences for Patty, as well as for her marriage. Their story is one of getting Nathan to see what is wrong with his treatment of Patty, which includes seeing what is wrong with himself.

We meet the last pair of parents at the family Thanksgiving dinner. When the youngest of the Buckman siblings, Larry, shows up, the only person thrilled to see him is father Frank. Frank grins with glee at Larry's grandiose gab about a hot deal he has cooking. When Larry's mother says that she hopes this isn't another get-rich-quick scheme, Frank defends Larry, gushing that "quick is the best way to get rich." Projecting his own fantasies of fast-buck success, Frank has encouraged in Larry a lack of discipline and willingness to work. Frank is himself a hard-working man, willing to spend free evenings laboring to restore a vintage automobile. However, like Nathan, Frank has vicariously projected a better future for his child, without paying attention to the kind of person Larry is becoming. Although Gil's relationship with Frank begins the film and is revisited toward its conclusion, Frank's fatherhood is most fully investigated with Larry.

Larry is so irresponsible as to have sired a child he didn't even know he had—a mulatto boy, about five, named Cool. Later, as Frank and Larry admire Frank's restored car, Larry's mother suggests the two of them take Cool somewhere. Frank is piqued at the intrusion, and Larry tells his mother to "plop him [Cool] in front of the T.V. It's what he always does." Larry soon hits his father up for money, which Frank seems only too eager to lend him, as if needing money is a sign of impending riches. Whenever Larry has needed financial help, Frank has had his wallet at the ready.

Frank's indulgent behavior of him has not resulted in Larry indulging his own son. Instead, it has created a self-centered person who neglects his offspring. Neglect marks the limit of inattentiveness. Gil, the oldest of Frank's children, is the antithesis of Larry (the youngest child) in his hyper-attentiveness to his children. *Parenthood* implies that the contrasts between the brothers are the result of the extremes of negligence and indulgence in Frank's treatment of each of them.

As might have become apparent, the film is male-centered, even to the point of focusing on Nathan as a parent, instead of his Buckman spouse, Susan. However, the male emphasis is not laudatory, and it indirectly serves to highlight Helen as the most interesting, stalwart parent in the film. With the exception of Larry, all the parents at least embark on moral improvement, but Helen comes further, more quickly, and in more trying circumstances than any other parent. To investigate the film's rendering of interpersonal adaptability, attentiveness, and humility, I begin with Helen because she most embodies these moral virtues of parenthood. We will also see how the realism that characterizes these virtues is manifested in Helen's resilient cheerfulness.

Exemplary Moral Growth—Helen

As the story gets under way, Helen's plan for Julie to go to college is compromised by Julie's romantic relationship with Tod. At first, Helen is dead against Julie's involvement with Tod, but when she learns they have married, she adapts to the situation. In the interest of her daughter's education and welfare, Helen has the newlyweds live in her house. Her flexibility and willingness to alter her preconceived plans in the face of changes in her children's lives is evidence of her social adaptability. Helen does not simply tolerate Julie's decision to marry Tod but exerts herself to promote the altered social relationships entailed by this decision. Where mere tolerance or endurance is passive, adaptability is the readiness to see and exploit the potential for improving personal relationships. It is needed whenever we must function in social relationships over which we have lit-

tle control. In neighborhood and work environments for instance, effort
can take us beyond merely putting up with one another to enjoying ami-
cable interaction.

Family is a paradigm context for developing the virtue of social adaptability because family members must live together, without choice. Even
when parents choose to bear and rear children, they soon find that they
must make choices in circumstances beyond their control. Although interaction among family members can nurture social adaptability in all of
them, life together tends to promote the virtue most in parents because
they are most responsible for harmony in the group.

Realizing the virtue of social adaptability is especially critical, yet difficult, for a single parent, such as Helen. Without a spouse, a parent has
fewer options and resources in dealing with her children. She must be attentive and flexible enough to balance divergent personalities and interests
on her own. Because Helen adapts energetically and is not simply tolerant
of her children and son-in-law, Tod, she is able to strengthen her relationships with her children, as well as help them. In her interpersonal adaptability, Helen recognizes how she is limited by her family, and she is able
to respond to the particular needs and choices of her family's members because she truly attends to them. The personalities, interests, and decisions
of family members dictate what specific accommodations will work best.
Possessing this virtue, Helen is resourceful in modifying her expectations
and behavior to meet the needs of her children and herself.

In the midst of Julie and Tod moving into Helen's home, Garry tells his
mother that he thinks he would like to live with his absent father. With
cinematic justice, the film mirrors the father's absence from Garry's life by
absenting him from our view, never showing his character on screen. In
her ex-husband, Helen must respond to a person and relationship over
which she has practically no influence. She knows Garry's father will not
want the boy to live with him, so absorbed is he with his new wife and
child. Putting aside her own feelings of rejection (registered in the cloud-
ing of her face and the catch in her voice), Helen gently tries to discour-
age Garry from calling his father. However, when Garry persists, she
doesn't spare herself the pain of watching, as Garry's telephoned request
to live with his father is brushed off.

Garry is shot in the foreground, making the phone call. Helen is seated
behind him, out of focus, and framed with Garry in the doorway—visually connected to her son as a behind-the-scene support, silently taking
part in the action with which he is preoccupied. Garry absorbs his father's

rebuff, mumbling "O.K." through his tears. Resigned to her ex-husband's insensitivity, Helen mutters his name, saying, "Oh, Eddy, shit." Helen had been hopelessly wishing that Garry's father would do right by him, even though it would have meant not having her child live with her. Helen has the humility to accept Garry's desire to move out of her home, as well as to understand that she cannot prevent the doomed overture to his father. All she can do is offer comfort, however little Garry welcomes it.

Helen soon discovers that what Garry has been furtively hauling around in a brown paper bag are pornographic video tapes. She quickly grasps that he cannot talk to her about his erotic desires and feelings. Again Helen demonstrates interpersonal adaptability, nimbly suggesting Tod as a confidant. She sees in Tod a potential big brother for Garry and seizes the moment to ask Garry in a whisper, "Would you like to speak to Tod?" The camera cuts comically to Tod acting goofy, wiggling his fingers as he looks at them through distorting glasses.

The humor is crude in that Tod is clowning around while Garry and Helen are dealing with a crisis. But the humor is also subtle in that it captures the way we cannot always tell from appearances who, or what, is going to be effective in meeting a crisis. The person who seems least likely to be helpful may be just the one whose help can be accepted, and Helen sees this—in an instant. Garry does speak with Tod and is reassured that his sexuality is quite normal, and not the perverse impulse Garry had feared.

Since Tod is available to Garry only because Helen was flexible enough to swallow her anger and disappointment at Julie's marriage to him, Helen's adaptability is building on its own fruits. She is able to improvise a solution to Garry's isolation because she had previously accepted Julie's marriage and devised a way to keep Julie college-bound. As a result of her work to make the best of the situation and experiment with living with Tod, Helen also benefits by putting herself in position to get to know who Tod is. Tod later confesses to Helen that he and Julie "look kind of stupid" in the haircuts they have given each other. This is the first time Helen has listened to Tod. Realizing that he has enough humility and good humor to laugh at himself, she smiles and thanks him.

Helen also reaps the benefits of Tod's presence by seeing a new Garry, or perhaps the Garry who had been walled off is coming out and into his own. Helen has the pleasure of Garry actually initiating conversation with her and the delight of seeing him horse around with Tod. The film casually deepens the theme of playfulness, moreover, by portraying Garry's roughhousing with Tod as a symptom of growing emotional health.

Looking out for her daughter and son, Helen is rewarded with richer, more open relationships with each child. Helen has adapted her situation to meet the needs of her children to which she has been paying attention, using whatever she finds at hand—her home for Tod and Julie, and Tod for Garry.

Social adaptability is such a critical virtue for parents because they are hemmed in on many sides in their relationships with their children. Children's stages of development, self-concepts, and relationships with other people constrain what parents can do for them. As Helen demonstrates, the virtue of adaptability involves taking social risks, as well as recognizing the costs of not taking them.

Against Julie's wishes, Tod returns to auto racing, with Garry enthusiastically in his pit crew. No sooner does the big race begin than Tod promptly crashes his brother's racing car. After his car is righted and his helmet removed, Tod asks Garry, "Did I win?" The wildly optimistic Tod hasn't even finished the race! When Julie says she can't accompany her family with Tod to first aid, Helen tells her that "this is marriage, now let's get in the truck." Garry looks on, mouth agape.

As Tod belittles himself for failing and destroying his brother's car, Helen reminds him that he is very important because he is going to be the father of her grandchild. She implies that flopping in this or that (occasionally ill-conceived) endeavor mustn't crush Tod. He will truly be a success if he does a good job in rearing his child. Buoyed by Helen's words, Julie embraces Tod and further braces him with, "I love you." Helen has rallied their flagging spirits. She not only adapts to Julie and Tod with energy and ingenuity, she also accepts their relationship and exerts herself on its behalf.

A somewhat surprised Garry takes in his mother's success in pulling the newlyweds out of their emotional skid. We can almost see his mind working to digest the significance of the tableau. After the foursome get off the truck taking them to first aid, Garry keeps gazing at his mother. He finally says, "You, like, saved their marriage." In the face of this accolade, Helen voices her skepticism with a joke. She gives their marriage "six months . . . four, if she cooks." Helen uses humor to point to a discouraging reality rather than to deflect attention from real problems and risks. Helen's quips never mask the truth of her situation or her children's. She wants Garry to see the shoals on which marriage can smash, but she also demonstrates for him her cheerful resilience in confronting them.

Helen also illustrates that the resilience of cheerfulness is double-edged. Helen's cheerfulness enables her to be resilient enough to continue to act by tapping her reserves of energy and resourcefulness.[13] Less obviously, the cheerfulness itself is resilient. Helen retains, or regains, her positive attitude toward her children and her own prospects, rebounding from adversity instead of being upbeat only when things are going well.

If she does not think they are going to make it, Garry asks, why does Helen help keep them together. Helen answers that "Julie wants Tod, and whatever you guys want, I want to get for you. That's the best you can do." Although Helen overstates the parental role in saying that she tries to get her children what they want, she nevertheless accurately expresses her commitment to her children. Above all, Helen shows how to balance cheerfulness and honesty. Helen is strong enough to resist the lure of cheery denial and refuses to deceive herself into thinking everything is fine just because she has helped Julie and Tod avert this one failure. She sees Julie's marriage to Tod for the frail thing it is and doesn't hide this from Garry.

The first extended conversation between Helen and Garry is about how and why Helen tries to help Julie and Tod. Helen captures the spirit of social adaptability in explaining to Garry the effort she makes to help her children satisfy their desires, even when she has misgivings about the desires. Parenthood also figures in the conversation in Helen's statement about Tod's impending paternity. The discussion implicitly raises the question whether Tod will be adaptable, or maintain a resilient cheerfulness, in response to his own child's unpalatable choices.

As if his mother's self-conscious concern for her children's well-being has struck a resonating chord, Garry expresses his wish for Helen's welfare. He tells her he's glad she's going out with the biology teacher, Mr. Bowman, remarking how "he's funny and he's the kind of guy that'd be nice to you." The movie hints at the possibility that parental devotion and attention to children may engender in them a regard for their parents as people with lives and interests of their own. Such regard could be the seeds in children of social adaptability toward their parents. At the very least, it signals a lack of the self-absorption so characteristic of adolescents.

Well-Intentioned Vice

Aside from Helen, the parents in the film succeed primarily in understanding their flaws or vices, which they then begin to try to correct.[14] The film uses the parents other than Helen more as her foils, to illustrate defects to be overcome, than to exhibit parental virtues. Because each parent presents an interesting and illuminating constellation of character failings, I have chosen to proceed from parent to parent rather than organize the analysis according to vice or character fault. My scheme makes for some dispersal and repetition in discussing the vices, but this seems preferable to examining each parent over and over as he or she exemplifies one vice after another.

As the characters embody different combinations of vices, where the vices recur they interlock in various ways, yielding different parental behavior and consequences for the children. This blending of vices also seems better captured by proceeding by character.[15] I begin by focusing on moral vices, exemplified in Nathan, and then shift to the auxiliary vices exhibited by Gil. However, just as Nathan's moral failure includes a profound lack of the auxiliary virtue playfulness, so does Gil's failure in auxiliary virtue have implications for his moral flaws.

Lack of Humility

Nathan's lack of humility indirectly makes him incapable of attentiveness and interpersonal adaptability. He is so enrapt with his program for Patty's brilliant future that he never thinks to pay attention to her needs or interests. Consequently, Nathan can see nothing to adapt to, no individual for whose sake he might have to modify his thoughts or behavior. When he looks at Patty he sees only the extent he has molded her and the goals of his pedagogy that are yet to be realized. Having been unable to secure a research grant earlier in his career, Nathan seems to be using Patty to meet his own ambitions through vicarious projection.

If Patty continues to be shaped by Nathan, she will be lacking in autonomy in thought and action: the ability to decide for herself what she wants to do, how to get what she wants, or who she wishes to be. Patty will be a stranger to herself, not knowing what she truly likes. Whatever Patty's own tastes and interests might have been, they will have been so overlaid by what her father thinks she should desire that Patty will hardly be able to find them. Proficient in all sorts of symbolic manipulations, Patty will be without a core of self-wrought values and commitments on which to base her prudential and moral decisions.

When we see Patty, we see a child devoid of spontaneity. Because Nathan plans her schedule in such detail and denies Patty the opportunity to act on impulse or whimsy, she seems emptied of the passions or desires that can so quickly move children. Patty appears on the screen as a programmed doll, not knowing what to do with herself unless following one of her father's planned lessons. She seems spiritless or dispirited. Contrasting with Patty is Gil's youngest child, Justin. Throwing himself into childhood with gusto, Justin loves to spin around, fling himself in all directions, and ram into things. Patty cannot fathom why Justin spins and flies as he does since his behavior appears purposeless.

The idea of doing something for the fun of it makes no sense to Patty. When she watches Gil do his movable thumb trick, for another example, she shrieks in fear, gravely afraid that his thumb has become detached from his hand. Patty's studies have left her completely literal-minded, unable to pretend or enter into the pretenses of others.

In these two brief scenes, the film reveals Patty's absence of playfulness and gently prods us to wonder what that deprivation bodes for her later life. Play enables children to try out possibilities. When they pretend, for example, children imagine scenarios that are not actual, and this enables them to project courses of actions and their consequences into an uncharted future. The ability to play out possible events in the imagination is crucial to the independent deliberations and problem solving denied Patty by Nathan's rigid regimen. Playing at made-up games and fabricating homemade stories contribute to the capacity of children to choose from among possible futures.

Patty's joyless life is a natural extension of Nathan's seriousness. Just as Patty is spooked by Gil's amateur magic tricks, so Nathan finds them stupid and boring. He mocks Justin's twirling and banging, envisioning a humdrum future for the little boy. Only when his wife, Susan, threatens to leave him does Nathan revert to the inspired suitor with whom Susan fell in love. He comes into her grade school classroom and begins singing a love song. His face is serious, as is his intent, but the act itself is playful—defying the norms and roles of adult behavior. He looks like a lovestruck student acting out his infatuation with the pretty teacher, and he wins his wife back.

Nathan's act of playful courting also illustrates the element of venture typical in play. Playing at games, or in made-up stories, includes taking a chance on an uncertain outcome. When children role-play in their stories, they have to improvise dialogue and action without the safety of a settled script or routine. The correlate of the freedom enjoyed in play is its attendant risk. As puppy playful as Nathan seems when he sings to Susan, his foray into her classroom takes courage. Nathan risks Susan's rejection and looking foolish singing to her in front of her students. The film suggests that adult playfulness is a token of the letting go and the risking essential in letting children go and grow up. Just as Nathan must let go of his pride and self-importance and risk looking silly and Susan's rejection, so must he let go and risk Patty's own choices. If play is instrumental to the development of children's autonomy, parental humility is entwined in fostering that autonomy.

In the scene of Nathan's schoolroom singing, *Parenthood* seems to propose that playfulness, and leaps of the imagination, are also needed to heal breaches in our deepest relationships. Family itself cannot survive unless the spirit of play informs it. Family needs play for jolly times like Gil's improvised role as a cowboy at his son's birthday party, as well as for such crises as Susan's rejection of Nathan and his martinet style of rearing Patty. The scene of Nathan's lyrical supplication of Susan embodies the film's overall tenor of playful, yet thoughtful, portrayal of the importance of family in the life of virtue.

Cheery Denial

Gil appears to be the most playful Buchman—full of jokes, party tricks, and joie de vivre. He is even decried by Nathan as being "too jocular" to take care of Patty in her parents' absence. But when we look more closely at Gil, we notice disturbing aspects of his play. We notice, for example, that it is bound up with his cheery denial. Gil is drawn into cheery denial, moreover, because he assumes too much responsibility for the happiness of his children. The film comically dramatizes Gil's hyper-responsibility during the Little League baseball practice.

Gil is the coach of Kevin's team and conducts batting practice for the boys. When Kevin yields to Gil's encouragement and tries to play second base, Gil lapses into a reverie of Kevin as valedictorian of his graduating college class. In the speech Gil imagines him giving, Kevin points out how his father got him "through his rough time, and that now he is the happiest, most confident, and most well-adjusted person in this world." Back on the ball field, however, Kevin immediately drops a pop-up Gil hits to him and blames Gil for pushing him into playing second base.

The film quickly cuts to a woman screaming, as an adult Kevin fires a rifle from a bell tower—Gil's crackling imagination taking a dark nosedive! This bleak fantasy of failed parenthood emanates from the same source as Gil's initial, glowing daydream about Kevin's future—his distorted view of the role he plays in his son's life. Gil's daydreams are not, however, the vicarious projection that motivates Nathan's relationship with Patty. Unlike Nathan, Gil is not projecting a particular set of goals he has for Kevin. He just wants Kevin to be happily well-adjusted, and his fantasies externalize his neurotic sense of responsibility for Kevin's happiness.

Gil's exaggerated, opposing projections of Kevin's future humorously capture Gil's exaggerated sense of parental responsibility. The creative play of his imagination perpetuates, rather than alleviates, the weight of fatherhood Gil bears. The fact that Gil can swing so quickly from glowing to gloomy projection also points out how he lacks the balance that a reasonable perspective would bring. The virtue of playfulness ideally provides parents with the ballast needed to weather the inevitable turbulence in their children's fortunes and in their relationships with the children.

The problem with Gil's jocularity and playfulness is that they don't penetrate his perception of his son or his role in Kevin's happiness. At the Thanksgiving gathering, Gil's sisters laugh at his sarcastic remarks. Their father, Frank, comments that they may think Gil is funny, but that as a child, he was "a serious little bastard." Appearances notwithstanding, Gil still is. When Kevin makes a game-saving catch at film's end, Gil struts, dances, and pounds the ground with ecstasy. The film enhances his humorous antics by shooting the boys and their parents in slow motion, to the accompaniment of mock-heroic music. The aftermath of Kevin's catch is cinematically rendered according to its overblown meaning for Gil.

Earlier, Gil had hired a professional performer, Cowboy Dan, to entertain at Kevin's birthday party. When Cowboy Dan is unable to come, Gil does a hilarious job pinch hitting, including improvising bathroom rugs as cowboy chaps and twisting balloons into a mess that Gil describes as intestines. Although it could be argued that he does adapt to the snafu, the adaptation is more technical than interpersonal, as Gil puts on a performance. Almost hidden in the hullabaloo is the fact that Gil feels it incumbent upon him to save the day. His humor and frivolity serve Gil's misplaced sense of duty to spare Kevin the criticism of his pals. Although "Cowboy" Gil's act is a success, it appears desperate—a way of keeping Kevin's worries at bay, discharging the endlessly proliferating duties of parenthood Gil mistakenly thinks are his.

Where Nathan programs Patty's life as her all-purpose guru, Gil is Kevin's rescuer. Each father takes on too much responsibility for his child's welfare. Even though Gil is free of Nathan's arrogance, he too lacks humility, a proper estimation of his abilities and station. Gil presumes more influence over and responsibility for Kevin than is realistic. Because assuming the responsibility for another person's happiness is incredibly onerous, Gil naturally gravitates toward cheery denial.

Gil's wife, Karen, helps him begin to acknowledge his character failings, which are difficult to isolate within Gil's genuine love and attentiveness. Gil and Karen rummage through a restaurant's garbage, searching for the expensive teeth retainer Kevin has lost in the restaurant. Alluding to how overwrought Kevin became when he discovered that the retainer was missing, Gil notes that Kevin is getting worse, more high-strung, "like a poodle." As Gil wonders aloud where Kevin gets his obsessive behavior, the film portrays him incessantly washing his hands at the restaurant's utility spigot. The audience is invited to laugh not in order to diminish the parental problems but to keep them in perspective. *Parenthood* seems to imply that if Gil could see himself as we do, including the humor of the moment, he would better appreciate his part in Kevin's difficulties.

Karen speaks to Gil's underlying cheery denial when she asks, "What did you think, that you'd dress up like a cowboy and coach Little League, and Kevin would be fine?" After denying that these activities of his were the means of denying the depth of Kevin's problems, Gil admits he did think as Karen suspected. In reply, Karen says, "Well, honey, you were really kiddin' yourself." Despite all his involvement in Kevin's life, Gil never addresses the boy's problems realistically, and he never discusses Kevin's feelings of insecurity with him.[16] Instead, Gil tries to create successful and fun times for Kevin. The flexibility and imaginative range so delightful in Gil's playing around is isolated there. His playfulness does not make him more supple in adjusting to Kevin's needs or situation.

The film leads us to conclude that to overcome his tendency to cheery denial, Gil must first see his sense of responsibility for Kevin as excessive. Relinquishing his hyper-responsibility requires the right perspective on his limited ability to control his son's future, the perspective conferred by humility. Until these interlocking vices are unraveled, Gil's playfulness is simply a way of trying to make things better for Kevin instead of realistically helping the boy deal with the causes of his anxiety. Gil's playfulness is a way of avoiding facing problems and actually keeps his son from facing his own nightmares.

Playfulness and Perspective

For a person whose playfulness truly permeates her outlook on life, we must turn to Grandma. Easily overlooked, as she almost blends into the background, Grandma unobtrusively illustrates how the spirit of playfulness can enable us to take things as they come, especially with regard to raising children. The fact that throughout the story Grandma accepts being shunted from the home of one grandchild to another, with apparent aplomb, subtly testifies to her elastic capacity for adaptability. In her one extended speech, she also offers Gil the playful perspective that will complete his recognition of his character defect and enable him to start dealing with parenthood without cheery denial. Before considering Grandma's allegory, I want to note brief moments in which the film inconspicuously represents her easy playfulness.

When Helen discovers the pornographic videotapes in Garry's room, she plays one on his television. As she watches, Susan and Grandma pause in the doorway to watch also. Without calling attention to it, *Parenthood* conveys that Grandma is moving from Susan's and Nathan's house to live with Helen. Susan and Grandma soon walk down the hall to get Grandma resituated, and Grandma sweetly remarks how the man in the video reminded her of their grandfather, her deceased husband. Not only doesn't the pornography faze Grandma, but it puts her happily in mind of her own sexual partner! Later, at Kevin's birthday party, Grandma is filling balloons with helium for the kids, inhales some of it, and delights in talking to them in the resultant high, squeaky voice.

Toward the end of the film, Gil and Karen are readying the family to go see their daughter in a school play. We discover that Grandma is now living with them when she has to interrupt her game of Nintendo to go to the play. She enters the room as Gil neurotically shares with Karen his fears about all that can go wrong for children. He cannot savor even Kevin's successful catch, noting that after all Kevin *could* have dropped the baseball. After Karen tells Gil that life is messy, Grandma, apparently out of the blue, starts talking about how Grandpa took her on a roller coaster when she was nineteen years old. She says: "Up-down, up-down. Oh, what a ride."

Grandma explains why she wanted to go on the roller coaster again: "It was just interesting to me that a ride could make me so, so frightened, so scared, so sick, so excited, and so thrilled, all together! But other people didn't like it and went on merry-go-round. That just goes around. Nothing." Grandma smiles mischievously and says she likes the roller coaster because she gets more out of it. Then she toddles off to wait for Gil and his family in the car.[17]

To Karen's praise of Grandma as a very smart lady, Gil replies with a snide remark. Karen becomes angry with Gil's dour sarcasm and reiterates that Grandma is wise. The film keeps Grandma's parable from assuming biblical proportions by being as playful with her as she is in her life. Gil asks an off-screen Karen, "If she's so brilliant, how come she's sitting in our neighbor's car?" Despite Grandma's apparent forgetfulness, Gil appears to be turning over in his mind the gist of her story. During the ensuing school play, Gil's youngest child, the spinning, head-banging Justin, rushes onto the stage to defend his sister from what he ingenuously perceives to be an attack. Justin soon wreaks havoc on the set and the play, bringing the "curtain down."

In the audience, Gil tenses up when he overhears another parent complain that Justin is ruining the play. But the sound of a crescendoing roller coaster and a swinging camera shot of the stage convey the onset of another of Gil's confections of the imagination. Screaming in the play's audience merges with fantasized roller-coaster squeals of delighted fright, as Gil fearfully peers over the imaginary bar of his roller-coaster car. He covers his eyes. When Gil opens them and lets go of the bar, he is able to smile. He smiles at Karen and touches her pregnant midriff, indicating that he accepts their new, impending parenthood and suggesting that he will learn to "let go" a bit and enjoy the ride. By showing how Grandma's story informs Gil's imagination in the midst of the chaos his youngest child has wrought, *Parenthood* implies that Gil has a fighting chance at incorporating his own playfulness into his child-rearing.

Realistic Perception and Personhood

Corresponding to the virtue of interpersonal adaptability are two contrasting vices, which are embodied in Frank, patriarch of the Buckman family. Besides neglecting Gil, Frank is guilty of unreflectively accepting Larry. Frank's uncritical acceptance of his youngest child most palpably expresses itself in indulging him so much that Larry lacks any of the virtues associated with independence or concern for others. *Parenthood* shows how unreflective acceptance both presupposes and perpetuates cheery denial and, consequently, a lack of genuine attentiveness, as Frank deceives himself about Larry's weakness and insincerity. Frank's rose-tinted portrait of Larry is mirrored in Larry's own unrealistically grand sense of himself.

In Frank's relationship with Larry, the film explores how the parent-child relationship persists into the child's adult life. Social adaptability requires of parents that they change with their children's passage into adulthood. Parental expectations of children, as well as ways of helping them, should be modified. The relationship is also altered when adult children have children of their own. Frank's failure to see Larry for what he is springs from Frank vicariously projecting dreams of fabulous wealth onto him. Larry's quest for the big score is the result of Frank feeding him a diet of unrealistic expectations. He has been taught to aim for success by wheeling and dealing instead of by working for it. But on this occasion, Larry's scheming has landed him in a life-threatening jam. Larry's predicament forces Frank to confront his son's shiftless nature and its source in Frank's failure to attend or adapt to the person Larry has become.

The film offers a variation of Aristotle's view of extremes as it traces the contrast between Gil's overwrought paternal diligence and Larry's parental fecklessness to the difference in how each son was treated by Frank. Some parental vices reproduce themselves, but others breed their complements. The brothers develop vices that complement, or invert, their father's treatment of them. As a father, Frank veered from the extreme of neglecting Gil to its opposite in overindulging Larry. Because he was ignored by Frank, Gil tends to be oppressively occupied with his children. Because he was spoiled by Frank, Larry is a self-centered, indifferent parent.

Larry's desperation soon leads him to take Frank's antique car to be appraised for possible sale. The threat to Frank's treasure awakens him to the truth that Larry is a good-for-nothing. Larry has gambled away the three thousand dollars Frank had given him, hoping to win enough to pay loan sharks the twenty-six thousand dollars he owes them. Incredulous, Frank asks: "What's the matter with you? You're not a kid anymore." In reply to Larry whining that he can't catch a break, Frank belatedly berates him for not getting a job.

Larry self-righteously retorts that his father's idea of success for him, of "making your mark," does not include the modest rewards of an ordinary job. Larry thinks he is too good to be a working stiff like his brother. He yells, "I am better than that. I am not Gil." As if scales are falling from his eyes, Frank's entire demeanor changes. The cheery denial that has characterized his view of Larry for so long is replaced with an undistorted understanding of his son's foolish self-importance and rationalized irresponsibility. Frank also appears to grasp how he has helped create Larry's careless conception of success.

Frank is like Nathan, trying to live out his fantasies through his child. In both cases, the father's conception of who he wishes his child to be dominates the child's upbringing. The film insinuates that beneath the glaring differences between Larry and Patty, the two share a lack of genuine personhood. Vicarious projection robs children of the chance to develop their own personalities and become their own person. Because *Parenthood* leaves the parallels between Larry and Patty so implicit, pausing here to examine them briefly seems worthwhile.

Although Larry appears to be extremely self-centered, there is very little self at his center. He lacks autonomy and the strength of personality it presupposes because he has been trying to achieve his father's idea of strike-it-rich success. Larry is a cacophony of desires clamoring for satisfaction, but he is essentially without a stable character. Larry's actions are rarely the result of thoughtful deliberations that express a conception of what he seriously cherishes or wishes to become. Rather, his will is but the "playground for different forces."[18] Except for immediate self-gratification, Larry has few of the ongoing dispositions of thought and action that make for a more or less enduring, determinate self.

Contrasting with Larry is the person Patty likely would become were Nathan's regimented tutelage to continue: a highly defined, structured individual who also is not her own person. She would have many entrenched habits—for work, language skills, motor activity, and mathematics. But Patty would not choose any interest or activity herself and probably would be incapable of thinking for herself. Clearly defined by externally imposed habits, Patty's rigid nature seems to contrast with Larry's lack of firm character, but both signal the absence of a true self. Each child's makeup results from the vicarious projections of parents on their children.

We see in Gil's youngest child, Justin, a child with a very strong, independent self. Recall that Justin, who is about Patty's age, likes to bump into things and roll on the ground. His parents allow him to choose his activities and develop a self from out of those choices. Gil doesn't try to manage Justin's childhood as he does Kevin's. When Justin misinterprets the action in a school play as harmful to his sister, he runs onstage to help her. Beneath the humor of the mistake and the ensuing pandemonium, *Parenthood* emphasizes the way Justin's will is his own. He (mistakenly) assesses the situation for himself and puts his fraternal love and moral outrage into action. Neither Patty nor Larry seem capable of doing something that comes so naturally to Justin. Neither has an autonomous foundation of convictions, social habits, and values to ground genuinely independent choice and conduct. Perhaps because Kevin absorbs so much of

Gil's anxious attention, Justin is growing up without the pressures inadvertently created by a hyper-vigilant parent.

Larry will be killed by the mobsters if he does not come up with the money he owes them. Frank does not want to desert his son, especially since he has unwittingly promoted the vices that have gotten Larry into trouble. But neither does Frank want simply to bail Larry out one more time. Faced with Larry's danger, Frank grows as a father and as a person. Perhaps less innovative than Helen's responses to her children, Frank nevertheless manages to steer a course between the errors of rescuing Larry and leaving him in the lurch.

Frank offers Larry a business proposition. Frank will loan him the money he needs to pay off the gangsters, but with conditions. Larry will have to come to work for Frank in his plumbing supplies business, paying him back a thousand dollars a month. While learning the business, Larry will also have to attend Gambler's Anonymous. At first, Larry seems to accept Frank's conditions and the constriction of regular work and discipline. Frank smiles and begins to get out of his chair, but Larry immediately wants to "add a wrinkle." Larry suggests that he go to Chile to assess a deal in platinum first. Should that not pan out, he glibly tells Frank, he'll come back and put the "Frank Buckman plan" into effect.

Frank's smile fades as his face registers understanding of the situation and unvarnished acceptance of it. Frank clearly sees that Larry is refusing his offer, taking the easy way out—out of responsibility for his debt and out of responsibility for Cool or the little boy's future. Frank has learned and has become a father without illusions, accepting who his son has turned out to be and his part in making Larry that person. It is not too late for Frank to change, although it seems to be too late for Larry. Where *Groundhog Day* presented an older man, the derelict, as beyond hope of change and revitalization, *Parenthood* shows the older individual capable of self-wrought moral growth. Frank has never deceived himself about himself, especially concerning his deficiencies as a parent.[19] His distortions were about Larry. Seeing Larry for who he has become, Frank is able to understand the depths of his own paternal defects and set out on a new course.

Even though Larry is the younger man, he is incapable of moral melioration because his delusions are about himself, and so he sees no need to change. Having announced his intention to leave for South America, Larry has to be reminded by Frank about Cool. Frank's "Don't worry about it (Cool)" has the ironic edge of someone who knows that far from worrying about his son, Larry has forgotten about him (reminiscent of Garry having to remind his father that Garry is still his son).

The camera cuts to Cool approaching Frank on the porch. In conversation with his grandson, Frank displays the courage to face the truth and deal with it honestly. Cool tells Frank that Larry is leaving, right away. He asks, "Is he ever coming back?" In a matter-of-fact tone, Frank answers, "No." Unlike his typical treatment of Larry in the past, Frank does not take the easy way, for Cool or himself. Instead of lying or hedging, Frank is direct. Just as he did not cushion the blow for Larry this time by unconditionally paying off his debt, Frank makes Cool a reasonable offer. He asks Cool if he would like to stay and live with his grandmother and Frank. Cool's quiet assent seems to point to a childhood of love, discipline, and direction. As a grandfather, Frank will make good in his second chance at parenthood.

Parenthood in Perspective

Even though *Parenthood* follows the wide arc of family relationships, it manages to present in depth how those relationships promote certain moral virtues and their corresponding vices—especially in the parents. It seems as if for every parent or child exhibiting a particular virtue, another family member is portrayed with the matching vice. The film explores these serious questions of character development with humor, both broad and delicate. Perhaps its ability to balance a comedic approach with serious content is meant to reflect *Parenthood*'s balanced depiction of family's influence on the acquisition of virtues and vices.

Stepping back and taking a larger perspective on the family, a philosophical version of the filmmaker's long shot, the film suggests that family members themselves must look at their shared lives with balance or equipoise. Nothing is so tragic that we cannot find an angle from which to laugh at it. Thus, Larry's life-endangering debt is portrayed humorously in a slapstick shot of him thrown, tumbling, from a moving car. When Larry tells Frank that the people in the car are friends of Larry's, Frank observes that friends slow down, even stop! And the funniest moments of the film are replete with substance, as Justin's vaudeville-like destruction of the set for his sister's school play discloses a little boy of grit and loyalty.

The balance of these elements in the cinematic depiction of parenthood is itself offered as a virtue of perspective. We need to be able to find humor in the most somber of moments and perceive important truths about the parent-child relationship in our times of levity. Although playfulness may be most directly productive of this perspective, it is greatly assisted by its auxiliary allies, cheerful resilience and humor. Even the moral virtues—interpersonal adaptability, attentiveness, and humility—can be seen, without too great a stretch of the imagination, to promote an outlook in which triumph and failure are kept in proper perspective, unlike Gil's glorifying and catastrophizing fantasies about Kevin! *Parenthood* indicates that if we are unable to maintain an even keel in response to our children and their entanglements, our familial life will be often out of focus or distorted.

Notes

1. Aristotle, *Nicomachean Ethics*, trans. Martin Ostwald (Indianapolis: Bobbs-Merrill, 1962), 1161b.

2. I do not ignore the fact that because of abusive relationships, or otherwise harmful parental treatment, adult children may need to sever familial connections. They may owe it to themselves. However, I am speaking of situations where such harm is not the case and the individual rejects family without this sort of justification.

3. George Nakhnikian, "Love in Human Reason," in *Midwest Studies in Philosophy*, vol. 3, *Studies in Ethical Theory*, ed. French, Uehling, and Wettstein (Notre Dame, Ind.: Notre Dame Press: 1978), pp.286–317, p.296.

4. Undertakings like work and hobbies also require that we pay attention to what is going on. But typically in these enterprises our attention is not attentiveness. We are not attending to the needs and interests of human beings out of concern for their welfare. Where we do, as in the case of doctors, ministers, and teachers, for example, the likelihood of distortion is not as great as for parents. For such professionals, the lower level of involvement and the modulating influence of a professional attitude help to keep the other individual in realistic perspective. This is why parenthood is such a fruitful context for the nurturance of attentiveness and can prepare us for these caring professions.

5. Just as preoccupation with possible futures for our children can interfere with realistic perception of them, so can past experience of them. We may fail to attend realistically to our children because impressions formed early on are clinging to us. We have pigeonholed our child as terrific in math and physically clumsy, for example, and so cannot adjust to his or her rejection of a scientific career for pursuit of modern dance.

6. Sara Ruddick, "Maternal Thinking," in *Mothering*, ed. Joyce Trebilcot (Totowa, N.J.: Rowman and Allangield, 1984), pp.213–230, p.217. As with all aspects of caring for children, Ruddick refers to the pertinent species of humility as "maternal." My adoption of the neutral term "parenting" is consonant with

Ruddick's meaning and usage insofar as she makes a point of noting that men are as capable of "mothering" as women. Ruddick cites with approval Iris Murdoch's claim that "humility is not a peculiar habit of self-effacement, rather like having an inaudible voice, it is selfless respect for reality." Iris Murdoch, *The Sovereignty of Good* (New York: Shocken Books, 1971), p.95.

7. Norvin Richards, "Is Humility a Virtue?" *American Philosophical Quarterly* 25 (July 1988): 253–259, 255.

8. The seemingly arrogant vice of parental rejection, mentioned earlier, can be the result of parents being unable to accept the fact that their role is diminished, perhaps now peripheral, where once, in their children's infancy, it was paramount and central. In *Parenthood*, Frank rejects Gil, his eldest child, out of a sense of helplessness. Frank admits that he hated Gil when he was young because for a week the doctors feared that the little boy suffered from polio. Frank's inability to accept the precariousness of his child's health and his own limitations with regard to it led Frank to an emotional rejection of Gil—a rejection he is perhaps just now overcoming.

9. Edmund Pincoffs refers to amiability and humorousness as "temperamental" types of "meliorating" virtues. By this, however, he has something different in mind from my notion of nonmoral virtues that are auxiliary to the moral virtues. For Pincoffs, meliorating virtues make life more tolerable, and the temperamental virtues are meliorative in that "the persons who have them are easier and more pleasant to live with." Edmund Pincoffs, *Quandaries and Virtues* (Lawrence: University Press of Kansas, 1986), p.87.

10. Ruddick, "Maternal Thinking," p.218.

11. Ibid., quoting Spinoza, *Ethics*, Book 3, proposition 42, demonstration.

12. Within *Groundhog Day*, the morally reformed Phil Connors also uses humor instrumentally, as a way to ease other people's embarrassment at his acts of helpfulness or, modestly, to mute his own accomplishments.

13. As recognized by Spinoza; see footnote 11.

14. I include only those parents who are depicted rearing their children. This excludes Grandma and her daughter, Marilyn, who is married to Frank.

15. Following Aristotle, there are two or more vices for each virtue, and examining all of them would make for an unwieldy discussion or a tedious compendium. Consequently, I shall address the particular vices exhibited by the characters in *Parenthood* and merely note in passing vices that contrast with those discussed, or variants of them.

16. An ironic light is turned on Gil's avoidance of Kevin's problems when, later, Frank comes to Gil to talk about his own problems with Larry! Frank's dawning awareness of himself as a parent who has been remiss may serve as a catalyst for Gil's self-scrutiny. Even as Frank realizes how and why he neglected Gil as a child, Gil begins to understand that he is now an overly worried and involved parent. Where Frank needs to move closer to his children's lives, Gil needs to step back a little and let go.

17. The film indirectly plays off the theme of the playful excitement of the amusement park in an earlier scene. Helen is returning from a date with Garry's biology teacher, Mr. Bowman, saying that she enjoyed the carnival. He replies, "You thought that was a carnival? That was my parents' house." No sooner does Mr. Bowman allude to the mayhem of parenthood than Helen's own three-ring circus explodes onto the screen. When she and Mr. Bowman open the door of her house, out scramble Tod and Garry, who spill onto the lawn, yelling at their rowdy play. They then bolt back into the house, whereupon Julie yells and storms through the house, angry with Tod for forsaking his job as a painter and resuming car-racing. Mr. Bowman's "my parents' house" is itself a hyperbolically playful way of emblematizing the pandemonium of parental homes—carnivals all!

18. Andreas Eshete, "Character, Virtue, and Freedom," *Philosophy* 57 (October 1982): 495–513, 498. In the language of Harry Frankfurt, Larry is a "wanton." He is unconcerned with "whether the desires which move him to act are desires by which he wants to be moved to act." Harry Frankfurt "Freedom of the Will and the Concept of a Person," in *Free Will*, ed. Gary Watson (Oxford: Oxford University Press, 1982), pp.81–95, p.88.

19. Recall how Frank confesses to being inferior to Gil as a father when he asks Gil for advice about what to do about Larry.

5
Language, Community, and Evil in *Rob Roy*

Linguistic Virtues

In the films we have been examining, the spheres of interpersonal life are private, comprised of romantic partnership, family, and friends. With Michael Caton-Jones's film *Rob Roy* (1995), we find virtue and vice displayed in the contexts of a tightly knit community and the wider politico-economic fabric of the state. This film also differs from the previous movies in presenting a protagonist whose character is firmly established. Rather than observing Robert Roy MacGregor developing virtues or overcoming vices, we see him exercise virtues he already possesses. He exercises them in concentric spheres of social life—nuclear family, clan, and state.

The film stands at the crossroads in our little collection, as the character of Rob Roy straddles two social worlds. Rob Roy derives his strength and virtue from life within the MacGregor clan, a paradigm of cooperative community. However, he must interact with the socioeconomic world beyond the clan, a cutthroat society shaped by grim material need, starkly monetary alliances, and power struggles among the nobility. This wider world of a barren and brutal political economy is the context of our remaining three films.

Rob Roy resembles *Parenthood* in that the social domain of both stories determines the class of virtues on which the film focuses. Just as *Parenthood* dwelled on virtues indigenous to family life, so does *Rob Roy* emphasize virtues crucial to cooperative community. They are virtues of

Rob Roy: Rob holds on,
blunting Archie's swordplay.

language use—linguistic virtues, so to speak. The relevant virtues and
vices correspond to moral standards of speech that make moral community possible. The character of Rob Roy, in particular, embodies a constellation of moral virtues that reflect standards of reciprocity, promise keeping, and truthfulness.

Corresponding to these moral standards of speech are the following
virtues: reciprocity informs respect; regard for promise keeping is found in
fidelity or integrity; and, of course, truthfulness is itself a virtue.
Reciprocity is captured in respect for other people in that respect compels
us to listen to what other people have to say and to vouchsafe to them the
same freedom to express their thought that we want for ourselves. In reci-
procal relationships, interlocutors are open to what one another has to say,
and participation in the conversation is extended to everyone affected by
what is discussed. Fidelity and integrity seem appropriate as the virtues
that dispose us to keep our promises. Fidelity is apt as a virtue of promise
keeping as it implies faithfulness to one's word, and integrity commits us
to the principles and conduct that define ourselves. Truthfulness is itself a
moral virtue. It involves resisting, or being free of, the temptation to lie,
distort, misdirect, dissemble, or omit relevant information when doing so
appears to serve our interests.

For the creation and sustaining of genuine moral community, the
group's members must habitually adhere to the moral norms regulating
speech and conform to these norms to a high degree. The cohesion and
unity of moral community require from its members a commitment to
inviting inclusive give and take of opinion (reciprocity), keeping their

word to one another (promise keeping), and saying what they believe (truthfulness). To the extent that the people of a town, tribe, or clan lack respect for one another, fidelity, and truthfulness, they cannot form a genuine community, and they will be cut off from the benefits of wholehearted cooperation. For example, these moral virtues of language use are essential for trust and for the social and material bounty that accrues to a society in which trust ripples through everyday interaction.

The influential work of Jurgen Habermas in discourse, or communication, ethics helps elucidate the philosophical theme of *Rob Roy*. As part of his model of democratic procedural justice, Habermas offers conditions necessary to agreement on basic ethical principles ("valid norms"), and these conditions define an ideal speech situation.[1] The grand Habermasian theory of communicative action, democracy, and valid ethical principles certainly exceeds the scope of my film interpretation. However, Habermas's portrait of the ideal speech situation, especially his understanding of reciprocity in discourse, clarifies the moral principles of speech to which Rob Roy adheres so fiercely.

The condition of reciprocity, sometimes referred to in discourse ethics as an aspect of justice, entails that all people "have the same chance to put forward interpretations, assertions, recommendations, explanations, and justifications," so that nothing previously said is exempt from criticism.[2] The first dimension of reciprocity, then, is inclusiveness. As commentator Edmund Arens puts it, "The principle of justice implies that nobody may be excluded from participation in the process of reaching an understanding."[3] In addition to inclusiveness, or as a condition of it, reciprocity protects individuals from coercion. "No speaker may be prevented, by internal or external coercion, from exercising his rights [to question the ideas of others or express his or her own opinions]."[4] "Internal coercion" refers to the ingrained ideological prejudices or indoctrination that can prevent individuals from forming, let alone voicing, their own views on issues that affect them.

Habermas's understanding of reciprocity, therefore, involves freedom "from" as well as freedom "to"—freedom from coercive force and freedom to express oneself. People are not to be prevented from, or intimidated out of, expressing their opinions; no topics are ruled out beforehand, and no one is precluded from participating in the discussion. All this is negative in thrust, to abjure unprincipled restrictions on who may participate, what they may say, and how they may express themselves. The determinants of reciprocity have implications for that other moral standard of speech—

truthfulness. The upshot of reciprocity is that the interlocutors are oriented toward truth, a readiness "to expose their assertions of truth to criticism from others . . . [to] mutually recognize each other as able to contradict one another . . . as being in a communicative, cooperative search for a mutual understanding of the disputed claims."[5]

The goal of the group seeking the truth is somewhat distinct from individuals, such as Rob Roy, being dedicated to speaking truthfully. But truthful speech would seem to be a necessary condition for the cooperative search for true principles or fair adjudication of disputes. Speaking truthfully is further connected with reciprocity by tacitly presupposing it. Explicating Habermas's views, David Ingram notes that "whenever we assert that something is true or right, we imply that all other persons should agree with us."[6] Since the agreement of other language users presupposes that they are included and able to express themselves freely in the conversation, making truth claims implies reciprocity.

Moral standards of speech should be distinguished from nonmoral linguistic norms that make communication possible, even among immoral people. Nonmoral linguistic norms include the rules of grammar and semantic reference, as well as context-sensitive language use, such as storytelling, theatrical speech, irony, and joke telling. These nonmoral norms enable us to convey shared meaning and subsequently to act on it. But these norms take us only so far. Some minimal version of the moral standards of discourse must be honored in ordinary social interaction, or very little could be accomplished through language. Without counting on some modicum of truthfulness, we could not reliably act on what we are told at all. If people did not more or less typically keep their promises, promise making and the interests served by it would not be viable.[7] And at least a semblance of reciprocity seems needed in certain critical contexts and at some levels of decisionmaking, or people would become disaffected and unruly.

Habermas views everyday commonplace conversation, which falls quite short of the ideal speech situation, as nevertheless implicitly informed by its moral standards. The principles that define the ideal speech situation are to some extent presupposed by run-of-the-mill communication. The underlying structure of everyday language "anticipates an *ideal speech situation*—in which full reciprocity, solidarity, and autonomy are achieved."[8] Socrates makes a similar observation in *The Republic*. He argues that social organizations, no matter how unvirtuous their members, must function within at least a bare-bones framework of justice in order to accomplish anything.[9] Otherwise, suspicion and double-crossing will prevent the cooperation necessary for achieving the group's goals. *Rob Roy* depicts and dissects social groups that honor moral standards of speech in varying degrees.

The film's portrayal of Rob Roy's character suggests that adhering to moral standards of speech is as necessary for a moral self as it is for a moral community. The linguistic virtues are important to an individual's overall moral character because his relationship to himself is mediated by how he speaks with other people. We cannot maintain our self-respect and integrity unless we exercise these virtues in social intercourse. In being true to other people, individuals are true to themselves, to what they believe and value. Rob Roy exhibits the linguistic virtues within his nuclear family, in the context of the clan's decisionmaking, and in dealing with acquaintances in the wider political state. Not only does he hold himself to what he says, fidelity to speech as fidelity to self (hence integrity), but Rob Roy is self-conscious about how speaking to other people entails a relationship with himself. He repeatedly cites his word or oath as surety and sees speaking falsely as jeopardizing his honor.

An oath or promise, for instance, is a linguistic representation we make of ourselves to the world. As such, we stand in relationship to ourselves even as we thereby put ourselves in relationship to other people. If we do not hold ourselves to what we have said in the past, if we are not true to our word, then we are not true to ourselves because we are not now continuous with who we were when we made the promise.[10] When we give our word to another person it is as if we are entrusting something of ourselves to that individual. Violating our promise not only breaks faith with the other person but is a breach with ourselves. As we will see, Rob Roy is willing to risk everything else he holds dear for the sake of keeping himself whole.

Consider the violation of the self contained in that most blatant disregard for truth telling, lying. When we lie, our own speech separates us from what we truly believe. The speech act fails to present the real self, for the real self is identified with the beliefs the person thinks are true. The content of the lie is antagonistic to what the individual is. Arnold Isenberg explains that "a man who lies, in a sense, opposes himself: he denies what he affirms or affirms what he denies."[11] An inherent end of speech is the communication of belief. Kant says that the liar "has a purpose directly opposed to the natural purposiveness of the power of communicating one's thoughts."[12] Because the liar necessarily shares in this "natural purposiveness" of language, he opposes himself as a language user and as a thinker whose cogency of thought depends on consistency in speech.

The relationship that all individuals have with themselves is mediated by their communications with other people, but the film offers Rob Roy as a paradigm of moral excellence that illuminates declensions toward its opposite pole. At the extremes of Montrose and Killearn, we see characters whose debased natures go hand in hand with their cavalier treatment of language. Their unprincipled inner life flows from their perfidy toward others. In between the lofty and base extremes, individuals such as Mary and Alasdair are merely generally moral. Their willingness to compromise promises and the truth corresponds to the more pedestrian morality of their characters—too easily angered and too easily shaken in their loyalty.

The virtues of discourse can also provide a basis for other moral virtues. Fidelity and truthfulness, for instance, can inspire courage. Someone who is deeply committed to keeping her promises may risk her own safety to fulfill the obligation incurred by giving her word. When we later examine *Aliens*, we will see that Ripley unhesitatingly puts her life in perilous jeopardy in order to rescue the girl, Newt. Perhaps Ripley's earlier promise never to leave Newt helps her screw her courage to the sticking point when time has almost run out for rescuing the child. In another historically based film, Fred Zinneman's *A Man for All Seasons* (1966), the courage of Thomas More is portrayed as directly stemming from his commitment to truthfulness. More risks everything he has, eventually losing his life, when speaking against his religious belief would swiftly and easily get him out of hot water.

Consider further how trustworthiness is likely to be aligned with truthfulness. It goes without saying that people who are true to their word are obviously to be trusted in their speech, but they are likely to be reliable in other areas of social life as well. Truthfulness may be but one manifestation of a broader trustworthiness, or the two virtues may simply dovetail, mutually reinforcing one another. Whatever the precise relationship, we can usually count on truthful people to be forthright or dependable in general, even when it may not be in their interest to do so. Conversely, people who habitually deceive or dissemble are not to be trusted in many respects. Recall how Larry, in *Parenthood*, habitually lies or distorts the truth to his own ends. His untruthfulness is accompanied by untrustworthiness, first, when he covertly tries to sell his father's vintage antique car, and later, when he takes no responsibility for paying his debts or rearing his son.

Truthfulness and fidelity to one's word can also collaborate with the virtue of tenacity or perseverance. Holding to the truth or holding oneself to a promise reflects the determination needed to maintain a firm grip on something important when doing so is arduous and painful. Loyalty is a figurative form of tenacity—persevering in a relationship when we might be justified or excused for letting it go. The film depicts Rob Roy as a stellar example of someone who is loyal, holding onto belief in the trustworthiness of a friend when no one else does. In the film's finale, Rob Roy literally exhibits a physical tenacity by holding onto Archie's sword barehanded, and thereby saves himself from death. I take Rob Roy's strength of will to hang on to the very thing that cuts him so badly as symbolic of less tangible forms of perseverance, such as loyalty, which save him from a kind of moral death.

In the area of moral psychology, *Rob Roy* explores the principle of likeness: People who possess virtues are able to recognize their presence in others.[13] Thus, Rob Roy is able to perceive loyalty and trustworthiness where his kinsmen cannot, and he can discern their absence from the knaves who threaten him. Rob Roy is best equipped to take the measure of individuals' linguistic virtues because they are most fully realized in him.

Contrasting with the virtues of language use are the vices of disrespect, faithlessness, and deceitfulness. Here we need to distinguish degrees of moral failure. Some individuals too easily yield to the temptations to compromise moral standards of speech from self-interest or to subordinate these standards to other values. There are also people who try to resist excluding other individuals from decisionmaking (lack of respect) or breaking their promises (lack of fidelity) and feel remorse at their weakness when their resistance is overcome. And still other people suffer from lack of self-knowledge, unaware that they manipulate the truth or the people with whom they interact. Most of us are guilty of such lapses in virtue at one time or another, but the three main antagonists in *Rob Roy* go further. They typically flout the moral constraints on language use without compunction, occasionally with glee.

To Montrose, Killearn, and Archie, language is merely an instrument, like a sword or horse, used to get what they want. Habermas categorizes such instrumental use of language as strategic, and although human welfare and social life require linguistic means, using language merely as a means to morally indifferent ends misses important moral aspects of language use. Employing language solely in the service of strategic reasoning overlooks its role in working toward general moral principles or situating specific decisions within a life's plan.[14] The wicked threesome in *Rob Roy* have no compunction about dissembling, lying, manipulating, coercing, or slandering. On occasion, these characters seem to enjoy thumbing their noses at linguistic norms, reveling in their violation for the sheer spite of it, and not simply to get something they want. I consider the clutch of vices that oppose moral standards of speech a kind of evil, especially as they here entail delight in immorality for its own sake.

As the film suggests, evil undermines the linguistic bedrock on which moral social life is built and makes those individuals who suffer from it unfit for moral community. We will see how the evil trio in *Rob Roy* are incapable of moral interaction, even (or especially) among themselves. In the story, the evil characters are symbolically incapacitated for speech, either by physical or social means, and are thereby cut off from moral community. Their evil destroys community by intentionally abusing the medium by which we constitute and maintain community—speech governed by standards of reciprocity (respect), promise keeping (fidelity), and truthfulness.

The film depicts an ever-increasing departure from the ideal speech situation as the plot takes Rob Roy from family and clan to the more impersonal politico-economic society. Restrictions on freedom and inclusiveness, which define reciprocity, and loss of commitment to truth and promise giving are portrayed as resulting from the influence of social power. The power is grounded in hereditary class-status, wealth, and military might. These three sources of power typically interlock and support one another, both in the film fiction and in human history.

Words, Words, Words

Rob Roy opens on the title character exhorting his men to pursue a ragtag band of tinkers who have stolen cattle, from the Marquis of Montrose (John Hurt), for which Rob Roy MacGregor (Liam Neeson) is responsible. When the sleeping thieves are overtaken, Rob argues for talking with them in the morning rather than slaying them where they sleep. For all his brawn and skill with dirk and claymore, MacGregor is at heart a man of words: for conflict, words of conciliation; for kinsmen, words for collective deliberation; for family, words of edification and love. *Rob Roy* begins the way Plato starts *The Republic,* posing the perennial choice in resolving human conflict—weapons or words, force or reason.[15]

Although killing sleeping men is easier than fighting them should words fail, Rob is committed to attempting reasoned speech. In response to why he opts for speech over sword, Rob says, "I know one of them." His decision seems to be shaped by the idea that acquaintanceship is like a faint copy of shared membership in community. On account of familiarity, we should try to treat the person in a manner approximating the treatment of one of our own, a truncated version of the reciprocity we accord members of our social group out of respect for them. Where his friends see merely opposition, Rob sees similarity, if not kinship.

Rob's speech to the thieves announces his duty to enforce the law and offers clemency to all but their leader, Tam Sibbald, who must pay the price of being in charge. Rob tries to arrive at a peaceful solution to a violation of property rights. When Sibbald attacks, Rob kills him easily but regretfully. He commands the remaining thieves to throw down their arms, "And you have my word that no one else will die." The importance to Rob of giving his word is elaborated upon as the story progresses; its role as mainstay of his linguistic virtues, and moral personality in general, becomes more prominent. Now brought low by circumstances, Sibbald played ball with Rob in happier days. Rob feels compassion for the thieves and later tells his wife, "Those tinkers weren't all born broken men, Mary. Some of them had kin and clan."

Rob's remark about the tinkers points to two other important themes in the film: the contrast between wholeness and brokenness of personhood, and the relevance of community to the difference between them. Through action and dialogue, the story offers images of, and commentary upon, the nature of being a whole person. We will see how and why Rob Roy is the most whole person because the most moral. His linguistic virtues connect him with a particular moral community, and this community sustains him in his wholeness. The tinkers were once whole, or at least had the potential for wholeness, when they were supported by kinsmen and clansmen. Cast adrift, they cannot be complete human beings.

In an unlikely parallel, the evil trio of Montrose, Killearn, and Archie are also incomplete or broken because they, too, are bereft of the moral nurture only a genuine community can supply. For individuals to have a chance at being whole, in the sense of fully realizing their human abilities, they must be part of a larger whole. The more moral that larger social organization, the better the chance of the individuals flourishing within it.

Mary (Jessica Lange) scoffs at Rob's comparison of themselves with the tinkers. "MacGregors are not tinkers," she avers. Rob proves more farsighted in pointing out that a harsh winter or two could easily land the MacGregors in similar straits. Rob's economic worry initiates the story, which follows a clear trajectory. Representing the clan, Rob borrows money from Montrose to buy cattle for profit, as insurance against hard times. Montrose's factor, Killearn (Brian Cox), and swordsman, Archie Cunningham (Tim Roth), conspire to steal the borrowed money. After Killearn manipulates Rob's man, Alan McDonald (Eric Stoltz), into taking cash instead of a note of credit, Archie kills him for the thousand pounds. When Rob Roy refuses Montrose's offer to cancel the debt for a slanderous lie against the Duke of Argyll (Andrew Keir), Rob and the clan must fight Montrose and his henchmen.

As noted, the outset of the story indicates the importance of speech in the individual's relation to others and to himself. The film suggests that Rob is right to try parleying with the tinkers, so long as he realizes that the rational, peaceful approach of language may fail and that force may be needed. The opening segment also introduces two subordinate characters in revealing, but inconspicuous, moments. Alan McDonald is first shown smelling cattle dung, as he estimates the tinkers' head start. McDonald is Rob's right-hand man, trusted to track the tinkers as he will later be entrusted to complete the loan for the cattle money on Rob's behalf. As good as McDonald's ability to draw inferences from the evidence of his senses, however, he will not be able to sniff out the trap in which Killearn and Archie ensnare him.

After McDonald gives his estimate of the progress of the tinkers with the stolen cattle, Rob's brother, Alasdair (Brian McCardie), recommends abandoning the pursuit. Speaking of the thieves, Alasdair says, "They're away and gone, the beasts sold." Although not especially telling in itself, the story will disclose that Alasdair's reluctance to continue after the stolen cattle is an aspect of his lack of fortitude and discipline. Alasdair lacks the proper will, perhaps because he doesn't have the judgment necessary to inform it. He doesn't know when to stay the course and when to retreat. Alasdair's inability to restrain his impulse to attack Montrose's soldiers, for example, leads to Rob's eventual capture, as well as to the death of a kinsman and his own demise. Alasdair's readiness to quit hounding the tinkers (who are soon overtaken) foretells a looseness in his moral frame, in sharp contrast with Rob's sound character.

The opening tinker episode also broaches the moral linguistic standards of truthfulness, promise keeping, and reciprocity central to the story and character of Rob Roy. Rob speaks truthfully to Tam Sibbald and, after killing him, gives his word to the other tinkers that no one else has to die. In addition, the pursuit party typifies the way the MacGregor clan upholds the principle of reciprocity—everyone enjoying free and equal candid expression of opinion. Although Rob lays out plans, his companions freely give their opinions, and Rob persuades with reasoned argument.

The clan's conversational modus operandi is repeated when Rob later proposes his idea to borrow money from the Marquis of Montrose to purchase cattle. He and the men talk things over. They agree on how the clansmen will later participate: bargaining in the purchase of the cattle, driving the cattle to sale, and finally sharing in the profit. The initiative is Rob's, but the effort is communal. The participants share in one another's ends, as Kant would say. They do so by virtue of being a community formed by trust and the commitment to fitting their action to what they say, so as to be trustworthy.

The concept of community is, however, confined to the clan, much as it was for Plato and his fellow Athenians. The film does not portray Rob Roy as a man of the Enlightenment and its universal order of equal participants. The thought never crosses his mind to include the tinkers in his circle, in an unrestricted exchange of ideas. Neither does Rob reason that the tinkers' poverty might justify their theft of Montrose's cattle or that he is in the wrong in upholding the nobleman's property rights. The horizon of Rob's moral vision is limited by his time and social context.

However, even when we aim for universal participation, for a public exchange of the ideas of all people, and strive to make social institutions accord with an ideal speech situation, we may need to distinguish our community of personal association from the wider world. Habermas himself concedes that specific normative obligations "do not extend beyond the boundaries of a concrete lifeworld of family, tribe, city, or nation."[16] The MacGregor clan exemplifies the importance of a history of shared daily life to one's group identification and allegiance, as "the identity of the group is reproduced through intact relationships of mutual recognition."[17] Given the limitations of Rob's context and the fact that the tinkers fall outside his clan, Rob articulates and embodies better than most fictional or real individuals the linguistic virtues that elevate a people to a moral community.

After their plans go awry and Rob is hunted by Montrose's men, the clan meets in council to discuss how to respond to the initial attack by Montrose's soldiers. Again, all the clanspeople, including the women, have a chance to speak their minds. Against the heated urging to fight Montrose's soldiers, Rob argues that the village lost homes and cattle, but "none were killed, none were injured." Retribution doesn't require taking life, and the MacGregors are greatly outnumbered. Instead, Rob proposes hurting the Marquis economically by guerrilla marauding. His reasoning prevails over the desire for vengeance, as the men and women of the clan are persuaded that this is best for the community.

The clan arrives at consensus on the social good through open, forthright discussion of the wrongs done to the community and its options for rectifying them. The clan meetings clearly center around strategy, pragmatic discussion of how to achieve particular group goals. More subtly, the meetings also demonstrate what Habermas calls "ethical-existential discourse," a form of communication that is "concerned with processes of individual or collective self-understanding and ascertaining identity."[18] Rob implicitly helps the clan understand itself. He points out the group's limitations, its possibilities, and what justice counsels doing in retaliation for the destruction of property, but not life.

The somber evening meeting by firelight contrasts with an earlier, merry bonfire gathering of the clan to celebrate the launching of the cattle venture. While the clan carouses, dancing and drinking, however, Archie is riding down McDonald to kill him and steal the cattle cash. The film artfully cuts back and forth between the community's bonfire bonhomie and Archie's cold-blooded ambush of the isolated McDonald. Infectious dance music alternates with the ominous thudding of horses' hooves. Juxtaposing the two events, *Rob Roy* cinematically renders the clan's future and how its vigor is circumscribed by violence. The plight of Rob and his kinsmen is wordlessly figured, suggesting that violence always lurks beyond the pale of the bright light provided by moral community and the moral standards of speech on which it rests. The parallel events intersect when McDonald's riderless horse enters the festive clearing, and the clan's spirits are appropriately dimmed by the grim irony of a future foreclosed even as they cheered its apparent unfolding.

The miniature society of family is also defined by speech. Rob engages in ethical-existential speech as he explicitly talks with his sons about the nature of moral character. He instructs them in the meaning of honor, a commitment as valuable to family and community as it is to the individual who steels himself to its demands. Rob commends honor as "a gift we give ourselves," which nobody can give or take away. It originates in the relation the individual has to himself and further defines the self by providing a moral measure or ideal by which to govern conduct. Rob tells his boys, "Honor grows in you and speaks to you. All you need do is listen."

Of course, honor itself cannot speak, but it calls for a mode of discourse that mediates the individual's relation to himself. The moral self is constituted by a morally alert self-consciousness and the speaking that makes that possible. The communing with himself that the man of honor engages in is mirrored in his communication with other people. That interpersonal communication must satisfy moral standards of speech or the individual's self-communion will be impaired and his honor jeopardized. Thus, among the desiderata of honor, Rob includes truthfulness in talking about other people: "You must never mistreat a woman or *malign* [emphasis added] a man, or stand by and see another do so."

Although no one can take our honor from us, we can throw it away by violating individuals directly by means of false speech or abusive force, or indirectly, by permitting their violation by other people. The virtuous man's self-understanding is mediated by moral standards of speech and the constraint they place on his actions. The story draws out the implications of living up to this self-conscious conception of moral selfhood for the individual, his family, and their community.

Rob amplifies upon the relationship among speech, honor, and moral selfhood during his contracting with the Marquis of Montrose for the thousand pound loan for the cattle. Montrose is happy with Rob's land as security but vexed by Rob adding that the money is further secured by his oath. When the Marquis questions his sense of honor, Rob adds, "When my word is given, it is good." Montrose snickers, complaining that MacGregor conveniently buys nobility cheap, with words. He disparages Rob's self-referential language, accusing him of using words such as "honor" to artificially inflate the value of words, as in giving an oath.

Here we see the inverted image of the likeness principle mentioned earlier: People who possess virtues are able to recognize them in other individuals. So lacking is Montrose in truthfulness and fidelity that he can see no virtue in being true in speech or in holding ourselves to what we say. The only attributes of people that matter to Montrose are extrinsic to their moral personality—titled wealth and land. Later in the story, however, Montrose implicitly contradicts himself. He demonstrates why he must value speech when he bargains with Rob to lie about the Duke of Argyll.

The importance of taking and keeping oaths develops another theme found in *A Man for All Seasons*. When Richard Rich perjures himself in court to condemn Thomas More, More tells him that in taking an oath before God a man holds his soul in his hands. The oath represents us to the world and to God. The implication in both films is that what we say and our willingness to stand by it, more than land or titles, make us what we are by symbolizing us. To represent ourselves falsely to the world (or God) is, in effect, to indicate that what we truly are is of little worth.

The titles, land, and money, by which Montrose sets such store, can be undeserved or circumstantial. The Marquis of Montrose no more deserves his lineage and inherited wealth than the hapless tinkers merit their poverty. Whether an individual keeps his word, however, is up to him and measures his moral worth. Without confidence in one another's speech, we cannot carry on as a moral community, which includes making fair contracts or trying men justly for alleged crimes.

The Organization of Evil

The tale of Rob Roy is populated with characters who exhibit a full catalogue of virtues and vices. We do not lack for examples of courage and recklessness, compassion and brutality, humility and arrogance, even wisdom and foolishness. Comparable moral portraits can be found in a number of insightful fiction films. *Rob Roy* is unusual, however, in its depiction of the distinctive good and evil grounded in moral standards of speech. Contrasting with Rob's linguistic virtues are the linguistic vices of the three principal evil characters. Although Montrose, Killearn, and Archie have plenty of such vices as malice, avarice, and spite, their corruption goes deeper, to the linguistic basis of moral social life. These characters do not simply overlook or compromise the moral norms that limit what we may and may not say. Rather, they mock the norms and eagerly transgress the limits they prescribe.

The three villains in *Rob Roy* are incapable of moral community because they are without respect for requirements of reciprocity, promise keeping, or truthfulness in the use of language. Alternatively, because they are not committed to something beyond themselves, such as family or clan or justice, nothing constrains their speech. Before we interpret linguistic vice in light of their use and misuse of words, we need to sketch the three faces of evil as depicted in the film. Embedded in the larger linguistic theme is a careful rendering of the organization of evil.

In representing three species of wickedness, *Rob Roy* shows how they interlock in joint enterprise. The temptation may be simply to rank the bad men according to the degree of their corruption, but this approach would miss how their different natures and temperaments fit together like parts in a destructive machine. The trio are arranged hierarchically, but not baldly from bad to worst. Rather, the conventional hierarchy created by birth, station, and wealth dictates proximity to the dirty work. The men who occupy the roles in this order hardly exhaust the varieties of evil, but they do delineate three clear types. The villains not only provide a counterpoint to the linguistic virtues of Rob but clarify the lesser immorality of characters who are merely morally flawed by being hot-tempered or weak-willed, for example.

The film wastes no time in setting out the antagonism between Rob Roy's virtue and the evil with which he must contend. The opening segment with the tinkers is immediately followed by the Marquis of Montrose wagering against the Duke of Argyll on a duel. Argyll's swordsman, Guthrie, is a lummox who contrasts smartly with Montrose's dandy of a killer, Archibald Cunningham. When Archie duels, he struts and poses, postures and smirks, flaunting his superior skill and the fine figure he cuts. But beneath his finery, Archie is a predator, taking women, money, and life without scruple. He is portrayed as a destructive force of nature, much the way archetypal gunslingers are in Western movies.

Archie's slicing and dicing of his fencing opponents is mirrored in the way his sexual sorties are more a tearing into the woman than a mutual physical passion or lovemaking. Leading Montrose's men in burning clan homes, for example, Archie gratuitously rapes Rob's wife, Mary. More than the sexual pleasure, Archie appears to enjoy dominating Mary and indirectly triumphing over Rob.[19] Thinking to stain Rob's honor, Archie hopes to goad him into a duel. Archie's animal cunning and taste for competition are thereby joined to his depravity in his rape of Mary.

He is depraved as only someone can be who has not been brought into the gentle concord of moral community. Archie's inhuman nature is indicated by Rob's reference to him as a "thing" and by Argyll calling him "carrion." The carrion reference may seem misplaced, since it is Archie who makes mincemeat of his fencing opponents, leaving them ready to decay. But it appears more apt if we think of Archie as carrion of the spirit, already dead in the sense of being unmoved by loyalty, friendship, or love, and incapable of receiving another person's love. Without compassion, affection, or even self-love, Archie proclaims himself a homeless bastard. He lives to satisfy his appetites for fine clothing, gambling, women, and bloodshed, aware that he exists outside the bounds and bonds of moral community. Archie is an evil variant of the man of action, sadistically executing the designs hatched and bankrolled by his benefactor, Montrose.

The scene of Archie fighting with Guthrie is duplicated in the film's climactic duel between Archie and Rob, at the end of which Archie holds

Rob's throat at sword's point just as he holds Guthrie's. The two sword fights frame the story, a story in which Rob typically tries to avoid fighting. The scene of the concluding duel also contrasts the lives of the nobility with the life of the clan, even as the clan's position had been contrasted with that of the tinkers in the film's first sequence. In quick strokes, then, *Rob Roy* displays the socioeconomic strata of the period within scenes of violent action, alluding to undercurrents of class conflict. The structure of the movie also sets off the animosity between Argyll and Montrose, who wager on the final duel as well as the opening sword fight.

The Marquis of Montrose exemplifies the evil of high places, happiest when embroiled in court intrigue, positioning himself in shifting confederacies of nobles. Like Archie, he is arrogant and spiteful, and needs to win. But he gets others to carry out his plans, as he manages his estate, finances, and underlings. Each kind of evil possesses an intelligence appropriate to it. Montrose's craftiness accords with someone above, and well back from, the fray, as if his lofty social position has also given him a higher perspective from which to judge his contemporaries and their actions.

Montrose personifies the evil variety of the well-born, deluded in thinking that birthright determines a person's true quality. He admonishes Archie to "remember [his] place, . . . that is all I ask of any man." When arranging for the loan, Rob speaks modestly of his station and ability, eliciting Montrose's approving, "To know one's place in the order of things is a great blessing." No possibility of reciprocity exists for Montrose, and he seems without respect even for others of his social class. People such as Archie and Rob are beneath him, and such nobles as Argyll are his enemies or potential threats. Montrose confuses caste status with moral worth because he thinks hereditary class structure *is* the moral order. Montrose is as much outside moral society as Archie is. Archie owes allegiance to nothing but his private appetites because he is an animal of prey, uncivilized in the sense of not being a citizen of a moral society. Montrose feels no compunctions about indulging himself because he thinks privilege puts him above others and their reproach.

Montrose's factor, Killearn, operates in the space between the lofty privilege of Montrose and the base feasting of Archie. Possessing neither Archie's animal ruthlessness nor Montrose's commanding status, Killearn must live by his wiles. Like a jackal, he scrounges for whatever he can find and snatches at the leavings of others. The film introduces Killearn asking Archie's wench, Betty, for postcoital sexual favors as she is leaving Archie's bedchamber. Killearn's salacious proposition is typical, as he survives and thrives on spoils—whether women, money, or simply the successes and misfortunes of others.

Where Montrose is the corrupt man of position and authority, and Archie the rapacious man of action, Killearn is the insidious version of the manager. He is the go-between, seeing to the details of plans, usually those of Montrose but sometimes his own. He isn't equipped to fabricate grand plans or execute any, but he is adept at conniving, cooking up sneaky schemes, and skimming what he can from whatever comes his way.

Killearn lives off the position and machinations of the Marquis and Archie's destructiveness. He is a looker and a talker, not a doer. Consider, for instance, how he tries to talk his way out of capture by Rob Roy. First, Killearn induces the thuggish Guthrie to fight Rob, and then he tries to weasel his way out of Rob's clutches. Similarly, confronted by Mary at the MacGregor's stronghold, he praises the nobility of her bearing as she walked from her burning village home. Mary refuses Killearn's oily compliment by precisely describing his vicarious participation in her rape: "You stood and gloated. You did all with your eyes."

Montrose aptly describes Killearn, his own administrator, as a "greasy capon." Apart from his lubricious manner, Killearn greases the engines of fortune as Montrose's factotum and oils the wheels of his schemes. He is capon-like in that he does not caper and crow like Archie the rooster, but only looks on with a leer. The scavenger takes what he can, even the sight of another's debauchery or cruelty. Killearn copies according to his abilities. His conniving is a lower imitation of his master's court intrigues, and his sexual pleasures are derived from Archie's callous exploits.

As with his cohorts, Killearn possesses an intelligence attuned to his evil. He is able to turn the affairs of other people to his profit. As indicated, he manipulates Rob Roy's lieutenant, McDonald, into taking a cash loan for the cattle instead of the agreed upon note of credit so that Archie can steal the money after killing him. Killearn's street smarts also enable him to figure out how things stand. After being abducted by Rob, he discerns that Mary hasn't told Rob of Archie's rape and that she may be carrying Archie's child. Killearn then tries to fashion an escape from his sexual surmise. His shifting eyes during this scene attest to how he is always looking for an advantage, always on the lookout for what might be available to preserve or further himself.

The evil of these men is not simple moral failure. Theirs is not the weakness of character that yields to temptation or passion or that cannot be steadfast when hard-pressed. The film illustrates such moral shortcomings in the character of Rob's younger brother, Alasdair. He is, by turns, quick-tempered and slow to vigilance. Indulging his anger by shooting one of Montrose's soldiers, Alasdair not only disobeys Rob and gets himself killed, but his lack of discipline leads to Rob's capture. Alternately, Alasdair is negligent, falling asleep on the watch for attack by Montrose's soldiers, and so is largely responsible for Mary's rape by Archie. Alasdair subsequently breaks his word to Mary by telling Rob of her rape and breaks his bond with McDonald, believing the rumor that he has run off with the thousand pounds.

These breaches of loyalty bespeak a lack of steadfastness or durability of resolve. But Alasdair is not wicked. His flaws fall within the moral sphere of community because he is committed to his kinsmen. Alasdair may fall short, but he intends to do right by the clan, and he tries to use language in a morally principled way. He yields to Mary's fierce demands for silence as much out of respect for what she has endured and her love of Rob as out of intimidation. Alasdair reveals the rape to Rob with his dying breath out of his persisting, but hitherto suppressed, respect for the truth.

Alasdair represents a lad of moral fiber with much potential, but who is as yet immature. Impetuous and unaware of his character flaws, Alasdair nevertheless is a caring person who is racked by the moral quandary in which he finds himself. In contrast, Montrose and his hirelings are truly evil, never bothered by a moral qualm, much less a crisis of conscience.

The Language of Evil

The three vicious characters in league in *Rob Roy* suffer the baseness of those who are beyond the pale, heedless of the limits of speech and action that build moral community. They are parasites, drawing nourishment from the organs of society, but outside its bonds of duty and fellowship. The role of speech in their lives defines their wickedness. In fact, their alliance necessarily teeters because common to them is the antisocial use of speech and disregard for its regulatory ideals.

The evil characters use speech merely as an instrument to achieve their private ends. Their lack of commitment to anything greater than themselves is reflected in the ease with which they turn language to their self-interest, saying whatever seems useful regardless of its truth or how it may conflict with their past assertions. They have no friendships, no fealty to anything beyond their appetites, such as family or clan, love or justice.

Without commitment to other people, Montrose and his lackeys are untrammeled by moral standards of language use.

In contrast, when Mary withholds the truth about her rape from Rob, she does so to spare him shame and to keep him from challenging the dangerous Archie in a duel. Speech is a medium for maintaining a loving relationship and for keeping the clan in tact. When the MacGregors make love, words are woven throughout: words of affection, words humorous, words erotic. Their passion doesn't shut off conversation but invites it. They look at each other, enjoying one another's expression, enhancing one another's subjectivity in full reciprocity.

Complementing the reciprocity that sustains the lovemaking and conversation of the MacGregors early in the film is an emotional scene toward the story's end, in which Rob and Mary ask one another's forgiveness. Mary awakens in the night to find the long-absent Rob sitting still by the fire. He has barely escaped the clutches of Montrose's soldiers, led by Archie, and is badly beaten. She begs Rob to forgive her for not telling him of the rape. Rob pleads to be forgiven for stubbornly, pridefully refusing to give Montrose what he had asked for: the slander of Argyll that Montrose had said would cancel Rob's debt to him.[20]

Not only do the MacGregor spouses treat each other with reciprocity by speaking identically to one another—apologizing and asking for the same thing, forgiveness. But their identical speeches presuppose reciprocity in expressing an understanding of the harm they have caused one another and in conveying that the spouse's feelings and welfare are at least as important as their own. None of the evil trio ever asks for forgiveness, nor do any of them seem capable of seeing the need for it. After their mutual pleas for forgiveness, Rob and Mary spare each other self-recrimination.[21] The theme of personal wholeness resurfaces when Mary points out that had Rob yielded to Montrose, he would not have himself: "Would you have stolen from yourself that what makes you Robert MacGregor?"[22] Recall, what Montrose had demanded from Rob was the compromise of honor entailed in the slandering of Argyll. Moreover, when Montrose sends Archie after Rob, he tells Archie to bring Rob back "broken but not dead." As we see, Rob's body is quite broken, but his character and fighting spirit remain intact.

The scene of the MacGregors' mutual solicitation and love retrospectively casts an ironic light on Rob's recent escape from Archie. Badly beaten and exhausted, Rob is on the ground, literally at the end of his rope, with which he is about to be hanged. In one agile motion, Rob leaps to his feet, wraps the rope around Archie's neck, and jumps over the bridge. The film presents a grizzly image of ironic reciprocity in the split-second during which Rob is suspended above the water by the very rope that strangles Archie, pinning him to the bridgeworks. Dangling over the river, Rob's weight pulls the rope tightly about Archie's throat. For Archie to be saved, the rope must be cut, thereby freeing Rob from bondage, into the flowing river. The enemies are literally tied together, the preservation of Archie's life reciprocally necessitating Rob's freedom.[23]

Rob and Mary are not perfect, of course, and the film is realistic in portraying exchanges in which their reciprocity is strained if not severed. For example, early in the story, Rob tells Mary his plan to borrow money for the cattle from Montrose. She reproaches him for getting too big for his britches, for thinking he can cut deals with the likes of the Marquis. Hurt by Mary's sour reaction to his project, Rob replies, "I didn't tell you my mind to be flayed for it." Here Rob distinguishes his speech, which includes Mary in his plan for their betterment, from her tongue-lashing, and breaks off conversation.

Mary's skepticism appears justified by the disastrous outcome of Rob's arrangement with the Marquis. Perhaps Rob was foolish to think he could be business partners with an arrogant nobleman. On this view, Rob's pride shuts out Mary's wise words, and the failure to maintain linguistic reciprocity is his. Mitigating against this criticism of Rob is the prudence of his economic concern for the clan, a concern that Mary unwisely dismisses. In addition, Mary does not point out to him that neither Montrose nor Killearn can be trusted and that Rob is gullible in believing they will deal fairly with him. Instead of giving reasoned argument against Rob's plan, Mary simply scoffs at his presumptuousness.

I began reflection on the film with its origins in the opposition between words and weapons. But now we should qualify that opposition by adding that the distinction between words and weapons only holds when language is bound by moral standards of use. When so bound, words establish and maintain human relationship: to deepen and strengthen family, friendship, and community; to reach accord with antagonists; to make contracts with acquaintances or strangers. When speech is not bound by reciprocity, promise keeping, and truthfulness, it is merely a means to whatever ends we happen to have. Under these conditions, words themselves can be weapons, used to injure or deceive, intimidate or manipulate. The wicked men in the story arm themselves with words.

Montrose and Archie speak to bludgeon, slash, and prick. Sometimes Montrose threatens or commands harm, sometimes he acidly condescends or derides. Archie's most cutting use of language occurs when Betty, the servant he has seduced, reminds him she is pregnant. To Archie's suggestion that she have an abortion, Betty replies that she loves him. Archie snidely retorts: "Love is a dunghill, Betty, and I am but a cock who climbs upon it to crow." Unlike Rob and Mary, who speak truthfully out of mutual love and respect, Archie is moved by disdain to tell the truth about himself. He would as readily speak falsely if it suited his self-proclaiming, because words are merely his vehicle for crowing and cutting.

The plot hinges on Killearn's deceptive, manipulative use of speech to steal the money Rob Roy borrows from Montrose for the cattle deal. Again, Archie is able to take the money Rob's man, McDonald, is carrying only because Killearn maneuvers McDonald into taking cash instead of the agreed upon promissory note. To cover up the murder and theft, Killearn cites an advertisement for the Americas that McDonald had been perusing, insinuating that he has absconded across the ocean with the missing money. Killearn's fabrications concerning the theft are so central to the complication of the plot that they can overshadow the variety of purposes to which he puts his virtuosity with language.

Besides the dissembling or deceiving speech designed to profit him, Killearn hops from flattery to blackmail in an effort to save his own skin. After Rob abducts Killearn for the purpose of bringing him to (clan) justice, Mary gets him alone and tries to pressure a confession out of him. Killearn begins by wheedling, telling Mary "how nobly [she] walked from that burning [cottage], like a queen." But Mary will have none of it and wants Killearn to sign a written confession in front of a judge to guarantee truthfulness. Killearn tacks into the wind. Having astutely deduced that Mary hasn't told Rob about the rape, Killearn threatens to tell him that she carries Archie's child unless Mary accepts his statement that Archie alone killed McDonald for the money. Even when he contemplates speaking truthfully, Killearn uses words to menace and still manages to anchor the truth to a lie.

Language is also Killearn's main medium of malicious play. First, it is a device for disturbing people's peace of mind and their social relationships. He delights in meddling and spreading false rumors simply to agitate people or to set them against one another. For example, Killearn tells Montrose of Archie's debts and peccadillo with Betty, ostensibly to entrench himself as Montrose's eyes and ears, but also simply to foment trouble between Montrose and Archie. Killearn never misses an opportunity to stir the pot, regardless of its likelihood of benefiting him materially. This is why Killearn suggests to Montrose that Rob Roy himself first ran off the cattle, only to recover them. He enjoys the air of incivility his rumor adds to the bargaining between Rob Roy and Montrose.

To his slander of Rob, Killearn shamelessly adds generous dollops of flattery, complimenting Rob on his bold signature, "worthy of a chieftain." Shortly thereafter, he belittles Rob to McDonald, suggesting that McDonald deserves a finer master. After all, his signature is nearly as bold as MacGregor's! Yet McDonald is no sooner out of earshot than Killearn's face, full of fawning smiles, becomes bitter with contempt. "Sheep shagger, baa aa," he bleats.

Nothing comes of Killearn's lie about Rob stealing cattle or the attempt to erode his relationship with McDonald. But his speech epitomizes Killearn's disdain for the truth. In still more oblique instances of Killearn's playing with language, he baits people solely for the sport of doing so and makes sly allusions that only he can appreciate. When Guthrie challenges Rob in order to avenge Tam Sibbald's death, for example, he tells Rob that they were close to being kinsmen because Guthrie "shagged his [Tam's] sister." Strictly for the sake of the jape, Killearn mutters, "Likely, so did Tam." During the transaction for the thousand pounds, Killearn registers McDonald's regard for the coin, saying to him, "It's a terrible shock, the sight of such a fortune within reach." Killearn speaks for his own amusement because this is indeed the small fortune brought within Killearn's very reach by dint of his murderous scheme with Archie.

Like Shakespeare's Iago, Killearn seems demonically driven to speak falsely and make mischief, reveling in the prospect of sowing discord and disrupting friendships regardless of whether he stands to reap financial benefit from the fallout. Not only does Iago also flatter and lie, misrepresent himself and goad people, but he, too, speaks often of money (although he has little use of it for himself), repeatedly telling Roderigo to "put money in his purse." Presaging the speechless fate of Killearn, Iago—that master of innuendo and verbal disingenuousness—concludes his part in *Othello* by refusing to utter another word![24]

Aside from using his own speech to cabal, demean, and threaten, Montrose also treats discourse in general as a commodity. During negotiations for the loan, he scolds Rob for trying to buy nobility cheaply, with words, as if words were of little worth. However, Montrose ironically vindicates the value Rob places on language when he later offers to forgive

Rob's debt of the thousand (stolen) pounds in exchange for Rob's false testimony against the Duke of Argyll. Montrose tries to buy Rob's speech, saying "I want your word against him." Montrose demonstrates that, in one way or another, all of us must practically value words. Although Montrose may not seem thereby committed to the genuine importance of truthfulness, he implicitly attests to it since the slander he wishes to purchase from Rob must be taken by others to be the truth, and it will have that cachet only because of Rob's reputation for honesty.

Montrose is nonplussed when Rob balks at dealing himself out of debt with a lie. He points out to Rob that "Argyll is nothing to you," as if the only good reason we could have for refusing to smear someone is that we have a personal relationship with him. Speaking falsely in itself is of no account. Montrose's tone quickly shifts from deal making to demanding, and thence to threatening. When he barks that MacGregor owes him, Rob replies: "I owe you money, nothing more." Rob declares that the requested slander of Argyll is as below him as it should be beneath Montrose. Standards of speech take precedence over MacGregor's monetary needs and Montrose's political interests.

Insulted by Rob's self-righteous rebuke, Montrose attacks Rob's right to speak, however veraciously, saying, "You misspeak yourself, MacGregor!" Of course, Montrose, who is oblivious to reciprocity, means that MacGregor has forgotten his place in the socioeconomic order. He is speaking out of turn. But from a moral point of view, how ironic an exclamation coming from Montrose, who is dealing for a slanderous lie. The irony latent in his language is lost on Montrose, who is incapable of stepping back and seeing himself as others might. In making Montrose the unintentional butt of his own words, the film implies that without respect for moral standards of speech, individuals cannot take an objective perspective on themselves. The principles of reciprocity, promise keeping, and truthfulness contain the social dimension of regard for other people as language users. When people such as Montrose employ language solely for private ends, they are locked in a private, and therefore myopic, understanding of themselves.

In the scene immediately following Rob's rebuff of Montrose, Mary echoes the nobleman's attitude. She exhibits her deficiency in the linguistic virtues by asking Rob, "What is Argyll to you?" Mary wants to know why Rob would defend Argyll against Montrose when slandering him would so easily save them, and the clan, from crushing indenture to the Marquis. Rob replies: "I do not defend him [Argyll]. I refuse to bear false witness against him." Rob's linguistic virtue is epitomized in his distinction between allegiance to truthfulness and alliance with Argyll. His statement and subsequent conduct, moreover, reveal that Rob's commitment to moral speech extends beyond family or clan. Perhaps truthfulness and fidelity to promises are universal values for Rob, but the scope of reciprocity can be limited by the misuse of physical, economic, or rhetorical power.[25]

Unwisely, Rob refuses to heed Mary's advice to apply to Argyll for help, saying that he is not being persecuted for Argyll's sake but for his own. When Rob later acknowledges that the burning of his home and the killing of his livestock exceeded what he thought Montrose would do in retaliation, we realize that his practical wisdom doesn't quite match his linguistic virtues. In fact, we will see that in forecasting the impact of Betty's possible testimony in court, Rob's faith in truth and honesty may actually keep him from being wise to the political, economic ways of the world.[26]

The film symbolizes how the evil men are incapable of communally constituted speech by rendering each of them speechless during conflict with the MacGregors. At the MacGregor camp, for instance, Killearn's neck is slit by Mary. When he comes out of the stronghold screaming that he's been cut, he is held under water by Alasdair, unable to protest further. For another example, Rob initially avoids imprisonment by putting a knife to Archie's throat and threatening to cut it. Once caught, Rob again frees himself at the expense of Archie's neck—his impromptu hanging of Archie at the bridge. Although Archie doesn't die, he is unable to speak until the film's conclusion. When he is finally felled by Rob's sword, Archie is hacked through the neck to his shoulder. No dying speech, only a gurgle, marks his demise. With Archie's death, Rob's debt to Montrose is canceled, and the Duke of Argyll has the last word with Montrose over his winning wager. Montrose simmers silently.

By incapacitating the speech of the three villains, whether physically or socially, *Rob Roy* intimates that evil undermines moral community linguistically. It sabotages community not by means of this or that particular vice, such as avarice or cowardice or sloth. Evil destroys moral community by intentionally abusing the medium by which we constitute and maintain it—speech governed by standards of reciprocity, promise keeping, and truthfulness. Genuine community requires participation by people who have the corresponding virtues of respect for one another as language users, fidelity to promises they make, and truthfulness. Without these virtues, individuals can neither define themselves as honorable nor represent themselves to others in ways that can be trusted. Lacking reliable communication, members of a society will not be able to enjoy intimacy, fellowship, or the fruits of cooperative action.

Speech, Truth, and Friendship

The villainous trio's lack of linguistic integrity is woven into two other moral deficiencies that characterize their evil. The first is their incapacity for love or friendship. The second is the failure to recognize or acknowledge the truth when they hear it. The film indicates that the linguistic virtues are necessary, though probably not sufficient, for relationships characterized by care or truthfulness. Montrose, Killearn, and Archie are all incapable of loving or befriending another person. Only Archie receives a declaration of love, and this from a young woman of a lower class whom he has seduced, and who is likely confusing infatuation with love. As we saw earlier, Archie greets Betty's declaration with contempt. Not only is he incapable of love, he laughs at it, seeing in its expression an opportunity, like swordplay, for preening condescension.

The three villains have no friends outside their association, and their little organization is itself riddled with dissension and suspicion. Early in the story, for instance, Montrose accuses Archie of contemplating defecting to Argyll to become his champion. Archie's smiling obeisance does not hide how much he chaffs at his subordination to Montrose. Later, Montrose tells Archie and Killearn that he knows the two of them are up to something, with the disappearance of McDonald and the thousand pounds, and not to play him for a fool. For his part, Archie threatens Killearn for informing on him to Montrose about his gambling debts and debauchery with Betty. And Killearn is so two-faced and self-serving that his allegiance to Montrose could be transferred to the highest bidder. Killearn is also eager to sell Archie out to the MacGregors to save his own skin.

Reciprocity is out of the question within the wicked coterie. Aside from the fact that each member is always jostling for personal advantage with regard to the other two, Archie and Killearn are clearly subservient to Montrose. He will always have the last word. As he tells Archie, "Remember your place, sir. That's all I ask of any man." Typical of most people during this historical period, Killearn accepts the socioeconomic stratification and seems to enjoy his role as assistant to landed gentry. Killearn carries the mind-set of hierarchy into his dealings with McDonald, for example, when he derides McDonald for not having a "finer master" than MacGregor. However, McDonald privileges reciprocity over authority by informing Killearn that he doesn't serve MacGregor; rather, MacGregor is his friend.

Recall the importance of interpersonal harmony on the Socratic analysis of group functioning in *The Republic*. Socrates points out that without some degree of justice, even a gang of thieves or bandits will not be able to cooperate enough to accomplish their goals, unjust though those goals may be.[27] The discord among Montrose, Killearn, and Archie is the result of the factionalism that injustice sows and of their shared conviction in one another's untrustworthiness. Integral to their injustice, and its social hallmark, is their unscrupulous use of speech. Nonmoral linguistic norms that ensure shared meaning and communication are not enough. To believe what they tell one another and to act in concert, a group's members must be able to count on a basic level of reciprocity, promise keeping, and truthfulness. Otherwise, mistrust undermines cooperation.

In contrast to the evil threesome, the MacGregor spouses have loving friendships with each other and with members of the clan. Mutual good will and trust flow from the reliability of their speech to create bonds of fellowship and moral community. The clan is an image of an interdependent society built on respect for moral standards of language and the behavior it calls for. Clan members work for one another, risk for one another, and share in Rob's openly offered plan for profit. It is just this sort of communion that Archie, Killearn, and Montrose are unfit for and would corrupt by their scorn for its moral foundations.

The divisiveness of the evil men can be heard in Montrose's chortling, "One must never underestimate the healing power of hate," as Archie regains his speech at the prospect of fighting Rob. Montrose's observation reproduces Archie's earlier prediction that Mary would come out of her burning hut because she is a hater. Montrose and Archie are sensitive to hatred in other people because they are so full of hate themselves. As a counterpoise to this relish of animosity, the film again offers Rob Roy's moral personality.

Rob generously speaks of including in his family and affections the child Mary is carrying, though it may well be Archie's. Because he is a caring person and committed to reciprocity, Rob does not allow his enmity for Archie to get in the way of making room in his life for his wife's baby. Rob's welcoming attitude toward Archie's misbegotten progeny is a sad, ironic commentary on Archie's disdain for the baby being carried by Betty, which he knows to be his. More generally, the camaraderie and trust that define the MacGregor clan contrast with the wary selfishness by which Montrose, Archie, and Killearn are tenuously allied.

Once captured and brought before Montrose, Rob claims that Killearn and Archie have plotted against him. To Montrose's demand for proof, Rob reprises the contract scene, saying, "You have my word on it." Told that it will take more than that, Rob points to Archie's nature and wonders whether Montrose can't "tell what is true from what is not." The term "tell" suggests that discerning the truth is the complement of speaking it, and another version of the principle of likeness is presented. A man who doesn't respect truthfulness in his own speech will suffer from one or another of two correlative defects. He won't be able to tell the difference between truthful and dishonest individuals, or he will be unwilling to acknowledge another's honesty and the obvious evidence of his own experience. Montrose's previous expressions of mistrust of Archie and Killearn indicate that his doubting Rob in this exchange is a sham. Montrose refuses to be ruled by truthfulness, whether he is speaking or listening.

On the other hand, Rob trusts in the truthfulness of what his friends say and their fidelity to what they say. He refuses to believe the rumor Killearn has planted that McDonald has run off to America with the cattle money. Exasperated at what she takes to be Rob's misplaced loyalty, Mary points out the strength of the temptation for anyone in McDonald's position—the sight of "a lifetime's wages in a bag." Rob explains his unswerving trust simply: "Because I know him. I know him more than half his life."[28] Rob believes that he, indeed, "can tell" who is true from who is not. Arguments grounded in abstract propositions about the temptations of people in general are no substitute for intimate knowledge of actual friends.

Mary persists, asking whether McDonald was "ever handed a thousand pound before." Rob puts the value of money in moral perspective, nevertheless employing a financial conceit. He quantifies his praise of McDonald, saying, "He was handed a hundred times more. He was handed trust, and he repaid in kind." Because McDonald repaid Rob's and the community's trust in words and the matching deeds, Rob now trusts his own judgment instead of giving credence to a plausible lie. His appreciation of the social bonds formed in living up to moral standards of speech steers Rob straight, past the falsehood in which Killearn has entangled others.

Montrose's counterpart, the Duke of Argyll, is also able to recognize and acknowledge the truth when he hears it. Complementing Rob's musing about Montrose's ability to discern or honor the truth, the Duke tells Montrose that he, Argyll, "knows the truth when he hears it"—that

Montrose has indeed tried to bargain with Rob to slander him. Argyll is not an especially virtuous man, but his respect for moral constraints on language is reflected in practical decency, as when he tells his champion Guthrie not to backstab Archie after Guthrie loses the opening duel to him. Against the odds and self-interest, Argyll also wagers Rob's debt to Montrose, willing to make it good if Rob loses in the climactic sword fight with Archie. As a fellow noble, Argyll's regard for truthfulness and fair play underscores Montrose's knavery. At the same time, Argyll's mere decency throws into relief Rob Roy's exemplary virtue.

In addition, Argyll is able to perceive Mary MacGregor's integrity and valor when she comes to him for help. When Argyll proceeds to tell Mary that Rob is a man much blessed by fortune to have such a devoted, strong wife, however, the film again employs a stark and dark cinematic wit. It cuts to a shot of a bloodied Rob, tied to a horse in Montrose's army, with a bit between his teeth. Rob is much blessed, indeed!

Linguistic Virtues and Harsh Reality

Rob's commitment to a moral ideal of language use leads him to great faith in its power, occasionally misplaced. Discussing Betty's potential testimony against Killearn and Archie, Mary says Betty won't be believed by those in authority and therefore can't help secure a conviction from them. Rob naively holds to the unassailability of truthfulness: "They [Montrose et al.] can say what they like [to impugn Betty's accusations], she'll speak the truth." Mary astutely replies that Betty is a servant and that she would be presumed vengeful because Archie has left her in the lurch, pregnant. To Rob, the truth is the truth, regardless of the various social forces arrayed against the weight of Betty's testimony. Mary is again sagacious, epigrammatically noting that to Montrose and other powerful nobles, "truth is but a lie not yet discovered."

Mary's insistence on the political and economic power of those who play fast and loose with language brings out the fact that adhering to a moral ideal of speech is often dangerous. For all his legal and linguistic scrupulousness in *A Man for All Seasons*, Sir Thomas More is finally executed. The perjuring Richard Rich, we are told, lives to a ripe old age and dies in his sleep. Just as there is a price for being a leader of men, as Rob tells the leader of the tinkers, so is there a price for commitment to moral principles in general, and to those governing language in particular. When Rob refuses to malign Argyll, he not only gives up the chance to get out of

debt, but he endangers himself, his family, and the clan. Rob had to remind Mary that it was not Argyll's welfare but speaking truly that was at
stake in his refusal. Rob's confrontations with Mary, as much as his run-
ins with Montrose, indicate how adhering to moral standards of speech
can conflict with our personal interests.

Even as abiding by standards of reciprocity, promise keeping, and truthfulness makes moral community and its joys possible, so can holding to
such standards threaten a community. Of course, the evil characters cannot face a choice between personal interest and integrity of speech. As
with all genuine principles or norms, principles of language use are independent of our particular interests and constrain our pursuit of them. But
for evil men, speech exists only to serve their interests; therefore, for them
no conflict between rightness in speech and self-interest can arise.

The film offers an image of a just resolution. Neither the MacGregor
clan nor Rob are destroyed by his linguistic virtues, but in reality, people
can suffer irreparably for having the courage of their convictions.
Upholding moral standards of speech is no guarantee of a benign outcome, *Rob Roy*'s edifying ending notwithstanding. As the film's historical
prologue indicates, the clan's narrow escape from disaster evidences the
actual decline and eclipse of clan organization of socioeconomic life in
Scotland. No matter how short-lived the MacGregor victory is, however,
their story captures deeper, enduring moral truths.

Were Rob to sacrifice his commitment to the moral standards that reg-
ulate his words, the clan would survive, but not as they had been. Their
lives would be better than the purely private, isolated lives of Montrose,
Archie, and Killearn, but they would become a society of merely decent
folk, such as the Duke of Argyll, Alasdair, and perhaps Mary. To be a finer
society, approaching an ideal community, they must be lifted by Rob's exemplary moral personality: his shining virtues of respect, fidelity to one's
promises, and truthfulness. Although Rob criticizes himself for jeopardizing the clan for the sake of his honor and its attendant linguistic ideals, if
he didn't embody these moral principles of discourse, the life of the entire
clan would be diminished.

The upbeat finale represents the mutual support of community and individual. Just as Rob's sterling nature elevates the moral life of the clan, so
do the clan and Rob's family sustain him. The strength Rob displays in
holding on to Archie's lethal sword derives in large part from the family
and community that make him whole, whereas the isolated Archie wants
to win solely for his own glorification and fortune. Rob is able to maintain

his strength of will in the face of bleak circumstances because the very community that he helps mold invigorates him with the extra determination needed to prevail. The closing shot of the film is the image that has kept Rob from giving up and letting go: the scene of Rob returned home, embraced by his loved ones.

Notes

1. Thus, Habermas writes: "Only those norms can claim to be valid that meet (or could meet) with the approval of all affected in their capacity as participants in a practical discourse." Jurgen Habermas, "Discourse Ethics: Notes on a Program of Philosophical Justification," in *Moral Consciousness and Communicative Action*, Studies in Contemporary German Social Thought, trans. C. Lenhardt and S. Weber Nicholsen (Cambridge: M.I.T. Press, 1990), pp.43–115, pp.92–93.

2. Jurgen Habermas, *Theory of Communicative Action*, vol. 1, *Reason and the Rationalization of Society*, trans. T. McCarthy (Boston: Beacon, 1984), p.177.

3. Edmund Arens, "Discourse Ethics and Its Relevance for Communication and Media Ethics," in *Communication Ethics and Universal Values*, ed. C. Christians and M. Traber (Thousand Oaks, Calif.: Sage, 1997), pp.46–67, p. 61.

4. Habermas, "Discourse Ethics: Notes on a Program of Philosophical Justification," p.89.

5. Arens, "Discourse Ethics and Its Relevance for Communication," p.59.

6. David Ingram, *Critical Theory and Philosophy* (New York: Paragon House, 1990), p.147. The agreement of rational individuals speaking freely in an ideal speech situation ultimately provides the basis for claims to universally valid norms.

7. This seems to be at least part of what Kant is getting at in his discussion of the perfect duty not to lie or make false promises. He argues that were the practice of making false promises widespread, the rule permitting it functioning in a law-like fashion, "No one would believe what was promised to him but would only laugh at any such assertion as vain pretense." Immanuel Kant, *Foundations of the Metaphysics of Morals*, trans. Lewis White Beck (New York: Bobbs-Merrill, 1959), p.40, para.423.

8. Ingram, *Critical Theory*, p.137.

9. *The Republic of Plato*, trans. and ed. Allan Bloom (New York: Basic Books, 1968), 352a (Book I).

10. This is not quite true in the case of someone who does not intend to keep his or her promise in the first place. In such a case, the individual would be continuous with him- or herself as an intentional promise breaker. However, then the breach with the self would be the break the liar suffers between what he or she believes and what he or she says. This breach is dealt with in the next paragraph.

11. Arnold Isenberg, "Deontology and the Ethics of Lying," in *Aesthetics and the Theory of Criticism: Selected Essays of Arnold Isenberg,* ed. William Callhan (Chicago: University of Chicago Press, 1973), p.262.

12. Immanuel Kant, *Doctrine of Virtue,* trans. Mary J. Gregor (Philadelphia: University of Pennsylvania Press, 1964), p.93, para. 428.

13. This principle is noted in passing in the discussion in Chapter 2 of Rita's imperviousness to Phil's successive manipulations in *Groundhog Day.*

14. See Jurgen Habermas's distinctions among pragmatic, ethical-existential, and moral discourse in *Justification and Application: Remarks on Discourse Ethics,* Studies in Contemporary German Social Thought, trans. C. Cronin (Cambridge: M.I.T. Press, 1993), p.6.

15. At the beginning of *The Republic* (327a), Polemarchus offers a mock show of force to keep Socrates from going home. Socrates suggests that an alternative to submission or overcoming the force is persuasion—deciding the issue through superior speech instead of superior force.

16. Jurgen Habermas, "Justice and Solidarity: On the Discussion Concerning 'Stage 6,'" *Philosophical Forum* 21 (Fall-Winter 1989–1990): 48.

17. Ibid., p.47.

18. Arens, "Discourse Ethics and Its Relevance for Communication," p.56.

19. Alongside the modern feminist view of rape as more to do with violence against women than sex is conceiving it as part of masculine competition. On this male-centered conception, men rape the women of other men to take the males' property and show dominance over them.

20. Rob does point out the thin line that separates the vice of stubborn pride or arrogance and the virtue of refusing to debase oneself out of integrity. Both the vice and the virtue involve valuing the self, but the virtue includes allegiance to something outside the self—objective moral standards, including standards of speech.

21. The exchange between Rob and Mary might recall the scene toward the end of *The African Queen,* in which Charlie and Rose, aground on the delta and in despair, keep one another from self-blame. Shortly thereafter, Charlie and Rose try to spare each other the life-threatening risk of going out on the lake in the African Queen to attack the German boat, the Louisa.

22. The view that an individual's unity of personality or wholeness of self is important enough to risk grave conflict with other people is anticipated in this speech of Socrates in *Gorgias:* "I do believe that it would be better for me . . . that multitudes of men should disagree with me rather than that my single self should be out of harmony with myself and contradict me." *Gorgias,* trans. W. C. Helmbold (Indianapolis, Ind.: Bobbs-Merrill, 1952), 482, p.50.

23. The scene of Rob's escape is especially rich in imagery. The rope that tethers Rob, while strangling Archie, recalls the rope Archie had strung across the road with which he unhorsed McDonald before pursuing him on foot. The im-

age of Rob apparently defeated by Archie, face down on the ground, presages their climactic duel, when Rob, brought to his knees, is at Archie's swordpoint.

24. Iago foreshadows his self-imposed silence, saying, "I had rather have this tongue cut from my mouth/ than it should do offence to Michael Cassio" (II, iii). Like Killearn, Iago loves to pun for his own amusement. Having been responsible for Roderigo spending all his money in his vain pursuit of Desdemona, Iago has the nerve to criticize him for lack of patience, punning on Roderigo's impoverished condition: "How poor are they that have not patience!" (II, iii).

25. David Ingram notes that on Habermas's view, concrete extenuating circumstances can justify departing from the controlling norms of the ideal speech situation. Ingram, *Critical Theory*, pp.155–157.

26. Rob's lack of phronesis need not concern us much here, except to note it for the sake of the analysis of the films in the next two chapters. Michael's practical wisdom in *Fresh* is the main topic of the next chapter, and the protagonists (Brody and Ripley) of *Jaws* and *Aliens* similarly display this virtue.

27. *The Republic of Plato*, 352a (Book I).

28. I might point out that the loyalty based on faith in a friend's character is different from the loyalty of standing by a friend whose character is flawed and who has done wrong.

6
Fresh Phronesis

Practical Wisdom

The film *Fresh* (1994) is about a street-wise, preadolescent black boy who sells rock cocaine for one drug dealer and transports heroin for another. In the time between his drug labors, Michael ("Fresh" to his friends) goes to school, strikes up a romance with a sweet young girl, and plays chess at the park—with strangers for money, with his father for instruction. Michael makes his way in a social world more like the predatory one inhabited by Montrose and his hirelings than the supportive clan of Rob Roy. Michael maneuvers, mostly by his own wits, through the social minefields planted throughout his neighborhood, drawing what strength he can from the tentative, tenuous relationships with members of his family. The context for Michael's virtue, then, is one in which social relations are worn thin by the selfish transactions of money, drugs, flesh, and violence.

In telling Michael's story, writer/director Boaz Yakin provides a penetrating portrait of Aristotelian phronesis, practical wisdom. Perhaps more than any aspect of virtuous character, including radical change such as we saw in *Groundhog Day* and *The African Queen,* practical wisdom has proven elusive and resistant to philosophical examination. This may be because phronesis involves making good decisions in particular situations, and so its philosophical exploration is best undertaken in the company of narrative illustration. Working with narrative enables the ethical theorist to keep in mind how the decisions of practically wise people reflect their specific histories while hemmed in by their particular circumstances. The film *Fresh* provides us with the narrative context to explore the concept of phronesis.

Fresh: Michael plays chess,
pondering life.

Typical of most moral virtues, phronesis is a matter of degree. People
are more or less practically wise, depending on their ability to keep learning from experience and apply what they learn in a changing world, as
they also change. Although phronesis does not require formal education,
it does grow through a kind of self-tutelage. An awareness of how people
succeed and fail is supplemented by a grasp of what is amenable to our influence as well as what lies outside our control. The extent to which people are capable of this species of perceptiveness is limited by their possession of good sense, understanding, and intelligence, regarded by Aristotle
as natural endowments.[1] Thus, the restriction of phronesis to a select few
is due to the delicate ability to develop and deploy a narrowly distributed
natural endowment rather than to privilege in education or training. We
shall see, however, that the film is sensitive to the emotional and intellectual nurture needed for these natural gifts to ripen into practical wisdom.

Phronesis begins in cleverness—knowing the means to particular ends.[2]
Additional moral insight is required to know which ends are good or noble, as well as how much various ends are worth.[3] Knowing the worth of
ends involves apprehending the value of things and being able to weigh
values over the course of a life, even if those values are incommensurable.
Although knowing the means to valuable ends may seem chiefly a mechanical matter, *Fresh* shows why it requires knowledge of human nature.
We must understand what people prize and how their interests relate to
our own ends.

Although Aristotle classifies practical wisdom as an intellectual virtue, it
seems reasonable to understand it as spanning the intellectual-moral distinction. The specifics of how phronesis partakes of morality and moral

virtue will unfold as we go, but here we should note that practical wisdom is needed to put moral virtues to their right use in various situations. What does being generous or just call for in particular circumstances—for example, in times of poverty rather than plenty, or during social upheaval rather than cultural continuity? In its most sweeping moral office, phronesis is responsible for making sure that acting on the specific virtues meets the needs of living a life that is good on the whole. What Richard Sorabji says of courage applies to any virtue: "So we cannot know what courage requires of us now without knowing what the good life in general requires."[4]

A person of phronesis, a phronimos, is alert to what is going on around him and is able to assess the significance of his experience.[5] Stanley Godlovitch points out that the individual with practical wisdom has "the ability to draw certain types of conclusion from experience."[6] He can sift experience for underlying truths about life, including those pertaining to virtue and vice. Practical wisdom then issues in directives about what the individual ought to do. Whereas understanding passes judgments, "practical wisdom issues commands: its end is to tell us what we ought to do and what we ought not to do."[7]

In order to decide what to do here and now, the practically wise individual must have some knowledge of what is generally good and bad. As implied in the need to be able to tell which ends are truly valuable and which are not, phronesis presupposes a correct conception of what constitutes a good life. The practically wise person is able to deliberate well not "about what is good and advantageous in a partial sense . . . but what sort of thing contributes to the good life in general."[8] The individual must then see how what is good in general can be realized within the framework of his own life. The individual's particular circumstances must be reconfigured as well as possible to fit the general understanding of a truly good life.

Kathleen Wilkes emphasizes how excellent people train their practical reason on the quality of their own lives: "Aristotle's claim is then that the best man is the man who exercises his rational capacities to their fullest *to gain for himself the best life possible.* He arranges and patterns his entire way of life upon the basis of his deliberative reasoning about what short-term and long-term goals and interests will bring him most eudaimonia."[9] A phronimos, therefore, must spend some time pondering what makes life worth living, with recurring recourse to his own experience and to what he notices about the impact other people's choices make on their happiness. Practical wisdom is responsible for the differing degrees of success people have in determining the nature of a truly good life. Most of us are presented with a smorgasbord of legitimate conceptions of living well, and practical wisdom is needed to choose from among them. Moreover, all of these beneficial life patterns must be distinguished from options that simply fall short. Phil Connors needed repeated experience of the same day in *Groundhog Day* to reassess his uncritical understanding of the good life precisely because he lacked phronesis. Youths in Michael's inner city typically witness a narrow band of putatively desirable lives involving exploitation, dominance, and violence. Michael is one of the few people, young or old, capable of seeing through the apparent allure of these life patterns to more enduring and rewarding possibilities.

But Michael has to project future scenarios for himself with which he has no direct experience, radical alternatives to what is daily evident to his senses. He must then be able to see which possible good lives can be realistically reached from his present circumstances—with his particular talents, needs, and proclivities. Phronesis therefore includes evaluating an array of living patterns, some of which are not part of one's immediate social context, and then seeing what is required to attain them from where the individual is, here and now.

This means that practical wisdom involves a considerable imaginative effort to explore "what it would be like to realize particular possibilities" and to assess those possibilities from a moral point of view.[10] The practically wise person must be able to play out what he can and cannot do in light of who he is and his current circumstances. But when John Kekes says that wisdom includes "knowing how to make a good life for ourselves in the particular context in which we live,"[11] he is only partly correct. For we must also deliberate for future contexts, anticipating what may befall us in the days to come, and this is indeed difficult to gauge.

On Aristotle's understanding, sound judgment lies at the heart of phronesis. The things that generally make life good—friends, education, and the wherewithal to make a moral contribution to society—must be translated into particular options.[12] Judgment is a process by which a decision is reached about what to do in a person's determinate situation. Given that I value the right sorts of thing, what should I do today to enable me to act for the best tomorrow and all the tomorrows that follow it?

The judgment demanded of phronesis is rare because details of what is good may be hard to discern, for example, determining whether an enjoyable companion is capable of true friendship. The requisite judgment is additionally hard to come by because translating what we know to be good in general into specific action is often perplexing, as in knowing what compassion calls for in a particular situation, with a particular acquaintance's distinctive difficulties. A phronimos is able to see how a particular string of actions can bring about a good that is presently merely latent in a situation or in a person. As David Wiggins points out, the individual must have some conceptual framework for connecting his ideal to the opportunities the world provides for realizing it,[13] and one might add, to the limitations the world imposes upon its realization. Noticing the opportunities the world affords includes seeing what exists qua opportunity, under the aspect of fruitful potential.

Judging what to do in different situations, therefore, demands sensitivity and adjustment to the particular. The practically wise individual streamlines a multiplicity of facts into handy generalizations by dint of what Aristotle considers intelligence. But eventually he must be able to apply this general understanding to ever new particular circumstances. "A man of practical wisdom [must] take cognizance of particulars."[14] Principles or precepts can be helpful only as crude rules of thumb because they cannot account for the distinctive textures of concrete situations or persons. The judgment in question is a perceptual discrimination concerned with apprehending concrete particulars rather than universals.[15] Unlike principles, perception responds to the fine-grained differences between specific situations.

Martha Nussbaum emphasizes that good judgment supplies a concreteness and flexibility superior to rules or principles. Citing Aristotle's use of an architectural metaphor, she argues that "good deliberation, like this ruler [flexible strip of metal], accommodates itself to what it finds, responsively and with complexity."[16] Like the architect's strip of measuring metal, the judgment that characterizes phronesis is supple, able to bend to the situation or wrap itself around the concrete details. In Shakespeare's *Henry V,* for example, we find a character who can adapt to the exigencies of military leadership and the requirements of romantic courtship with equal facility. Henry is able to shift from inspiring his outnumbered, war-weary men to heroic fighting at Agincourt to wooing the French princess with playful, gentle affection.

Practical circumstances are not amenable to tidy encapsulation in rules because they are ever-changing and complex.[17] The changing nature of practical circumstances entails indeterminacy or indefiniteness in their arrangement. We are presented with open-ended variety and complexity from situation to situation. This makes the appropriate choice context dependent, relative to the way just these people, events, and circumstances come together. But practical situations are rarely so cut-and-dried that they neatly mark off their temporal and social parameters for us. Therefore, a secondary sense of indeterminacy burdens the deliberating individual with ascertaining a situation's span of time and with deciding which people should be counted as part of the situation.

Excellent choice is a matter of fitting one's goals and values to the complex requirements of concrete situations. Their complexity stems from variety of elements as well as the many different ways these elements can be combined—by events or in the thinking of the individual making the choice. Change and complexity are the natural concomitants of the irreducible particularity of practical life. The concrete situation may even contain some "ultimately particular and non-repeatable elements."[18] The phronimos must have the imagination necessary to improvise in the face of novel situations. Rules can only deal with what has come before.

Imagination has to extend to envisioning new actions, complicated by the fact that we usually act in conjunction with the actual and potential choices of other people. The practically wise person seizes upon the significant aspects of the particular situation and sees how its novel possibilities can be adapted to his unique, and perhaps transient, needs and abilities. In sum, practical wisdom enables people to reach good decisions about unrepeatable, complex combinations of changing components of open-ended situations.

Aristotle maintains that considerable experience of life is needed to see what is important in this welter of detail and to be resourceful in deciding what to do. Practical perceptiveness comes only through a long process of living and choosing; consequently, young people cannot have much of it. Only experience can bestow the intuitive insight (nous) that enables immediate grasp of the possibilities inherent in this, rather than that (slightly different) situation. Offering a prepubescent boy as a model of practical wisdom, as *Fresh* does, therefore, runs decidedly against the Aristotelian grain. I hope to show that Michael's dominant traits, such as his powers of observation and reasoning, make him a plausible paradigm of phronesis. Added to this are the way inner-city youths of today live lives of more concentrated experience and the fact that the film presents, after all, a fiction. As with any fiction, we will find Michael representative of a budding phronimos, Aristotle notwithstanding, to the extent *Fresh* tells a believable story.

Another presupposition of practical wisdom is good moral character. For one thing, the ability to act on what we perceive as the best course of action requires such virtues as self-control and patience—to act at the right time; resourcefulness—to summon the appropriate means; and courage—to face the appropriate risks to which right action sometimes exposes us. Most of these virtues take root early, largely through the individual's upbringing, but perhaps also through one's natural tendencies. The ability to be decisive or resourceful, for example, may require more than childhood training. A natural alacrity of mind or aptitude for noticing the usefulness of what happens to be at hand may be essential to develop these virtues.

We have been speaking of executive virtues, the virtues that enable us to execute our plans by putting our decisions successfully into action. Executive virtues are complemented by the substantive virtues, which provide the moral ends and values also ingredient to practical wisdom.[19] The individual must have the right values so that he can sort out the competing conceptions of the good life and adequately discriminate its components. These seem most dependent on childhood upbringing, yet even here, such virtues as compassion or kindness may be grounded in a natural sensitivity to the plight of other people. The individual's values and character properly orient him in particular situations. They discriminate within the stream of experience to pick out what is important for sustained attention.

Moral character can explain why the majority of people may miss seeing a situation as the practically wise person does, for example, as an opportunity to right a wrong, deflect criticism from a vulnerable individual, or to defuse a volatile confrontation. Martha Nussbaum explains why values and character are not merely a matter of intellectual comprehension. They necessarily involve the motivational and selective activity of the appetites and passions.[20]

The intuitive perception that marks the practically wise individual's practical choices is determined by intellect, emotion, and appetite operating in concert.[21] The notion of salience can provide us with a summary term for the subtle and multiple psychological influences that lift to prominence certain features of a situation, giving them importance for thought and action. What has salience for us results from our character and values, which are informed by our dominant desires and emotions no less than by our central beliefs. Our perception is driven by the match of objects in the world with what we want. "We would not have been able to perceive those ethically relevant features without passional reactions."[22]

Salience then is an essential component of the phronimos's distinctive appreciation of concrete situations. Situational appreciation involves a gestalt that draws together disparate pieces of an event or setting into an intelligible pattern and also bestows a feel for what is worthwhile in that gestalt.[23] Perhaps the gestalt is organized around and by means of this worthwhile crux or core. Most people typically fail to see what is actually worth acting upon—at least in complicated and tangled circumstances. The salutary influence of salience and the capacity for situational appreciation enable the practically wise individual to regularly perceive, assess, and decide perspicaciously when faced with new situations. He makes choices as if operating with an instinctive feel for the right path to take. Perhaps we value competitive sports as much as we do because the athlete's split-second decision to run in one direction instead of another, or to throw the ball to one teammate rather than to another, affords so clear an exhibition of this instinctive capacity. However frivolous the ends of sports may be, we usually know whether they have been attained with greater certitude than we enjoy with regard to the moral goals of practical life.

Practical wisdom enables us to cope with harsh facts of life that simply cannot be avoided. John Kekes considers contingency, evil, and conflict between our values to be life's "permanent adversities." We all must suffer these obstacles to the good life, but wisdom can facilitate coping with them.[24] Among the contingencies that life deals out are illness, accident, and injustice. Bad things happen to good people, and bad people are sometimes quite well off. Although virtue is no guarantee of a good life, living a good life is sometimes the result of moral virtue. Moreover, some measure of practical wisdom seems essential to understanding and then adapting to the bad luck that is bound to hit even the most fortunate of us.

Practical wisdom also enables us to recognize and deal with evil, in others and in ourselves. Because Michael is sensitive to the diverse evils that surround him, he is able to contend with them successfully. Through repeated shots of his steady gaze, *Fresh* conveys that Michael is able to look evil in the face, even his own, without blinking. Michael is portrayed as possessing what Herbert Morris characterizes as essential components of wisdom: "To appreciate that there is evil in the world, to hold no illusion about it, . . . to have experienced many of its manifestations, to have seen . . . what allows for [evil's] . . . being overcome, to see all that makes for good and to give it due weight."[25] The wonder of Michael's story is tucked within his clever manipulation of the wicked, powerful drug dealers—in his penetration into the fissures of their hard-baked personalities. He is also able to discriminate between genuine evil and simple frailty, as found in his father, sister, and friend Chuckie.

In addition to contending with evil in ourselves and other individuals, practically wise people are clearheaded in choosing between the lesser of two evils. After all, sometimes we are simply boxed in by the contingencies mentioned earlier, and even the best available choice is morally unpalatable. Instead of responding with incessant gnashing of teeth, despair, or procrastination, the phronimos will accept the deal of the cards and act as best he can.

Choosing between conflicting values is also unavoidable because pursuing one desirable thing may preclude trying to attain something else of value. How does one decide between a vacation involving the cultural opportunities of a big city and enjoying nature in a mountain retreat? Because entire ways of life are incompatible, deciding among them is even more difficult. Thus, wholeheartedly raising a family excludes being an explorer or hopscotching the world as a news journalist. Similarly, a single-minded dedication to science or art rules out the roundedness of a life filled with community commitments, sports, culture, travel, and hobbies. Kekes notes that these conflicts are not simply due to unfortunate circumstances or conditions.[26] Rather, they are built into the nature of being human and valuing what we do in the world as we know it.

Moreover, some of the values that are incompatible are incommensurable. No reasonable comparison is possible because no common measure is available.[27] Practical wisdom enables us to accept that we cannot have it all, and it also equips us to project which values are most suited to our natures or what shape we should try to give our natures. The former keeps us from corrosive regret over roads not taken, and the latter calls us to paths of happy moral development. The three kinds of permanent adversity merge insofar as we are thrust into the midst of evil by life's contingencies, which contingencies also force us to sacrifice some good things in order to pursue what seems most valuable for ourselves and those we love. Such is Michael's challenge in *Fresh,* and the joy of the film is seeing how his phronesis gives him the cunning, strength, and insight to tear a hole in the ubiquitous evil of his world through which he and his sister can flee.

A Boy's Life—On the Streets

In what follows, we will see how the character of Michael (Sean Nelson) exemplifies the practical wisdom we have just sketched but also deepens our understanding of it. The story illustrates how practical wisdom involves a marriage of judgment, imagination, self-control, and the ability to put thought into action. Michael's character also suggests that practical wisdom necessarily incorporates specific moral virtues. In addition to digesting explicit words of advice, for example, Michael accurately assesses people and their strongest desires and understands what a good life amounts to. To appreciate the contours of Michael's practical wisdom, we must examine his concrete options within the world of the film fiction. The plot is brimming with complication, thick as it is with characters and incidents, but it is fairly straightforward in outline.

The story is divided in two by a tragic turning point in Michael's life and his understanding of it. In the first half of the story, Michael navigates nimbly through his daily spheres of drug dealing, school, and family. The movement of the plot results from the intersecting of these spheres. Michael runs heroin for Esteban (Giancarlo Esposito) and pushes rock/base cocaine for Corky (Ron Brice), supervised by his lieutenant, Jake (Jean La Marre). A small-time drug dealer, James, supplies Michael's sister, Nicki (N'Bushe Wright), with heroin and enjoys a sexual liaison with her. Nicki goes to live with James, leaving the home where Michael's grandmother and saintly Aunt Francis take care of a passel of cousins, including Michael. The other member of Michael's family is his father (Samuel L. Jackson), with whom he plays chess and from whom he receives sage advice.

The story pivots on the killing of a lovely young girl Michael likes. Jake, Michael's street boss, accidentally shoots the girl in the schoolyard, in the course of intentionally killing a sparkling basketball player for showing him up. We realize that the girl's death at Jake's violent hand is a crucial moment in the story because of what transpires in the second half of the film. Michael so orchestrates events that the two narcotics kingpins incapacitate one another, doing away with Jake and James in the process. The goal of Michael's scheme is to extricate his sister and himself from their crippling circumstances, freeing them to start a new life.

Using his secreted savings to buy base cocaine, Michael switches it with the heroin that he is transporting for Esteban. This subterfuge enables him to frame Jake for stealing from and undercutting Corky, their mutual boss. After duping Corky into killing Jake, Michael tells him that James is the distributor for the compromised cocaine. With this move, Michael stages a showdown between Corky's gang and Esteban's troops. Caught in the cross fire is James—who has a narcotic-erotic hold on Nicki. Planting Esteban's original heroin for the police to find, Michael finishes Esteban off.

The film opens with an upward angle shot of a nearly empty prairie. The wide prairie is bifurcated by a paved street pointing toward a deep blue sky with puffy clouds. On either side of the street, buildings begin to fade into view. The camera pulls back, lengthening the roadway prospect, as it fills with more buildings, streetlights, traffic signals, and then a brick wall. The wall enlarges into the clean corner of a building, which is immediately littered with paper, garbage, and graffiti. The camera moves over a sidewalk on which sneakered feet, and then jeans, stride into view. We finally see the full figure of a near-adolescent black male walking with a knapsack. He is the title character, no more fresh than the city in which he walks.

As Michael walks under an el, we view a full-blown cityscape, and its sounds replace the gentle music that harmonized with the earlier shots of the simpler town. The urbanization of the town into a bustling, dirty metropolis reflects the gradual sullying of Michael by his environment and the erosion of his innocence. We are given to understand that this is a boy of the streets and that he is wise to their ways. The early prairie vista may also foretell, with a displaced, backward glance, the more tranquil and hopeful life to which Michael will take his sister at story's end.

The technique of unfolding the city's development through superimposed or faded-in, layered images suggests several other layers of meaning. We can view the city's increasing density and expansion as representing Michael's ability to grow as a chess player and as a player on the streets. Filling in the cityscape creates a sense of a personal biography, accruing meaning over time. As we watch a simulation of time-lapse photography convey the history of a locale, the film inserts Michael within a historically defined social context. The practically wise individual exercises his perceptive insight within particular settings that limit his range of choices. The unfolding movie frames illustrate how possibilities are narrowed by choice. The wide open prairie, like a clean canvas, gets filled in one way rather than another. Even as every choice an individual makes opens up further possibilities for him, so does it block his access to other undertakings.

Michael's special qualities are established from the outset through a series of business transactions. Although we never see him shine in school, we know he values it because he repeats, "I gotta get to school," in each early drug-dealing episode. The tension between Michael's street job and his formal education is later ironically figured by the image of heroin hidden in the dummy textbooks he transports in his knapsack. Michael's joking reference to the textbooks, "Yeah, I'm a crazy 'A' student," can then be heard as a bitter reminder of his missing out on school, but also as a veiled allusion to his brilliance as a student tutored by the rough streets.

Michael demonstrates his intellectual superiority to the drug personnel who fill his morning by his ability to school himself through his trafficking with them. The education involved in phronesis is not so much of the formal stripe as it is the product of keen observation of people in the hurly-burly of everyday life. The Hispanic woman from whom Michael is picking up packets of heroin prattles on about telling her daughter to "wait for that Michael, he's gonna go far, to a very far place." The flattery does not keep Michael from noticing that she is short one packet.

As Michael listens to the dealer make excuses for misplacing the heroin, the sound of a train clacking along tracks accompanies a close-up of Michael's world-weary, wistful face—immediately superimposed over a faint shot of train tracks. The shot reinforces the woman's assertion that Michael will go to a very far place. The seed of the story's outcome takes root in Michael's daydream of departure, since he will in fact travel out of the sordid life the dealer's apartment and conniving transaction represent. When the woman directly locates the twentieth square of heroin, we are led to believe that Michael suspects her of trying to cheat him and perhaps distract him by appealing to his vanity. By catching the dealer shorting him, Michael demonstrates the correctness of her estimation of his superior abilities. Michael registers needle tracks on the woman's arms with a slight, disapproving corner-of-the-mouth wince.

At his next stop, Michael exchanges hostilities with a teenage boy, culminating in Michael challenging him to a fight to silence his derogatory comments about Nicki. This brief standoff conveys Michael's loyalty to his sister and his toughness, as the teenager is clearly older and bigger than he. The film begins to explore the specific virtues that are essential to practical wisdom. Not only do virtues such as loyalty and courage inform wise judgment, but such virtues are needed to act once a judgment about what is worthwhile has been made.

In the schoolyard, Michael flirts with the cute black girl who will soon be shot to death by Jake. As Michael speaks to her of becoming rich, we again hear trains on the soundtrack and the faint image of tracks this time emerges into full, clear view. The film segues to Michael walking down the actual tracks to the hole where his money is stashed. He does not splurge on the clothing, trading trove, or recreation so attractive to most emerging adolescents but squirrels his pay away. He possesses the virtues of frugality and foresight, since he may need the money for something really important later—such as buying cocaine for his scheme to turn the drug lords against each other.

Michael's maturity repeatedly distinguishes him from his young friends. While his pals banter about trading cards and comic books, Michael looks intently across the playground at the object of his affections. Michael rarely smiles because he is serious: about getting to school on time, about being paid by his bosses, about saving his money, and about the pretty girl. The film makes Michael's practical wisdom plausible by realistically portraying him uninterested in the hijinks, hobbies, palaver, or values of the kids around him. With his self-possessed watchfulness, Michael appears to be a young man in a boy's body. Although all youths in the inner city lead lives of more concentrated, adult experience, we witness Michael as one who takes it in with extraordinary thoughtfulness and acumen.

During the first scene of Michael playing chess with his father, his father scolds Michael for wasting his time playing chess in the park for money. Over Michael's protest that he's just won twenty dollars, his father philosophizes that "time ain't money . . . anything lost can be found again, except for time wasted." Taking a swig of alcohol, the father seems to be sad proof of time wasted, a promising talent squandered. He is incapable of turning his fine chess mind to everyday, practical use.

Perhaps chess anesthetizes the father to reality, the way alcohol does, a diagnosis suggested by the similarity of the brown bags in which the father keeps his booze and his chess set. On the other hand, Michael applies the analytic powers of intellect he hones playing chess, as well as his father's chess wisdom, to real circumstances. Michael's father has also overlooked something else that, once lost, cannot be found again—innocence. Michael displays unrelieved resilience in transmuting the ugly incidents that wear away his innocence into nuggets of practical wisdom.

Michael's father is clearly disappointed that his son is not playing on the school chess team and tells Michael that he is watching the world pass him by. The father's emphasis on playing chess for the school signifies his concern for Michael's education, a priority that he has clearly impressed upon his son. The father also urges Michael to think and to "lose his attitude." He wants Michael's chess play governed by reason, not emotion fueled by vain posturing. Instead of being absorbed in himself, as the film shows so many of his peers and bosses to be, Michael should pay attention to his competition and figure them out.

As they play a game of chess, Michael's father asks him, "What kind of player am I? Am I an offensive or defensive man?" The father answers his own question: "Neither, I play my opponent. If he likes to attack, I force him to defend himself. If he's a cautious man, I draw him into dangerous waters." The father's principles are abstract, referring to types of players. Michael will have to recognize instances of the types outside the game of chess and then apply the principles with the suppleness of the architect's flexible metal strip. Like the astute chess player, Michael will adapt his game to the personalities of his opponents in real life. He will force Corky, who likes to attack, to defend himself, and he will draw the cautious Esteban perilously out of his depth.

Maturity Versus Machismo

Chuckie is one of Michael's schoolyard pals. And although he possesses some positive qualities such as enterprise and grit, he is used in the story as a foil for Michael's moral strengths. Whereas Michael keeps his own counsel, Chuckie spouts off to everyone how terrific he is and how much he will accomplish. Whereas Michael digests and applies the insights of other people, Chuckie scorns Michael's prudent advice at his own peril. Most blatant is Chuckie's callousness and machismo, a variation on the "attitude" Michael's father admonishes him to get rid of. Both traits are in strong evidence in Chuckie's plans for Roscoe, the pit bull he shares with Michael.

The movie underlines Chuckie's perverse understanding of manhood and manly strength by cutting from his lauding "Punisher" as the most intimidating comic book action hero to his training Roscoe for dogfighting. Michael argues with Chuckie about using Roscoe to fight other dogs, and while Chuckie protests that he wants the money to be made on wagering, Chuckie obviously also likes the idea of training a dog that can kill other dogs. Chuckie tells Michael that everyone knows he earns drug money, so how come Michael doesn't look spiffier instead of looking "ratty" and "nappy." Chuckie boasts of the running shoes and gold he'll buy with the dogfight money he expects to win.

We glimpse the depth of Michael's maturity against the shallowness of Chuckie's pretensions and aspirations. Michael will save his money unmindful of the scorn of his peers for not decking himself out in adolescent finery. Moreover, Michael is sensitive to Roscoe as a vulnerable creature deserving of care and affection. All the while he argues with Chuckie over Roscoe's fate as a professional fighter and listens to Chuckie's grandiose designs, Michael is petting an obviously affectionate Roscoe happy to be stroked and fondled. Michael wants the dog as a pet. Chuckie sees Roscoe as a way to riches and reputation.

The film suggests that egocentrism and brutality go hand in hand. Because he thinks only of himself, Chuckie can be cruel without a second thought, in this case, to an animal. Chuckie's brutality, and the tough-guy ambitions that accompany it, will deafen him to Michael's cautionary words, costing Chuckie his life. Michael's objection to having Roscoe fight indicates his fundamental commitment to care rather than exploitation. Aristotle would say that in his upbringing, Michael has been imbued with the virtues of responsibility and care. The film implies that Aunt Francis's gentle love has conspired with the father's gruff affection and respect for natural gifts to nurture this sensitivity in Michael. The intelligence and understanding of human nature that Michael has also inherited from his father have been molded and channeled by virtues that keep him from the self-centered obtuseness of Chuckie.

Recall that the practically wise individual faces novel situations with an intellect informed by desire and emotion. Desire and emotion supply discriminating force, helping to determine which features of a situation are picked out. The attractive and repulsive are "marked out" for us by the way things present themselves to our desires and passional interests.[28] Michael's opposition to Chuckie's newly hatched plan to fight Roscoe, therefore, is conditioned by his aversion to the dog becoming violent and having its affectionate nature debased. Because Michael's desire is for a friendly, gentle dog, he tries to deflect Chuckie from his intentions.

Nevertheless, Chuckie prevails over Michael and will pit Roscoe against other dogs because Michael refuses to find him work with Esteban. Michael refuses on the grounds that Chuckie acts "like a stupid little kid." But it is precisely because Chuckie is foolish that Michael will soon get him a job with Esteban. He will incorporate Chuckie's braggadocio into his strategy to sabotage the drug bosses. Chuckie will resemble the knight in chess, which piece Michael likes for its "crazy jumps." Even though "the knight is his friend," his father tells him, "you're gonna have to use him, just like you use the others [pieces]. If he falls by the wayside, well, that's just life's little game, ain't it?" Chuckie will literally fall by the wayside because he doesn't listen to Michael.

Michael is motivated to get Chuckie a job with Esteban to keep him from fighting Roscoe again. Attending Roscoe's initiation in the fighting pit, Michael tries to dissuade Chuckie, telling him that Roscoe is scared. Even though Roscoe clamps his jaws on his adversary's neck and wins the fight, Michael is despondent. He shakes his head and makes his corner-of-the-mouth frown amidst the shouting, settling of bets, and Chuckie braying Roscoe's praises. Michael tells Chuckie that Roscoe won't fight again and offers to offset Chuckie's loss of fighting money with a job running drugs for Esteban. Like Michael, Roscoe has lost his innocence to the world of violence and greed.

When we later see Michael shoot Roscoe with one of Chuckie's ill-advised guns, we might think Michael has become callous, or we can view him as taking the morally difficult but correct course. Killing the product of Chuckie's avarice, cruelty, and grandiosity, Michael is destroying an animal whose loving nature has itself been killed off.[29] Roscoe is beyond reform, having been corrupted by Chuckie, and Michael is symbolically terminating his own connections with the evil in his environment that had been corrupting him.

Phronesis includes awareness of evil in oneself. Michael seems aware of the need to stop the spread of his own evil, such as his impulse to berate and slap a pitiable female junkie. Using Chuckie's gun, Michael is destroying that aspect of himself represented by Roscoe. On a more practical level, Michael is solving the problem of Roscoe's future. With Chuckie dead and Michael leaving town, who will care for Roscoe? Anyone who would care for him would do so only to continue to exploit him in the fighting pits for profit. The thought of such a violent future for Roscoe, one bound to end in his bloody death, is intolerable to Michael.

Cleverness Combined with Moral Insight

If Michael's execution of Roscoe symbolizes his opposition to the destructive forces in his environment and in himself, then Michael has self-reflectively arrived at an understanding of evil. He has had to reach a decision about his life faced with the inescapable price exacted by choices involving wickedness. As John Kekes sees it, evil in the world can force us to choose to "collaborate with unsavory people or withdraw and remove a curb on their power."[30] For Michael, the choice is between continuing in his complicity with evil, including standing by as his sister is ravaged by drugs and paramours, and doing battle with evil, at the cost of human lives. What brings Michael to see his options in light of this permanent adversity is the schoolyard shooting of the girl he is so fond of.

During a basketball game in the schoolyard, a gifted player embarrasses Jake, who oversees Michael's dope peddling for Corky. Michael watches studiously as the hot-tempered, muscular Jake knocks down the younger ballplayer, only to suffer the indignity of having the boy swiftly steal the ball from him and make a basket. The agile athlete next bamboozles Jake with a staccato of dribbles and feints, slides around him, and scores easily. The camera dwells on Michael's concerned face. Unlike the star basket-ball player, Michael can sense trouble brewing. The ballplayer is too wrapped up in his own game, too enamored of his own skills to pay attention to Jake's growing humiliation and anger.[31] When Jake's mates tease him for letting the boy toy with him, Jake boils over and shoots the superb ballplayer for showing him up, and a stray bullet finds the lovely girl who had been walking across the schoolyard expressly to chat with Michael. She would not have been taken from Michael had she not been on the way to be with him.

This incident is the story's turning point because the lessons Michael draws from it prompt him to reexamine who he is and what he wants from his life. Michael sits by the dying girl, holding her wounded neck, as the blood and her little life flow away, until a paramedic removes him. Having refused to help the police identify Jake as the killer, Michael is next seen naked in a fetal position on a white sheet, like the one that covered the dead girl. When he awakens, Michael begins to formulate his master plan, as if reborn with the possibility of a better life, determined to devise the means to achieve it.

We will understand that Michael has received bruising education from the girl's accidental death in that other permanent adversity, contingency. The girl just happened to be in the path of Jake's enraged shooting. Contingency converged with evil and an innocent life was lost. Michael discovers that where evil envelops us, contingencies magnify its direct, intended effects, such as the direct effects of drugs on Michael's sister, Nicki. Michael is one of the morally wise people who have "not been crushed by what they have confronted, but have emerged . . . victorious, capable . . . of affirming rather than denying life."[32] The moral dimension of Michael's phronesis yields his assessment of the prevalent evil and its convergence with the unavoidable contingencies of life. The clever dimension of his phronesis enables Michael to map out a plan to turn the evil against itself; however, even this cleverness requires insight into human nature and the ability to interpret his father's chess savvy in light of that insight.

Back at Aunt Francis's home, Michael sets up a chessboard, the working model for his game plan. The image suggests that phronesis includes the ability to envision the whole—to take in the significance of the parts for one another and for the total design. Michael's ability to see how events can unfold over time is complemented by his immediate grasp of a situation, giving him a temporal completeness that matches his spatial understanding. Devising his plan on the matrix of the chessboard, Michael takes the offensive in his relationship with the drug dealers.

To go on the offensive, Michael has had to interpret criticism of his chess playing as shedding light on a wider flaw in his character. Michael had been unable to mount an attack against his father because he was unwilling to risk losing his pieces. His father accused him of "hoardin' . . . playin' each piece like losin' it hurts. You want my king, you got to come get my king. All these other pieces are just a means to do it."

Through Michael's character, the film discloses how responsiveness to criticism and openness to change are essential to practical wisdom. The father's commentaries on the anatomy of Michael's chess game, which we can assume have been ongoing, have shaped Michael's natural reflectiveness. He is disposed to examine himself critically and change himself—in this case, to overcome his reluctance to take the risky initiatives needed to get what he wants. As a result of his introspection, Michael is able to see more clearly his relationship to the three permanent adversities.

How well does the metaphor of chess capture the realities of contingency, evil, and conflict of values? Chess is unlike life in that there are no contingencies in the rules for how the pieces move, but which pieces are moved and where they are placed is contingent on the particular opponents. How opponents play a particular game is contingent on the intersection of their skills and personalities. And as the game progresses, more or less novel positions can emerge on the board. Evil is translated as the character defects that prevent individuals from playing to their potential, and conflicts arise because reaching the goal of checkmate requires sacrifice of favored pieces or exposing one's position to attack.

Michael must take stock of his particular situation and who his adversaries are. The powerful Esteban and Corky are at once analogous to chess opponents as well as to pieces on the board.[33] Once Michael decides what is truly important to him, he will have to figure out what he must sacrifice to get it. The story shows Michael having to sacrifice Chuckie, the relationship with his father, and his stash of cash.

Fresh emphasizes how well Michael is able to grasp the weaknesses of other people in addition to his own. The camera gives us those close-ups of Michael's disapproving little mouth shrug when faced with the needle marks of the Hispanic heroin supplier and when he watches Roscoe kill his rival. Less graphically, Michael perceives the moral weaknesses of his sister, father, and Chuckie. Chuckie is easily impressed with flashy appearances—clothing, money, violence—but lacks understanding of what has enduring worth beneath the surface of things. However intelligent about human nature Michael's father is, his defeatism and indolence render him incapable of using his profound insight outside the imaginary world of chess. And Michael's sister is riven with self-hatred and lack of self-respect, seeing herself through the exploitative eyes of the men who run her life.

When the girl Michael cares for is killed, he is moved to take control of his life. Its contingencies and evil are such that Michael must set violent forces in motion against each other, his version of "knowing how to make a good life for ourselves in the particular context in which we live."[34] The particular context is an urban war zone in which people's lives are determined too often by unpredictable violence. The chess board schematizes how Michael will seize the concrete particulars of his life "in a confrontation with the situation itself."[35] The convolutions of Michael's scheme turn on deceptions involving drugs and James, the small-time drug dealer who is Nicki's demon lover. By making James appear dangerous to both Corky and Esteban, Michael spurs them into mutual destruction.

Michael's strategy begins by introducing Chuckie to Esteban. Loud, loutish, and boastful, Chuckie seems an odd choice as Michael's backup on the big heroin run Esteban has planned. But Michael foresees that Chuckie will brag of being in Esteban's employ and spread the false information that they will be carrying cocaine for him. We see Chuckie strutting about with a retinue of followers, and a close-up of his face fills the screen. Chuckie's broadcast will invite Corky's boys to ambush the little couriers, just as Michael plans.

Michael surreptitiously replaces the heroin he has picked up from Esteban's supplier with the rock cocaine purchased from another drug operative, Hector. With a loud pop, the screen is brilliantly lit with the flash from a bank of oversized headlights atop a gang vehicle. When Corky's boys move in, Michael tells Chuckie to just drop the backpack with the drugs and run. But heedless Chuckie wants to shoot it out. Chuckie is killed because he is foolish, so foolish that he can't recognize someone with practical wisdom.

In the previous scene, Chuckie had come close to being taken into custody by a transit officer for defying his orders. After Michael talks the official out of pursuing the matter, the man tells Chuckie that he should learn "some respect from [his] friend." Although the officer means respect for police authority, we can see how his phrase also suggests respect for the authority of Michael's good judgment. Taking the admonishment one step further, Chuckie also hasn't learned to respect what is genuinely good, in himself and in (Roscoe's) simple animal nature.

Chuckie is further unlike Michael in that he lacks knowledge of his own limitations and abilities. Lack of self-knowledge helps explain why Chuckie's imagination takes the form of fantasy rather than realistic creativity. Chuckie pictures himself turned out in expensive running shoes and gold jewelry, enjoying the fruits of his lucrative dog-fighting venture. In contrast to the person with phronesis, the fantasist indulges himself in a degenerate form of moral imagination. Chuckie's brutality may contribute to the fantastic image he has of himself and his place in the world. Brutal individuals tend to distort their perception and understanding of the world in order to enjoy an image of themselves as tough.[36] Like the knight who is liable to fall by the wayside, Chuckie falls in the street, curbside. The violent scene ends with Michael running, superimposed over a shot of the neighborhood—a cinematic rendering of Michael's imminent flight from this precinct of destruction.

Understanding, Flexibility, and Imagination

The rest of the story illustrates how Michael's phronesis integrates moral understanding, flexible judgment, and imagination. He must put his grasp of human nature into effect, adapt himself to concrete circumstances, and see how events that are yet to occur can be coherently meshed. In motivating diverse drug dealers to behave as he wishes, Michael exhibits an understanding of specific forms of evil and how each man's personal weakness ripples through his evil. Michael's understanding of other people includes seeing himself through their eyes. Imagining what he looks like to Corky and Esteban, Michael sees that they do not perceive him as a threat. He enjoys a provisional immunity from suspicion because he is an unlikely maestro of an expensive, devious trap and because both drug bosses trust him.[37]

The inflated views Corky and Esteban enjoy of themselves reinforce their underestimation of Michael and their faith in him. To doubt what Michael tells them would belie the accuracy of the drug kings' long-standing judgment of him as dependable and loyal, and so make them feel foolish. As mentioned, Michael's father gives him abstract principles about how to treat the aggressive and cautious types of adversary. But to apply this tactical advice outside the realm of chess, Michael has to see to whom it applies, and understand how it applies to them in the particularity of their characters and situations.

Even more, Michael must imagine how the advice can be adapted to these particular men for a situation that does not yet exist. Michael has to be like Aristotle's architectural strip of flexible metal in bending his father's typology to fit just these individuals in their possible, and not just in their actual, circumstances. Finally, Michael must envision concretely creating the novel circumstances in which Corky and Esteban eliminate one another and James is erased from his sister's life.

The finest of strategies will fall flat unless the individual plumbs the natures of the people he must influence in order to succeed. Jane Austen incisively describes this practical insight in *Persuasion:* "There is a quickness of perception in some, a nicety in the discernment of character, a natural penetration, in short, which no experience in others can equal."[38] Laying out his grand strategy, Michael sees how his drug bosses can be brought to confrontation by their opposite temperaments—Corky's aggression and Esteban's caution. The smaller pieces are equally understood and deployed: Jake's temper, the greed of Hector the cocaine merchant, Chuckie's machismo, and the police detective's consuming desire to bust Esteban.

But Austen's notion of "quickness of perception" also operates literally in Michael. To put his dodgy scheme in motion, Michael has had to sacrifice his savings to buy rock cocaine from Hector, who is reluctant to give him the drugs. Pretending to be Corky's emissary, Michael quotes Corky as saying that he won't forget the friends who helped him when he was in trouble. Pausing deliberately, Michael adds, "And he won't forget the people who didn't." When Hector still balks at handing over the drugs on consignment, Michael flashes his thick bankroll. Michael slips smoothly from reassuring Hector to tapping a vein of fear in him, only to wrap up the deal by appealing to his greed.

Explaining himself to the three wholesalers of narcotics (Hector, Corky, and Esteban), Michael must improvise his speech to suit their immediate and shifting reactions. He has to read his opponents and strike the right notes to play them, in Hamlet's poetic phrase, like pipes.[39] Michael understands what is called for on the spot because he has the perception of the practically wise individual: "'Perception' can respond to nuance and fine shadings, adapting its judgment to the matter at hand."[40] Michael is able to read the behavior of these men as nuanced and shaded because he has figured out what makes them tick.

The film deepens our understanding of what goes into this practical perception. To arrive at an accurate estimation of another individual's character, the phronimos must be receptive to perspectives other than his own. Such receptivity requires the individual to set his own nature aside and see things as the other person is likely to see them. Because Michael is very different from those with whom he contends, he must step out of his normal viewpoint to appreciate their desires, interests, and emotions.

Brought to an irate Corky, Michael feigns trepidation at "betraying" Jake. He tells Corky that he wasn't running base, or rock, cocaine for Esteban after all, but for Jake, who was cutting in on Corky's action. In this way, Michael puts offensive men on the defensive. Both Jake and Corky are aggressive, violent men, who now feel besieged. Earlier we saw Corky become furious with a card-playing gang member for continuing to play the game "behind his back" while he spoke with Michael.[41] Michael has grasped Corky's distrust of apparent friends and fear of double-dealing subterfuge and now mobilizes these emotions to turn him against Jake.

Michael claims that Jake built his bankroll for the cocaine by skimming from Corky and buttresses his story with the widely known fact that Esteban hates cocaine ("too confrontational") and wouldn't traffic in it. Michael explains Chuckie's boast, that they were carrying the cocaine for Esteban, as the result of misleading him in order to protect Jake, but that Michael didn't expect Chuckie to talk so freely. Desperately defending himself, Jake hits on the truth—that Michael used his own money to buy the cocaine. But it isn't plausible that such a small fry as Michael could have five thousand dollars, and Jake is doomed. Off-camera, we hear Corky lash Jake to death with his large-linked chain.

Michael has amassed and concealed his wealth by being frugal and tight-lipped. Michael's phronesis is reinforced by his habitual self-control. Unlike the people who surround him, Michael is able to delay gratification, whether in spending his money or pushing his game plan to fruition. Besides the many people in the movie who crave the quick satisfactions of drugs and sex, Corky and Jake immediately gratify their hot tempers with eruptions of violence. Michael is always composed, his emotions and desires in sync with his thoughts and long-term goals. Instead of impulsively reacting to Jake shooting the girl he likes, for example, Michael painstakingly plots Jake's retribution. Having maneuvered Corky into murdering Jake, Michael dexterously positions him to attack James by implicating James as Jake's cocaine distributor.[42]

Reporting to Esteban, Michael uses the truth, that Corky's boys jumped him and Chuckie, to frame Corky. Michael claims that Corky is tired of running cocaine, wants to live well like Esteban, and so is trying to horn in on his heroin trade. Cautious Esteban is drawn still more deeply into dangerous waters when Michael points out that Nicki has gone to live with James, who has allegedly thrown in with Corky for money and protection. Esteban is enamored of Nicki and knows that James has a hold on her. The threat to his sexual relationship with Nicki turns up the heat on Esteban, roiling his thought with anger, fear, and jealousy. His game is all but ruined.

Michael hits just the right notes to push Esteban toward a reckless path of confrontation with Corky and James because he has divined Esteban's character. The film elaborates upon the imaginative aspect of practical wisdom by showing Michael's insight into the imaginations of other individuals. To his ability to imaginatively concoct a plot in which to entrap his adversaries and his capacity to project a fresh start for his sister and himself, *Fresh* adds Michael's ability to sympathetically enter into the moral imaginations of those who would control his fate. He grasps what they envision for themselves as a good life.

Speaking of the moral imagination, John Kekes notes how it must include an emotional element, guiding the individual to appreciate the values harbored in the possibilities he envisages for himself.[43] Michael takes the affective element of imagination a step past his own future preferences and choices. He intuits the affective element in others, perceiving the appeal or distaste particular possibilities have for them. If the moral imagination involves engaging the affective pull possible scenarios have for ourselves, as Kekes suggests, then Michael seems blessed with a meta- or inter-moral imagination. It is grounded in judgment about human nature and invigorated with sympathetic attunement to the heart's desires and dreads of other individuals.

Michael's father has said that when he encounters cautious chess players, he draws them into dangerous waters. Esteban is self-confessedly cautious, having told Michael that smack (heroin) is the way to go: "The clientele is stable and peace-loving, the competition is nonconfrontational," unlike the cutthroat competition over cocaine, to which the volatile Corky is naturally drawn. The silky Esteban advises Michael to find his niche, cool and safe. Esteban has also explained to Michael why he is so attracted to Nicki, even though he has a wife and children. When Nicki is on heroin, Esteban purrs, she gets "soft and pure, and I am holding my very own virgin, my Madonna."

Nicki tells a curious Michael that she prefers James to Esteban because Esteban looks at her like a queen, when in fact she is nothing. To

Michael's retort that Aunt Francis thinks she is something, Nicki complains that being loved by a saint doesn't count: "Aunt Francis loves every damn dog in the street the same as she loves me."[44] In answer to Nicki's self-deprecation, Michael tells her, "*I* love you." The only time Michael utters this word, it stills and silences his sister. Nicki looks pensively at him, as if just discovering how solid his devotion to her is. Her look of appreciative wonder is repeated at the conclusion of the story when Michael tells the police detective who arrests Esteban that the new life with which the state is to provide him must include his sister.

Michael's father describes Nicki looking like an angel in her childhood and asks Michael if she is still beautiful. Michael expresses pique at his father's nostalgic reverie, and perhaps dismay over Nicki's presently fallen state, by telling his father that "them niggers be all over her."[45] His father gets angry, ostensibly with Michael using the word "nigger," but probably more for puncturing his idealized portrait of Nicki. Nevertheless, hearing his father laud Nicki's beauty doesn't make Michael feel envy, an emotion that could naturally obscure his love and commitment to her.

Michael keeps his perspective, unlike Esteban, whose judgment is funneled through a mythologized lust for Nicki, or Corky and Jake, whose decisions are dictated by their anger. Although several people tell Michael how unattractive he is, the image of his sister as a once regal angel may inspire him to see restoring her to health as a worthwhile undertaking. In such films as *Parenthood* and *Groundhog Day*, we saw how playfulness and humor enable us to keep events and ourselves in balanced perspective. We also saw how characters, such as the Marquis of Montrose in *Rob Roy*, lack a proper conception of themselves because of their self-centeredness.

Michael is able to maintain an uncannily clear view of himself, his relationships with other people, and the unstable power structure of his social world. Perhaps chess playing helps him keep things in perspective. But if so, it's not because chess is a playful pastime for Michael. Echoing Michael's loss of innocence is the fact that chess is not a game for him. It is a way for him to make money, sharpen his mind, and finally, plot out his life. However, chess may enable Michael to distance himself from his life's entanglements and take a larger view of things. Using chess to represent people and events, chess functions for Michael as art can, to extend or implement imagination. Through criticism of his chess playing, in fact, Michael has been led to reappraise his typical defensive response to the dangers posed by people in his life and to deal with the dangers now by going on the attack.

The father's criticism of Michael "hoarding" his pieces included Michael permitting attacks on his queen to disrupt his game strategy, treating the queen "as if she were the last lady on earth. The queen is just a pawn with a lot of fancy moves. When you see you're playin' a man who feels naked without his lady, use her, jump in there and take her. Tease her, threaten her, and he won't be able to think about his game anymore. That's when you make your real move." Michael's phronesis enables him to extrapolate from chess to the real world, to perceive Esteban as a man who is naked without Nicki.[46] To lure Esteban into checkmate, however, Michael must find a way to make the threat of Nicki's loss palpable to him.

Michael therefore speeds things up, distorting Esteban's judgment. Michael has learned from his father that people who make smart decisions when there is ample time often make mistakes when pressured, when the "clock" is on them. His father has told Michael that various great chess players beat him, but if the "show was put on speed," if heat was applied, he'd "chew their ass." With accelerated images of Corky, James, and Nicki flitting across his mind, Esteban is drawn into drowning waters.

At this point in the story, Esteban and Corky each believe that James poses a threat. Michael has positioned James like a chess piece apparently poised to attack in opposite directions, but actually functioning as a stationary decoy. The use of James to fulfill several functions at once suggests how the person of practical wisdom is able to see something from more than one angle at the same time. After James, Corky, and assorted henchmen are killed, Esteban returns to the apartment where he keeps Nicki.[47] Michael completes his plan by calling the police detective, planting Esteban's gun and heroin for him to find. With Esteban's arrest, all those who held Michael and Nicki in thrall are disposed of. Michael cuts a deal with the police to get himself and Nicki out of the city and into a new life.

Nature and Nurture, Character and Judgment

By adroitly juxtaposing Michael's phronesis with his chess playing, the film portrays phronesis as a gift of nature requiring cultivation. *Fresh* intimates that practical wisdom presupposes a natural talent, such as found in prodigies of chess, mathematics, and music. Aristotle views the common sense and intelligence that are aspects of practical wisdom as natural endowments.[48] Stanley Godlovitch speaks to the innate aspect of wisdom by contrasting it with the virtues that anyone can work at acquiring, such as moderation, generosity, and perseverance. "Wisdom sits alone. We cannot rehearse or practice it. We cannot be prompted to assume it."[49] I would add that to develop these natural abilities constitutive of practical wisdom, the individual must expend considerable effort. Michael must exert himself in paying close attention to the people around him, drawing correct inferences about their personalities, and envisaging a worthwhile future for himself and Nicki, as well as the means of realizing it.

In addition, *Fresh* endorses Aristotle's view that whatever the extent to which an individual is blessed by nature, the aptitude still requires the right sort of nurture. Michael clearly has inherited his father's intelligence and ability to judge people. This natural endowment is then nurtured by the father's instruction, the aunt's loving kindness, and Michael's own alacrity in learning from street life. Even cleverness, the instrumental facet of phronesis, seems to be built on a natural base developed in childhood. Not everyone has the ability to recognize, or fabricate, the means to achieve their goals, and those who have this ability usually cultivate it with the help of other people. Beyond cleverness, practical wisdom involves discriminating morally worthy purposes from among the many ends we could have. And this power of moral discrimination depends even more on proper upbringing.

Because phronesis is necessarily connected with moral goodness, we might question the morality of Michael's plan. Many people are killed in order for him to accomplish his purposes. Blunting this objection is the fact that with the exception of Chuckie, all who die are evil, themselves responsible for much more suffering and death than Michael instigates. The death of Esteban's and Corky's henchmen is incidental to Michael's design, and some of the gang members do survive. Michael's goal is not the loftier one of ridding the neighborhood of all its parasites. If it were, the portrayal of his character might be less plausible.

We should also remember that circumstances always limit the practically wise individual in what he can accomplish and how he can accomplish it. Michael cannot disentangle himself and Nicki from the drug dealers without their death or arrest, and he cannot accomplish everything he must strictly on his own. After all, "man is essentially a social animal, and thus he has interests, desires, demands, and pursuits that require the cooperation of others."[50] With no voluntary assistance to be found among his acquaintances, Michael must secure the unwitting "cooperation" from as mixed a bag of individuals as Chuckie, Esteban, the police detective, and Hector.

Isn't Michael guilty of irresponsibility in bringing about Chuckie's death, as a school friend alleges? Although causally responsible for

Chuckie's death, Michael is less obviously morally responsible for it.[51] Michael's behavior certainly puts Chuckie in the path of a danger he would not have otherwise risked, but Michael takes explicit, repeated steps to protect Chuckie. We can also defend Michael by pointing out that Chuckie is a lost cause. The combination of his own foolishness and bravado makes him more than merely susceptible to the violence that surrounds him. It destines him to an early end. Yet even so Michael could be faulted. If he thought Chuckie would listen to him, drop the drug bag and run, he was mistaken. Here we do well to bear in mind that phronesis doesn't entail perfection. Those who are practically wise may make mistakes, just as those with particular virtues may fail to achieve the ends those virtues tend to promote.

The foundation of phronesis is the right assessment of what matters in life—what is worth sacrificing and for what it is worth being sacrificed. Throughout the first segment of the film, we sense Michael's enlarging appreciation for the cumulative meaning of the failure, loss, and destruction around him. To his father's sad life, Michael adds his sister's self-hate and addiction. Smaller accretions include Michael's hostile interactions with a pitiful female junkie on the street and one of Esteban's jealous underlings, as well as the awareness that he is not repaying Aunt Francis's love and worry about him. Jake's schoolyard killings are the final layer of toxic sediment. We feel the cumulative weight of these layers of loss build as Michael weighs their meaning for his life.

Michael sees the evil of the life around him and his need to free himself from it, but not without a price. He turns his back on a life of easy money in which he would be a king. Both Corky and Esteban have told Michael that he'll soon be their main man, their money man. His future is assured as a drug lord. A lesser person could easily rationalize the girl's death in the schoolyard and Nicki's addiction as the unfortunate fallout of ghetto life, which, in a sense, they are. Such rationalization would allow the individual to be swayed by the prospect of big narcotics money, prestige, and power. But Michael refuses this easy way and his all but guaranteed success.

In choosing an open-ended future with his sister, Michael displays courage. Fear of life outside the inner city, fear of having to make it in a new environment by new rules, could weaken resolve or block the liberating decision from ever taking shape. Without the courage to act on the fruits of practical wisdom, the individual with phronesis is hardly better off than people who lack it. Courage might be essential to having phronesis in the first place. The film invites us to wonder whether practical wisdom includes courage and, more broadly, the strength of character needed to resist temptations and overcome trepidations. Although seeing what is good and how to get it can be incentives for doing what is difficult, they can only supplement existing willpower. Would we say of someone lacking the virtues needed to act on practical wisdom that he nevertheless possesses it?

Whether courage and strength of will are inherent in phronesis or are its indispensable auxiliaries, Michael is able to act on what he understands and values. Conversely, Michael's phronesis makes his risky actions instances of courage. In fact, Michael risks everything—his money, his standing with the drug dealers, Chuckie, probably his life as well. But he risks it all for what is truly worthwhile. Richard Sorabji explains why practical wisdom is necessary for courage: "Courage is not a matter of facing any danger for any reason. But of facing the right danger for the right reason . . . [which] depends partly on . . . what kind of life we should be aiming at."[52] Michael is courageous only because he is wise enough to determine what a good life is and to see which dangers he should brave from that larger perspective.

Fresh implicitly shows us Michael choosing what kind of person he wishes to become and what kind he doesn't. He doesn't want to become irascible (Corky), defensive and covetous (Esteban), narrow and cynical (his father), macho-posturing (Chuckie), or self-loathing and dependent (his sister). What he wants for himself in a life outside the housing projects is informed by what he presently values. We see how Michael properly esteems what is genuinely good in other people: his father's intelligence and seriousness of purpose; Aunt Francis's gentleness and compassion; the talent of the young basketball player; his sister's beauty and potential for a good life; and the sweetness of the slain schoolgirl.

Michael seems to understand how Nicki's passive degradation and Chuckie's attempts at being a big shot both stem from lack of legitimate self-respect. He strives to help his sister regain her self-respect because Michael understands the importance to us of respect for ourselves and others. He perceives that using creatures capable of pleasure and pain for gain is wrong—whether other people or animals. Through the personal example of his sister, Michael appreciates how narcotics and prostitution exploit people, and he instinctively rejects Chuckie's training of Roscoe as degrading to the animal. Michael also possesses the good sense not to try to save those who can't be helped, such as Chuckie and his father.

Michael further exhibits phronesis in realizing what he will have to give up to achieve his immediate and long-term goals. Thus, he unflinchingly sacrifices what is good only extrinsically, such as money or the esteem in which others hold him, as a means to more important ends. But Michael is also strong enough to give up what he recognizes as less worthwhile, but nonetheless intrinsically good, the relationship with his father. At the park to play chess with his father for the last time, we see Michael cry. In a film filled with ironies, the most poignant occurs in the closing moments. Michael's father chides him for keeping him waiting in favor of playing what he supposes are his "little boy games." In masterminding his scheme, Michael is able to absorb his father's chess wisdom and apply it to real people and situations in ways his father could never dream of. To do this, Michael must assess the strengths and weaknesses of those around him in order to manipulate them to his advantage. His practical wisdom includes the foresight to deliberate carefully when he has the time, thereby preparing for choice and action when time is fleeting.

Telling Michael that he won't always be there to hold his hand, the father is abashed by Michael's tears and his almost voiceless, rasped sobbing. We realize how much Michael is forgoing in severing his relationship with his father. The conflict between good things is deep, and Michael's decision is made harder because, as the closest thing to a mentor Michael has, the father is a kind of shelter. Just as only the sweet girl evokes smiles from Michael, so his father is alone responsible for Michael's tears. The last shot of the film is of Michael crying, leaving a lasting impression not only of sadness but of the underlying strength of character needed to make such a painful choice for what is ultimately for the best.

Of course, the portrait of Michael in *Fresh* doesn't exhaust the meaning of phronesis. What I have argued is that the film pulls together strands of practical wisdom as articulated by such philosophers as Aristotle. By realizing them in the character of Michael, it develops our understanding further, adding fresh insights to ancient wisdom about phronesis.

Notes

1. Aristotle, *Nicomachean Ethics*, trans. Martin Ostwald (Indianapolis, Ind.: Bobbs-Merrill, 1962), p.166, 1143b.

2. Aristotle considers cleverness "the power to perform those steps which are conducive to a goal we have set for ourselves and to attain that goal." *Nicomachean Ethics*, p.169, 1144a.

3. Philippa Foot, "Virtues and Vices," in *Vice and Virtue in Everyday Life*, 2nd ed., ed. Christina and Fred Sommers (Orlando, Fla.: Harcourt, Brace, Jovanovich, 1993), pp.216–231, p.219.

4. Richard Sorabji, "Aristotle on the Role of Intellect in Virtue," *Proceedings of the Aristotelian Society* (n.s.) 74 (1973–1974): 197–229, 207.

5. I shall follow Aristotle and use the masculine pronoun because our paradigm, Michael, is male.

6. Stanley Godlovitch, "On Wisdom," in *Vice and Virtue in Everyday Life*, 2nd ed., ed. Christina and Fred Sommers (Orlando, Fla.: Harcourt, Brace, Jovanovich, 1993), pp.262–284, p.271.

7. Aristotle, *Nicomachean Ethics*, p.164, 1143a.

8. Ibid., p.152, 1140a.

9. Kathleen V. Wilkes, "The Good Man and the Good of Man," *Mind* 87 (1978): 553–571, 568.

10. John Kekes, *Moral Wisdom and Good Lives* (Ithaca: Cornell University Press, 1995), p.101. Although Kekes distinguishes moral wisdom from practical and philosophical wisdom, I draw on a number of his observations about the former in sketching an understanding of practical wisdom. There is a large area of overlap between moral wisdom and phronesis proper, if only because, as Kekes acknowledges, "moral wisdom is [also] practically and contingently oriented" (p.17). The details of the distinctions Kekes draws need not detain us, so long as we note their importance to him and that all my references to Kekes' thought are originally couched in terms of "moral" not "practical" wisdom.

11. Ibid., p.54.

12. Aristotle, *Nicomachean Ethics*, 1141b.

13. David Wiggins, *Needs, Values, Truth* (Oxford: Blackwell, 1987), p.237.

14. Aristotle, *Nicomachean Ethics*, p.166, 1143a.

15. Ibid., 1090b, 1109b, and 1113a.

16. Martha Nussbaum, *The Fragility of Goodness* (Cambridge: Cambridge University Press, 1986), p.301.

17. Ibid., pp.302–304. Nussbaum distinguishes among mutability, indeterminacy, and particularity; however, I think a strong case can be made that mutability and indeterminacy follow from particularity.

18. Ibid., p.304.

19. For a more detailed discussion of executive and substantive virtues, see the discussion of virtue in Chapter 1.

20. Nussbaum, *Fragility of Goodness*, p.307.

21. Aristotle, *Nicomachean Ethics*, 1113a, 1113b.

22. Nussbaum, *Fragility of Goodness*, p.308.

23. David Wiggins uses the term "situational appreciation" in a more narrow way to refer to the ability to fit a generalized ideal conception to the objective conditions within which the individual exists. *Needs, Values, Truth*, p.237. As the reader can see, I understand the notion of situational appreciation more broadly.

24. See Kekes, *Moral Wisdom*, especially Chapter Three, "Permanent Adversities," pp.51–72.

25. Herbert Morris, *On Guilt and Innocence* (Berkeley: University of California Press, 1976), p.161.

26. Kekes, *Moral Wisdom*, p.58.

27. Bernard Williams argues for a lack of common standard on the grounds that there is no highest value or a basis for translating different goods into a common referent or principle to provide a preference ordering. *Moral Luck* (Cambridge: Cambridge University Press, 1981), pp.77–80.

28. Nussbaum, *Fragility of Goodness*, p.308.

29. A possible word play adds a cops 'n' robbers piquancy to Michael's execution of Roscoe. Since "roscoe" is old-fashioned slang for a gun, Roscoe the dog is killed with Chuckie's roscoe, the use of which is crucial in bringing about Chuckie's own demise.

30. Kekes, *Moral Wisdom*, p.59.

31. We are reminded of an earlier scene in the school gym during which this gifted ballplayer had dribbled around people and shot beautifully. The gym teacher had reprimanded the boy for "hogging the ball," so taken was he with his own talent that he ignored his teammates.

32. Morris, *On Guilt and Innocence*, p.161.

33. The dual role of opponent as chess piece is made explicit at the end of the film, when Michael's father asks him if he is ready to be king by beating him at chess.

34. Kekes, *Moral Wisdom*, p.54.

35. Nussbaum, *Fragility of Goodness*, p.304. Whenever Michael ponders his chessboard configurations, we hear synthesized harpsichord music against background beeps emanating from the video games played by Michael's cousins. Not only does the cerebral counterpoint of the harpsichord contrast with the more childish beeping, setting Michael's maturity apart, but the synthesizer is a subtle update of a traditional instrument of refined taste. Michael's inner-city machinations and manipulations are a recontextualized version of traditional practical wisdom.

36. See Mary Midgley, "Brutality and Sentimentality," *Philosophy* 54 (1979): 385–389, 385 and 387.

37. Earlier, Esteban tells Michael that he has won a bet on Michael's integrity. A confederate of Esteban's had mistakenly assumed Michael had stolen the conspicuous twentieth packet of heroin which he had misplaced. Michael's return of the missing packet to Esteban confirms his trustworthiness.

38. Jane Austen, *Persuasion*, ed. Andrew Wright (Boston: Houghton Mifflin, 1965), p.197.

39. Shakespeare, *Hamlet*, Act III, Scene ii.

40. Nussbaum, *Fragility of Goodness*, p.301.

41. In this scene, Corky ironically tells Michael that he'll speak to Jake about *his* temper! Undeterred by Corky's flash of disproportionate anger at the card player, Michael disdains the money Corky proffers and insists on the hundred dollars that Jake has withheld from him. Echoing Esteban's sentiments, Corky foretells that when Michael is bigger, he'll be "the man." And of course, we are

acquainted with Jake's hotheadedness from his shooting of the basketball player whose excellent play infuriated Jake.

42. The film is filled with ironic turns on Michael's intelligence. When Corky confronts Michael over the cocaine, for example, he tells Michael that he's "just a little kid, in way over his head." Of course, Corky is reacting to Michael's moves exactly as Michael had anticipated. Corky's observation resonates with the re-mark of the detective at the station house where Michael is questioned after Chuckie's murder. There, the policeman tells Michael that he is either innocent or a "helluva lot smarter than [he] looks." Michael will soon use the home phone number the detective gives him to put Esteban away.

43. Kekes, *Moral Wisdom*, p.113.

44. Here the film raises the paradox of agapic or neighbor love. While loving other people unconditionally, regardless of their attributes or relationship to us, is a virtue for the loving individual, the recipient nevertheless desires to be loved as special, for the unique person she is. The tension between giving and receiving selfless love is nicely dramatized in Mary Gordon's novel, *Final Payments.*

45. Michael seems to have an instinctive distrust of sentimentality, just as he is repelled by (Chuckie's) brutality. Like its opposite counterpart, brutality, senti-mentality also fosters and relies upon a distorted image of ourselves, but in the case of sentimentality, the image is of someone filled with kind, gentle, and noble sentiments.

46. The film may be also making a subtle allusion to the fact that the only time Michael sees Esteban naked is when he is with an undressed, drugged Nicki. Michael seems riveted by the sight of his somnolent sister with her lover.

47. Michael watches the shooting showdown perched atop the hood of Esteban's car, calmly eating a candy bar. Having played the role of (film) director, Michael now assumes the viewpoint of the audience. He hears snatches of Esteban's jealous accusations of James and catches glimpses of Esteban striking and shooting James in the upstairs windows—framed as by a movie or television screen.

48. Aristotle, *Ethics*, p.166, 1143b.

49. Godlovitch, "On Wisdom," p.279.

50. Wilkes, "The Good Man," p.558.

51. Moral and causal responsibility should be distinguished. If I receive the kidney you need because I am ahead of you on the recipient list, I contribute causally to your failing health or death. But I am not morally responsible in the sense of being blameworthy for your condition. Similarly, if Michael had not lined Chuckie up with Esteban for the drug run, Chuckie would not have been killed when he was. However, Chuckie bears the moral responsibility for putting himself at risk, first, by accepting the job, and later, by not following Michael's prudent directives.

52. Sorabji, "Aristotle on the Role of Intellect," p.207.

7
Character in Crisis: Reluctant Heroes in *Jaws* and *Aliens*

Moral Completeness

In this chapter, I widen the lens of analysis to include two films because I think comparing them not only enhances our appreciation of each but also sheds light on what is distinctive about the virtues of the protagonists of both films. Similarities between the mythically proportioned monsters and their relentless attack on humans account for only the most obvious affinities between Steven Spielberg's *Jaws* (1975) and John Cameron's *Aliens* (1986). Additional parallels in plot, theme, and characterization should broaden our understanding of why the morally good person is uniquely equipped to overcome both natural danger and human vice. The stories pit individuals of apparently ordinary ability against spectacular creatures from beyond the hospitable landscapes of civilization—the briny deep and deep space. The pair of confrontations are structured to show how great danger can evoke heroism from people who, though morally good, would rather evade danger than fight it.

In fact, a virtue central to these unlikely heroes is precisely the good sense to recognize the destructive forces they are up against. The films contrast these wary protagonists with colleagues who eagerly plunge into battle with the beasts. In this contrast, we see how completeness of virtue enables individuals unprepared for such combat to succeed where experts fail. Chief Brody in *Jaws* and Flight Officer Ripley in *Aliens* possess a

Jaws: Brody, about to face the shark and recommend a bigger boat.

Aliens: Ripley comforts a frightened Newt.

constellation of bright virtues, but they are fully expressed or realized only in the crucible of catastrophe.

The first thing to note about these individuals is that their virtues are representative of the conscientious citizen or Everyman. These morally well-rounded characters act for the safety of other citizens, and they themselves function as model citizens, forced into heroism. Brody and Ripley do not possess the larger-than-life virtue of the extraordinary ruler, glorious warrior, or saint. In Aristotelian terms, they are not "great-souled" people, who are high-placed rather than commonplace; not merely generous, but magnanimous; self-sacrificing more than public-spirited. People of extraordinary virtue believe themselves worthy of great things, mindful of their ability and station.[1] Such magnificent individuals are typically blessed with high birth, wealth, or power, which enable them to exhibit their nobility with deeds of great scope and lasting impact.[2]

Recall how self-assured and self-consciously principled Rob Roy is in initiating plans for his community's welfare, defying authority he finds un-just, and teaching his sons about honor. Although not actually highborn,

Rob Roy wears his position of political leadership confidently, physically and morally dwarfing the other characters in the story. Rob has a sense of his superior ability to fulfill his stewardship of the land and the people who live on it. On the other hand, the morality tales told by *Jaws* and *Aliens* concern the virtue of Everyman taken to its limit—an ideal to which all citizens can aspire in their own sphere of life because the main characters are not so far above the ordinary that we cannot identify with them.

The morally complete person possesses the classic array of virtues. Many of the virtues that make the individual so valuable as a citizen orient him or her toward other people. The other-regarding virtues include compassion, justice, generosity, and courage. Since the heroes in our films fully realize their virtues in conflict with extremely dangerous enemies, courage will naturally be paramount. But before discussing such other-regarding virtues, I want to consider virtues related to the self, if only because so many other-regarding virtues depend on them.

The virtues that have the self as their object are self-regarding in a way that mirrors the other-regarding virtues. Two important self-regarding virtues that our films explore are self-knowledge and humility. Moreover, the films indicate how these two are necessarily connected. An important dimension of self-knowledge is self-awareness: the transparency of the individual to him- or herself, which contrasts most markedly with self-deception. Self-deception enables people to dissolve, rather than resolve, a tension between what they want to do and their moral convictions. The self-deceiver "completely ignores . . . those features of his behavior that make it wrong. For example, he chooses not to think about how what he does might harm someone."[3]

Self-deception typically proceeds by people embracing false beliefs about themselves (such as our benign motives), about other people (their malicious intentions), or about circumstances (no hard evidence that our action is harmful). By providing themselves with a distorted interpretation of a relevant portion of reality, people who deceive themselves are able to avoid recognizing the moral wrongness of what they do even though "in some sense" they know that it is wrong. Self-deception always serves the individual's interests by smoothing the transition from moral self-obstruction to fulfilling one's desires.

Herbert Fingarette insightfully observes how self-deception involves a two-tiered cover-up. Self-deception not only covers up the fact that the behavior is wrong, but it also conceals from the person the fact that she has judged it to be wrong.[4] The individual actually believes what she says because she has deceived herself about herself. Fingarette argues that people who resist self-deception possess "moral courage," interpreted by Ron Milo as "the courage to stand one's ground with respect to maintaining one's moral convictions against the onslaught of contrary desires and emotions."[5] Despite the temptation to redefine a situation in order to yield to desires and emotions that violate one's moral convictions, some people are able to maintain a steady view of themselves.

But here we should side with Aristotle in noticing that the person of Fingarette's "moral courage" is at one remove from the truly virtuous person. She is merely continent or self-restrained because it takes an effort of will to do what is morally right,[6] just as the person who lacks true generosity has to force herself to give. For the truly virtuous person is not assailed by desires and emotions that run counter to her moral convictions in the first place. The virtuous person enjoys a moral-psychological harmony such that emotions and desires accord with the moral views supplied by reason. Should a desire or emotion arise that is later recognized as conflicting with the requirements of morality—say, because it is unjust or unkind—it would be extinguished by the recognition. For example, once the virtuous individual noticed that her off-color jokes were upsetting a fellow worker, she would cease to want to tell them.

The lure of self-deception, then, calls attention to the two standard Aristotelian alternatives to moral failure or wrongdoing: continence (successful struggle against temptation) and virtue (no temptation against which to struggle). People who manage to resist cravings for excess amounts of food, for instance, are better off than those who yield to gluttony because they do, after all, heed reason. But those who successfully struggle against their desires are inferior to individuals who desire the right amount, as their appetite has been fully penetrated or educated by reason. The virtuous individual is so far from self-deception that her self-perception is safe because she has no struggle with the impulses that prompt self-deception.[7]

Of course, self-knowledge extends beyond merely being free of self-deception. A person might not be self-deceived and still fail to know himself very well. Self-knowledge can probably proceed indefinitely: from simply knowing what one's moral beliefs are to understanding how one came to have them and the extent to which they are defensible. Self-knowledge also includes a grasp of one's true motives and feelings, as well as a realistic assessment of one's responsibilities and abilities. *Jaws* and *Aliens* are especially good at conveying the pivotal place of knowing one's responsibilities and abilities in the virtuous life. Here again, self-deception comes into play. The films contrast their virtuous protagonists with people who deceive themselves about their abilities or their responsibilities toward others. Both *Jaws* and *Aliens* portray overweening desire for money as the force prompting self-deception about moral responsibility.

The virtue of humility is a tributary of self-knowledge. Individuals who have an overall modest perspective on themselves, wary of self-aggrandizement and slow to flatter, are likely to be clear on their abilities and duties. If we keep in perspective our talents, accomplishments, and virtues—how they compare to truly gifted or great-souled people, for example—we will not exaggerate our abilities or strengths. Conversely, perspicacity about ourselves promotes our humility. If we see clearly what we can do and where we come up short, we won't get a swelled head. Self-knowledge and humility share a realistic view of the self and the world and so reciprocally support one another.

Not all self-related virtues are self-regarding. Besides virtues that take the self as their object, such as humility and self-respect, there are virtues that are of or about the self. In these virtues, the self figures prominently in defining what the virtue is about, but as the subject rather than the object of the virtue. Perhaps what is curious about these virtues is precisely that the self is not the focus of attention or concern, despite the virtues consisting in the person's relation to him- or herself. For example, self-reliance and moral independence are virtues about the self, but in neither one does the individual attend to him- or herself.

Self-reliance seems essential to moral completeness. Self-reliance is shorthand for a well-knit web of virtues. Resourcefulness, decisiveness, initiative-taking, and perseverance, for example, work in concert to make people self-reliant. These traits of character are of instrumental value, enabling us to accomplish things, alone and with others. In this, its more obvious sense, self-reliance is the complement of cooperativeness. A virtuous person is able to work with others, share ideas, give and receive criticism, and modify her views in light of what other people say and do.

When combined with cooperativeness in the right way, self-reliance yields leadership—the ability to give direction to willing, supportive colleagues. We might also notice that self-knowledge indirectly contributes to self-reliance. People who know their strengths and weaknesses can play to their strengths and remedy or compensate for their deficiencies. Only action that reflects these strengths and weaknesses can be self-reliant because the individual does not come up short due to overestimation of ability, nor does he shrink from undertaking what he can accomplish.

However, there is a deeper sense of self-reliance than the instrumental one we have been considering. Virtuous individuals are morally independent or self-reliant in taking their moral bearings from themselves. Certainly, they listen to the views of other people and take them seriously, but in the end their own moral standards and convictions carry the day. The moral independence that characterizes truly virtuous individuals fuels an unobtrusive sense of self-worth and confidence. These individuals have a strong sense of their commitments and obligations and resist plausible denials of responsibility. Thus, when a woman who is distraught over her son's death by shark attack blames Chief Brody for not closing the beaches, he accepts the responsibility, refusing the denial proffered by the mayor. Although the reluctant heroes of *Jaws* and *Aliens* make no fine speeches about an inner sense of honor, as Rob Roy does, they possess a quiet integrity that runs throughout their narratives. They keep themselves intact by holding fast to their moral principles and acting on them, regardless of opposition by other people or of temptations to take the easy way out.

A final self-related set of virtues are those that characterize the good student. Both Brody and Ripley possess the virtues of learning that make acquiring new information, understanding, and skills enjoyable. Brody and Ripley are inquisitive: eager to seek out information, ask questions, and assimilate what they learn. They quickly and instinctively look into new domains or dimensions of the world when their circumstances make it wise to do so. The student virtues imply an objectivity—an openness to what is not subjective, of the self.

Good students respect the objective world and find it worth investigating. This marks one of the ways in which the virtues of inquiry presuppose humility, the person seeing him- or herself as a supplicant, asking for what the objective world has to offer. In order for good students to grow intellectually and gain knowledge, they must have the humility needed to recognize the gaps and limitations in their understanding for what they are and then to take responsibility for these deficiencies. The desire to overcome one's intellectual shortcomings and a willingness to labor for this goal are concomitants of the humbling regard for all that the world has to teach.

The intellectual appetite of the apt pupil is enlivened by a mind that is good at making deductions and drawing inferences and is resourceful in knowing how to seek out what is lacking. The good student knows how to ask the right questions and how the answers to them can be incorporated into what is already understood and put into practice. These intellectual strengths mesh with practical wisdom. Although it is possible to be a good student without phronesis, phronesis does seem to require considerable powers of inference making, learning from experience, and applying what is learned to novel situations. All the inquiry therefore is for practical ends and is not invested in learning strictly for its own sake—which, instead, characterizes the purely intellectual virtues. Because the learning is subservient to accomplishing something practical, the individual must be able to choose morally good goals and morally worthy means to them. The excellences of intellect that define Everyman, therefore, must be interwoven with practical wisdom.

As with Michael, in *Fresh*, Ripley and Brody must figure out how to solve difficult problems in order to reach worthwhile goals. All of these featured characters must use whatever means they find available, often improvising, to secure cooperation from other people and defeat their opponents. But unlike Michael, Ripley and Brody do not have to use their practical wisdom to reassess the course their lives are taking and redirect it wholesale. Instead, their practical wisdom enables them to hit the mean in dealing with their particular tight spots. The stable understanding of the good life enjoyed by Brody and Ripley informs their daily, critical decisions.

Richard Sorabji describes this aspect of phronesis as enabling a person, "in the light of his conception of the good life in general, to perceive . . . what virtue . . . require[s] of him, in the particular case, and it instructs him to act accordingly."[8] The natural impulse to give, for instance, is not enough. We need practical wisdom to tell us what and how much to give and on whom to bestow our largesse. More to the point in these films, we need practical wisdom to tell us when and how to fight. Thus does Ripley time and again counsel the Marines to retreat or forgo fighting the aliens, appreciating the danger and the lack of resources for successful engagement. Her larger aim always includes saving the lives of the Marines as well as exterminating the aliens.

With the application of phronesis to the practicalities of fighting, we arrive at the virtue of courage, in particular, and the other-regarding virtues, in general. Like all moral virtues, courage involves hitting the mean between extremes of excess and deficiency. Unlike other virtues, however, Aristotle describes the mean or median for courage along two axes: one involving fear and one involving confidence. The courageous individual feels the appropriate or medial amount of fear, which is determined by human nature.[9] We feel fear at the perception of danger to ourselves because we desire to avoid harm (injury or death). The disvalue of the harm is weighed together with its probability of occurring.

Confidence is an expectation that what brings safety will be close at hand, while what produces fear will not exist or will be far away.[10] It seems plausible to interpret Aristotle as implying that the right (medial) amount of confidence depends on correctly assessing the chances of attaining safety in the face of the perceived danger. There is also a correlatively weighted value on this confidence side of the ledger or scales—the value of the goal to be achieved by the contemplated (courageous) act.[11] The paradigmatic goal for Aristotle is the safety and survival of a city, or community, at war.

David Pears helpfully describes the uniqueness of courage as arising from incompatibility between values: "courage is a virtue exhibited in predicaments in which two different values conflict with one another."[12] The value of the individual's safety (or the disvalue of harm to him) is in conflict with the value attached to the goal of the contemplated act, such as preserving human life or the independence of a nation. These conflicting values must now be assigned probabilities of being realized. Consequently, there are two pairs: one pair of valuations, and a pair of probabilities respectively assigned the valuations. To the value of X is attached its likelihood of occurring and to the value of Y is attached its likelihood of occurring. The value of the goal to be achieved has a corresponding probability, and the disvalue of harm to the agent also has a probability.

This twofold interpretation rightly allows for courageous people to choose not to fight. The value of a goal may be seriously outweighed by the disvalue of the anticipated harm, such as saving a cat at the risk of ten human lives. Or the odds may be too lopsided, as in a high probability that many people will be hurt or die, coupled with very little chance of saving lives. At one extreme, which clearly enjoins forbearance or withdrawal, is the combination of high risk of great loss for little chance of small gain. Courage enters the picture when the goal is indeed very valuable and the individual's safety is dicey. The courageous individual tries to increase the odds of achieving the valued goal and decrease the probability of harm to himself (or others).

Sometimes, of course, the goal is so valuable, such as saving an entire community, that even with bad odds in achieving it and strong probability of death in striving to attain it, the courageous individual takes the gamble.[13] Fear is properly tempered, therefore, by the value (and sometimes likelihood) of the goal to be achieved. Our desire to avoid harm will be outweighed by the desire to achieve the good. When the medial fear is outweighed, "it may still rightly modify the way in which the agent tries to attain the external goal."[14] I take this to mean that the courageous person is more diligent in preparation for, or circumspect in the approach taken toward, attaining the valuable outcome.

The cowardly mercenary, on Aristotle's account, overestimates his chance of attaining safety in his current encounter, based on previous success. The mercenary revises downward his chances of avoiding harm when the crisis comes and so flees the fight.[15] I would add to this that the mercenary typically has little or no commitment to the valuable goal to be achieved by the risky act, which is to say that the mercenary does not himself value the goal. Consequently, the shift in odds against him, or his perception of the shift, is sufficient to prompt his flight. For it is precisely in valuing the goal that fear is modulated in courageous people.

Let's conclude our outline of the individual well-rounded in virtue with mention of another central other-regarding virtue—justice. Aristotle tells us that justice and injustice concern allocating such divisible goods as honor, money, and safety.[16] These goods are competitive in that if one person gets more, another individual typically gets less. The just individual looks to distribute goods impartially, without undue regard for his own benefit, based on some independent principle of desert. Aristotle argues that unjust people are greedy (pleonexia); they want "more"—more than they have, more than other people have, more than they are entitled to. Because the goods are competitive, the vice of injustice entails that the unjust person wants more at the expense of others.

Aristotle's association of injustice with wanting more certainly seems open to dispute. We could point out that unjust particular acts may be the result of jealousy or the desire for revenge as much as the motive of gain; however, the unjust characters in *Jaws* and *Aliens* nicely fit Aristotle's model of injustice motivated by greed.[17] We will therefore skirt the niceties of Aristotelian exegesis and the general connection of injustice with greed and work within Aristotle's framework of people whose injustice is driven by greed.

The greed of the merchants in *Jaws* and of the Company managers and Carter Burke in *Aliens* eventuates in other people receiving less safety than they deserve and less than they would otherwise enjoy. Brody and Ripley are so indifferent to their own gain as never to be tempted to treat other people unjustly. Justice is such a part of their moral fabric that Brody and Ripley habitually spurn opportunities to yield to the importunings of greedy people who invite the protagonists to acquiesce in their injustice. Moreover, the sense of justice ingrained in Brody and Ripley commits them not simply to reject injustice but to compensate for the injustice of others by taking on greater responsibilities for themselves.

Obviously, the improbable heroes of *Jaws* and *Aliens* do not embody every virtue—the films wouldn't have room to dramatize them if they did. For instance, neither Brody nor Ripley is especially generous, friendly, agapic, or witty. But they possess the central or cardinal virtues, as well as others, and display them in such an exceptional degree, or with such exceptional grace under fire, that they serve well as exemplars of morally complete individuals. All that remains for them is a monumental challenge to bring their characters to full bloom. The films supply the challenge overtly in the form of their toothy monsters and implicitly in the greed of the vicious individuals whose behavior looses the terrors on innocent citizens.

Reluctant Heroes on Alien Turf

The plot structure and dynamic of the two movies is virtually identical. In each story, the protagonist perceives and warns of a great danger, which those in power either ignore or explain away. Once the monstrous threat is acknowledged, Brody and Ripley accompany their more skilled, knowledgeable, and experienced cohorts on a journey of search into alien environs. Bloody engagements en route to the climaxes of the movies display their respective beasts' cunning and ferocity, until they are finally vanquished by the brave protagonists in a fight to the death.

In *Jaws*, Chief Brody (Roy Scheider) is a former New York City policeman transplanted to an island off the coast of Long Island whose resort business depends on summer tourists. When a young woman is reported missing and body parts are washed up on the beach, Brody's instinct is to close the beaches. But his worry about the safety of swimmers is rebuffed by the mayor (Murray Hamilton) and the town's leading merchants. Subsequent shark attacks enable Brody to force the mayor to subsidize the shark hunt, which will include the former Navy man who owns the boat, Quint (Robert Shaw), and a scientific expert from the Oceanographic Institute, Matt Hooper (Richard Dreyfuss). Both Quint and Hooper are amazed at the size, speed, and intelligence of the great white shark they soon encounter. Quint's ship is eventually so incapacitated by the shark's ramming and chomping that it can't provide protection for the three men. Quint is eaten alive by the shark, and Hooper barely escapes from a futile shark-cage venture. Clinging to the drooping crow's nest spar, Brody is able to shoot the shark, succeeding where the experts of experience and technical knowledge have failed.

Flight Officer Ripley (Sigourney Weaver) also triumphs over her primeval adversary in spite of the failures of people with more fighting experience, training, or technical knowledge. The managers of the Company are angry with her for costing them an expensive spacecraft (in the previous film, *Alien*[18]) and dismiss her warnings about the alien creatures, blithely claiming no evidence of their presence. The Company makes money colonizing distant planets, such as LV426, where sixty-odd families have been living and working for some twenty years. One of the Company's profit-makers is the terra-form equipment, which creates atmosphere needed for colonizing otherwise uninhabitable places. Carter Burke (Paul Reiser), a company bureaucrat, soon recruits Ripley to join a reconnaissance crew of Marines by promising her reinstatement as a flight officer and the chance for her to overcome her recurring nightmares.

Once on the planet, the Marines are ferociously attacked and overmatched from the outset by hordes of insect-like, crustaceous creatures. The main plot developments involve Ripley befriending an orphaned girl, Newt (Carrie Henn), and Burke increasing the risk to all but himself in his venal attempt to bring gestating aliens back to earth for profit. To add to the crew's difficulties, the nuclear reactor on the planet is quickly melting down, and the earthlings have precious little time to get clear of it. Amidst the planet's destruction, Ripley engages in hand-to-hand combat with the alien queen and finally launches her into outer space.

The central movie elements found in *Jaws* are all present in grander scale in *Aliens*—whether monster or political economy, human antagonist or cinematic excitement. The beach resort locale and mercantilism of the merchants of *Jaws* is elevated in *Aliens* to outer space and intergalactic, postplanetary capitalism. The small-town avarice of the merchants is magnified in the corporate greed of the Company and Burke. Most obviously, *Aliens* populates its story with an army of lethal beasts, and their queen is certainly more menacing than the great white shark in *Jaws*. Technical developments in moviemaking provide a realistic portrayal of the space monsters in both detail and size. It's as if the changes in moviemaking and political economy during the decade separating the production of the two films is reflected in their relative proportions. The fact that about half of the story in *Jaws* occurs in the town, before the nautical voyage, seems representative of the domestic size and pace of the film.

The menace of the aliens and their queen and the otherworldly circumstances in which Ripley finds herself require that she do more things more of the time than Brody is called upon to do. Because she must do more than Brody to prevail, Ripley's virtues are broader in scope and greater in magnitude. But as with the obstacles and dangers each leading character must overcome, the gap between Ripley and Brody is more a separation of magnitude than of kind. They are kindred characters, reluctantly pressed into service against apocalyptic predators. In each case, the hero battles with the consequence and symbol of an underlying economic, human predation. The alien creatures are a thinly veiled trope for the human vice that exposes innocent people to their saw-like maws.

Brody and Ripley are thrust into deadly predicaments because of the political economies that control their societies. The irony of the pair of heroes being supercitizens, exemplifying civic virtues on behalf of their fellow citizens, is that there is little genuine community in the town of Amity and none whatsoever in the futuristic setting of *Aliens*. Here, too, *Aliens* goes one better than *Jaws*. The weak bonds of shared commercial interests in the social setting of *Jaws* give way to nothing but contractual economic relationships (and duplicity) in *Aliens*, in which the only nexus between people is money, except for the pumped-up camaraderie among the space Marines. The life-and-death challenges Brody and Ripley overcome draw out the virtues they already possess, but which await fulfillment.

The opening shot of each film establishes alien habitat: starry outer space in *Aliens* and treacherous ocean waters in *Jaws*. The music accompanying the underwater shots in *Jaws* soon becomes identifiable as the menacing shark theme, composed primarily of an insistent cello joined by an alarum of horns. Spielberg thereby chillingly and economically supplements his comparatively limited cinematic palate of horror. On planet LV426, alien eggs endanger the colonizing families. On the beaches of Amity, the shark threatens the families frolicking in the water. Images of water symbolize how the humans are not naturally at home in these surroundings, though they try to domesticate them. The trio in *Jaws* are literally at sea. When Quint pridefully, angrily destroys the ship-to-shore radio, Brody yells, "Where are we now?" Significantly, his immediate reference is to place—the perilous sea, not directly to their loss of communication. The expedition in *Aliens* is eventually enveloped in the watery atmosphere of LV426, which even permeates the interior of the colonized compound. They are almost adrift on the drizzly planet, tenuously connected to their civilization by a tricky remote-control spaceship landing and rendezvous.

In both films, pursuit of the humid monsters draws humans off solid terrain. The ocean and the constantly dripping rain of LV426 are the elemental environs of their respective primeval creatures. The shark is prehistoric, unchanged in millions of years. The aliens are ahistoric, living out of our time, in another world. Each creature is almost indestructible. Neither shark nor alien queen can be captured or preserved but must be annihilated. So basic is their destructiveness that they can only be defeated by utter devastation.

The stories depict their monsters as bent simply on survival. For both the aliens and the shark, humans provide nourishment and a means of procreation. Alien offspring gestate in humans, and so are temporary parasites, eventually killing their hosts. The great white shark feeds directly on human flesh, enabling it to thrive and reproduce. As Hooper says in *Jaws,* the shark is a miracle of evolution; all it does is "swim and eat and make baby sharks." Neither the alien crustaceans nor the shark is evil. They are forces of nature, using human beings for their own survival and the perpetuation of their species.

After the initial fatal encounters of humans with shark and aliens, the subsequent killing of people is brought about by humans. If the people of Amity didn't continue to swim in the shark's waters, the shark would pose no threat. If the colonists did not invade the aliens' space, they would not be imperiled. Neither seaside recreation nor space colonization is essential to human life, reproduction, or welfare. In the recreation and colonization, moreover, unwitting people are endangered to further economic interests of selfish, callous individuals. The evil of human greed creates the framework within which the virtuous individuals must battle destructive forces of nature. *Aliens* and *Jaws* suggest that expertise and experience in doing battle cannot repulse the threat loosed on innocent people by unrestrained economic appetite. Only individuals with civic virtues can salvage human welfare from the jaws of avarice, which are alien to true human happiness.

In each story, social context and human enemies match and mesh with the physical contexts and natural adversaries of their heroes. The political economy in each society furnishes the heroes with their human antagonists. In *Aliens,* the ubiquitously powerful Company cares only about making a profit and minimizing financial loss. The economic self-interest is crystallized in Carter Burke who, we discover midtale, has caused the deaths of the colonists on planet LV426 in an attempt to make a bundle of money for himself and the Company. On a smaller but psychologically more detailed scale, the merchants of Amity will go to practically any lengths to keep the beaches open in order to profit from the tourist trade.

Self-Deception Versus Self-Knowledge

In the style of an action movie, *Aliens* wastes little time in getting to its frenetic battles and pyrotechnics. Ripley vainly tries to convince the managers of the Company that aliens really do exist. They take her warnings seriously only when communication from the colony mysteriously ceases and their economic investment appears to be in jeopardy. Because of its smaller scale and more homey locale, *Jaws* has the narrative room to explore the moral psychology of vice. The first half of the story remains ashore, where it patiently imbues its portrait of greed with subtle hues of self-deception. Unlike Ripley, Brody displays much of his virtue before his expedition is underway.

As *Jaws* doles out evidence and glimpses of the shark in bite-size portions, we see Brody wrestle with layers of the mayor's denial. After the first shark attack, Brody is readying signs announcing that the beaches are closed when the mayor tells him they can't be sure a shark is the cause of the mangled body. The medical examiner changes his previous tune and concurs with the mayor, who emphasizes that they "need summer dollars." The self-deception is soon punctured when, with a sea full of bathers, we get the signature underwater shot of people's legs and hear the shark theme on the soundtrack. A boy goes down and blood colors the waters. At the quickly convened town meeting, Brody asserts that the beaches will be closed, only to be undercut by the mayor adding "only twenty-four hours."

Although Brody protests that he "didn't agree to that," he accedes to the mayor's wishes. We can fault Brody for not having the backbone to stand up to the financially motivated merchants; however, the impression the film gives is that Brody is fairly new on the job. Not only is he unsure of the precise peril the shark poses, but he is uncertain of his authority. For example, Hooper upbraids Brody for failing to notify the Coast Guard after the first shark attack and for not phoning to check out the local waters. Brody realizes that he has not discharged his duties as police chief and is abashed. When a large shark is caught by a local fisherman, Hooper is skeptical this is the rogue shark, and he urges that they cut the shark open to see if the missing boy is inside.

The mayor's reaction to Hooper's request for confirmation accentuates Brody's commitment to the truth and his self-awareness. We see the logic of Hooper's argument leech away the relief Brody had just recently enjoyed. Brody admits that an autopsy is the "only way to be sure," but the mayor tells him that he doesn't want everyone gathered to see the little boy spill out of the shark's belly all over the dock. We know that the mayor wishes to maintain the belief that supports his interest in keeping the beaches open because he orders the disposal of the shark's unexamined carcass. That night, of course, Brody accompanies Hooper to dissect the shark, and the informal autopsy verifies Hooper's disappointing hunch.

Later, in a desperate stratagem of self-deception, the mayor points out that Hooper cannot produce the shark tooth he claims to have extracted from the hull of a ship adrift. The size of the tooth would allegedly confirm that the captured shark is not the killer they are after. The mayor harps on the technicality of the missing evidence in order to cling to his self-serving falsehood. The film thereby presents a dual mechanism by which people can suppress or ignore dealing with conflict between what they want and their moral convictions. First, the mayor tries to prevent action that could disconfirm the desirable belief; then, he insists on the production of disconfirming evidence he knows is unavailable. The mayor looks even more foolish in insisting that Brody catch the kids who have vandalized a town billboard by painting a shark fin into the picture of a bather. The film thematizes the mayor's attempt to eradicate this visual depiction of the truth by making it symbolic of his entire effort to whitewash the danger still besetting the town.

In contrast, Brody wants to know the truth about the identity of the killer shark and strives to do what is right by closing the beaches. True, he is the chief of police, but he is beholden to the town leaders for his job, and he could just as easily play along with the mayor instead of badgering him to examine the shark, listen to Hooper, and forfeit a portion of the summer tourist revenues. Brody not only looks squarely and clearly at the truth about the shark, but he has an uncompromised view of himself as well.

In addition to acknowledging his negligence in failing to call the Coast Guard, Brody takes responsibility for leaving the beaches open when the bereft mother of the boy who is killed by the shark slaps Brody. She correctly accuses him of knowing about the girl killed earlier, yet letting people swim, and thereby jeopardizing her son's life. Weeping, she simply states, "My boy is dead." The irony, of course, is that Brody wanted to close the beach immediately but bowed to business pressure. The mayor assures Brody that the woman is wrong to blame him, but Brody replies, "No, she's not." Although he would be justified in defending himself,

Brody takes responsibility for not protecting the citizens. His independent sense of right and wrong keeps him from ducking responsibility, just as it impelled him to try to close the beaches and to discover whether the captured shark was indeed the one they were looking for.

Cautious Heroics

The heroism of the central characters is given depth by their concern, wariness, and qualms at tackling the formidable beasts. The caution of Brody and Ripley is informed throughout the stories by their student virtues and phronesis. The moral irony fortifying both narratives is that the very individuals whose caution would have saved innocent lives are willing to risk their own necks to prevent greater destruction. After the first fatal attack, Brody sets out to learn about sharks. He reads, asks Hooper questions, and figures out that splashing shoreline bathers are the ideal magnet for attracting the rogue shark and that it will linger so long as this food supply lasts. Brody quickly grasps that it is just the wishful thinking of the self-deceived mayor and his cronies to believe the shark will attack and then leave. The problem of the shark attacks is a chronic one.

On board the boat, Brody continues to learn and draw prudent inferences. He learns the tying and untying of knots—this last the hard way, by letting two canisters of compressed air get loose. But in the process, Brody also learns that the canisters are explosive, and he will use this information to defeat the shark. The film foreshadows this finale with a visual-verbal coupling. Mocking the fancy equipment of the college-educated Hooper, Quint, whose education has come from the rough and tumble of a seagoing life, wonders what the compressed air is good for. He laughingly answers himself, saying that maybe the shark will eat it! The image of the tank of compressed air is paired with Quint's talk of the shark swallowing it, pointing toward the moment when Brody will thrust the tank into the shark's mouth. Once Brody gets a close look at the shark, he worries aloud that Quint's "gonna need a bigger boat." Ever the wary pursuer, Brody correctly gauges the shark's superiority—something the two experts fail to grasp or acknowledge.

Brody's initial talk of radioing shore for a bigger boat is heard in the background of the more knowledgeable dialogue between Quint and Hooper. But after the shark attacks the boat and water pours in below decks, Brody's concern for safety moves, with urgency, to the fore. He picks up the radio to get some help but is interrupted by Quint's order to put out a small fire. This scene is soon repeated with dire variation, when Quint smashes the radio with which Brody is about to call the shore. When the shark goes underwater with two barrels attached to his thick hide by harpooned rope, Quint says that "it's incredible." Brody appreciates the shark's power and speed and asks Hooper, "Why don't we start leading the shark in to shore, instead of him leading us out to sea?"

To the prudent ideas of radioing to shore for help and bringing out a bigger boat, Brody adds a wise strategy he can only have arrived at using what he has recently learned about the nature of sharks, his experience of this particular shark and their boat, and his good sense. Being a confirmed landlubber has stood Brody in good stead. Thoughts of shore are never far from his mind, whether it be to radio for help or to lead the shark back to land.

Brody had been cautious on shore, pleading for the closing of the beaches. Whereas the mayor and the merchants took foolish risks with people's lives from greed, Quint and Hooper now underestimate the shark from their respective positions of expertise. Quint is the salty dog whose knowledge rests on experience. Through much firsthand dealings with sharks, he knows their ways and believes his talents are more than a match for this great white shark. Hooper has had some small experience with sharks, but his primary expertise comes from study. He is the academic technocrat, replete with underwater shark cages, poison darts, and shark-tracking devices.

The film illustrates how Brody's student virtues enable him to learn from both Quint and Hooper and to learn in the manner distinctive of the expertise of each. Like Quint, Brody learns from his own direct experience of the dismembered victims ashore and in the nautical pursuit of the shark. Like Hooper, Brody learns by reading up on sharks and asking questions of those who know more than he does. But what he learns is filtered through his phronesis and humility. He is ever vigilant and always aware of his own limitations, both moral and technical.

Although Ripley has had direct experience of the aliens, she has been in hypersleep for over fifty years and has to catch up with new technologies. Ripley speedily assimilates technical information about spacecraft and weaponry and, on the foreign planet, thinks to ask for computer blueprints of the compound so that she can devise a barricade plan to protect the party from attack. When the landing shuttle (the "dropship") crashes and several Marines emotionally disintegrate, Ripley keeps a cool head and hits on the idea of bringing the other shuttle down by remote control. She not only intelligently processes what she is told but also asks precise and clear questions whose answers enable her to think up practically expedient solutions to their problems.

With regard to enemies, human and alien, Ripley is adept at drawing the right inferences. From what she knows of Burke, she divines his scheme to impregnate Newt and herself with gestating aliens in order to smuggle them back to earth undetected. Ripley infers that Burke would have to dispose of the surviving Marines to make his plan work and perceptively outlines what his explanation would have been. Having figured out the reproductive pattern of the aliens, Ripley wonders aloud, "So, who's laying the eggs?" She realizes that there must be a queen for the alien colony, and her question hints that she anticipates a still more potent adversary in the queen. The film certainly sets us up for this eventuality.

Ripley is cautious not only with her own skin but she invariably thinks of the safety of others. During several skirmishes between the Marines and aliens, Ripley adamantly implores withdrawal or retreat. And her definitive solution to the existence of the alien colony is to "nuke the site" from orbit. Indeed, when she originally agrees to accompany the Marines as an advisor, she asks for Burke's assurance that the mission is to destroy the aliens, "not to bring back, not to study." With treacly sincerity, Burke avers, "You have my word on that." Along with Ripley, we will realize that Burke is honest only when talking about money, such as the millions of dollars to be lost if they destroy the installation as Ripley recommends.

Ripley's motivation for joining the party of Marines seems less noble than Brody's motivation for joining the shark hunt. Brody feels compelled to go out of a sense of his responsibility to the community. Brody declares, "It's my party. It's my charter," when Quint expresses the desire to go it alone. We discover how much Brody's decision costs him when, out of his earshot, his wife tells Hooper how much Brody hates the water and boats. Brody was motivated to leave New York City out of a sense of civic responsibility. He has come to Amity, after all, because in a small town one cop can make a difference and not be overwhelmed by the tide of crime encountered in a large city.

Ripley decides to confront the aliens to overcome her demonic dreams and "to heal herself, to redefine herself, to reintroduce herself to society."[19] Burke has also promised her reinstatement as a flight officer if she takes the assignment. However, we see that she is also concerned for the safety of the vulnerable colonists. Ripley is visibly upset when a Company executive tells her that families have accompanied the engineers to the planet, and she is later pained by the Marines joking about the "dumb-ass colonists." We should conclude that although probably a subordinate consideration, Ripley hopes that she might be of value to the Marines in protecting innocent civilians from the aliens. Civic concerns do seem to move Ripley toward the danger.

Ripley is reluctant to go on the mission, telling Burke that she wouldn't be any good to him and that she's "not a soldier." In fact, the professional soldiers, the Marines, clearly hold her in low regard, smirking at her warnings of what they are up against in the aliens. Ripley earns their grudging respect with action. First, by demonstrating her facility with a mechanical loader, and later, with a rapid-fire rescue of the Marines surprised and besieged by aliens. The Marines are cut from the same cloth as Quint, all swagger and tough talk. Like the Marines, Quint enjoys flaunting his ruggedness and shows a disdain for Brody that echoes the Marines' contempt for Ripley. Ripley also must endure a less prepossessing version of Hooper, and his more formal education, in the person of Lieutenant Gorman (William Hope).

In the shuttle craft, or "dropship," taking them from the spaceship to planet LV426, Ripley asks the lieutenant how many drops he's made. Gorman's answer of forty is less than comforting when he clarifies that this is only his second combat drop, the others being simulated. Once they've landed and are approaching the complex, the lieutenant's formal training is evident in his commands to deploy the Marines, always in textbook formation. Ripley's caution is in early evidence when she wisely corrects the lieutenant's assertion that the "area is secured" simply because no evidence of danger has been unearthed. We may be reminded here of Brody's skepticism that the beaches are safe (secure from sharks) merely because no shark has been spotted.

The lieutenant alternately freezes and panics when confronted by novel circumstances, the exact contexts in which Ripley shines. Time and again Ripley demonstrates the invaluable and unteachable virtue of practical wisdom, or phronesis—the ability to bend one's judgment and decision-making to fit the particular concrete situation.[20] The lieutenant's ineptitude highlights the quick-wittedness, decisiveness, and flexibility of Ripley's phronesis.

Courage

In the areas of leadership and courage Ripley truly outstrips Brody. Once on the planet, Ripley quickly assumes practical command of the expedition. She remains with the lieutenant and Burke in the armored ground car monitoring the Marine patrol, which has entered the Company compound. Within the compound, dripping resin deposited by the aliens mimics the outdoor drizzle. Just as the boat in *Jaws* will take on seawater, the interior precipitation of *Aliens* signals the infiltration of an alien ecology into fabricated human habitation. Looking at the monitor screen, Ripley asks the lieutenant what the Marines' rifles fire. She infers that if they shoot, they will destroy the (nuclear-powered) cooling system, since the Marines are "right under the primary heat exchangers." Not only does the lieutenant miss the connection and attendant risk, but he proceeds to bemoan his resulting loss of options.

When aliens attack the reconnoitering Marines, Ripley immediately assesses the increase in danger to them along with the plummeting odds of their attaining safety. She tells the lieutenant to pull the patrol out of the area. He becomes discombobulated, first complaining that he ordered the Marines to hold fire (because of the threat to the cooling system), and then woodenly quoting deployment protocol, ordering the Marines to "lay down a suppressing fire." As the lieutenant whines on the intercom for his sergeant to talk to him, Ripley barks, "He's gone," and repeats, "Get them out of there." The lieutenant swings from paralysis to panic, yelling at Ripley to shut up and tearing the intercom out of her hand. Lieutenant Gorman thereby mirrors Quint's more absolute interruption of communication—his smashing of the ship-to-shore radio on which Brody presumes to speak. Like Quint, the lieutenant isn't willing to consider the wise words of other people and becomes angry when his authority is challenged.

As the command post receives images of shooting, shouting, flailing Marines, the enervated lieutenant catatonically recites their names: "Hudson, Vasquez, Hicks." Ripley realizes that even if he has at last understood the precariousness of the Marines' position, the lieutenant is incapable of the necessary action. He mumbles, "I told them to fall back." Ripley springs into action, seizes control of the ground vehicle, and fashions an impromptu, dashing rescue. The soundtrack swells with mobilizing martial music, as Ripley goes to get the Marines instead of sitting and talking.

In this crescendoing sequence, we see Ripley's prevalent wariness supplemented by her practical wisdom in discerning the danger of rifle fire to the nuclear cooling generators. Her analysis of the threat posed to the Marines leads her first to urge retreat and then to take the action crucial to saving their lives. Ripley's caution and prudence combine with her virtue of decisiveness to afford the mission a temporary reprieve. But from this point on, the reconnaissance squad will be on the run, led by Ripley as they scramble for their lives.

Brody's more mundane leadership provides an instructive alternative to Ripley's dazzling mastery over a barrage of dangers. For example, Brody is responsible for bringing Hooper to Amity from the Oceanographic Institute and for giving him the opportunity to autopsy the captured shark. He also instigates the shark hunt by browbeating the mayor into signing a voucher to hire Quint and his boat. And although Brody is clearly a third wheel onboard the ship, he asserts himself as best he can by trying to radio for help and by suggesting that they draw the shark toward shore. Brody demonstrates his leadership most forcefully while on land, before directly confronting the shark, where he has more authority and better understands what he must do. On the other hand, Ripley comes into her own away from the safety of earth, after the landing party is attacked by the aliens.

Brody exhibits his courage, first, in going out on the boat, and later, by remaining calm in the face of a bloody attack. It is striking that when he rhetorically asks, "We're gonna sink, aren't we?" we hear no fear in his voice. The ship has begun to founder, and the shark is clearly winning the day. Brody also stays steady in taking aim at the shark as it comes for him in the film's finale. Not given to joking, Brody's humor keeps him on an even keel. Having lodged a canister of compressed air in the shark's mouth during their previous tête-à-tête, Brody tells the oncoming shark to "smile, you son of a bitch," so he can hit the canister and blow the sea demon to kingdom come. The Brody we see at the end of the voyage is no longer the scurrying, scared rookie seaman who first left shore.

Quint is the leathery, weathered seafarer, exemplifying Aristotle's conception of professional soldiers, whose "experience enables them to be efficient in attack and in defense."[21] Just as the mercenary is confident because of his superior skill and experience, Quint's confidence also comes from previous success in hunting sharks, evidenced by all the relics of shark jaws with which his home is adorned. Quint additionally resembles a mercenary in demanding ten thousand dollars from the town to rid it of the shark. He has no commitment to the town or its safety. But Quint behaves rashly in destroying the ship's radio when Brody tries to call for help, matching Brody's humility and common sense with his hubris and foolishness. Even as Brody carries civic life with him, represented by his mindfulness of land and what it represents, so Quint is the mariner, contemptuous of the town and the boat's communion with it.

When Quint belatedly announces that they will draw the shark into shallows to drown it, he heedlessly races the engine. He ignores Hooper's warning of damage to the engine, becoming irate and obstinate. It is not clear whether Quint is stubbornly asserting his captain's authority or if he is panicking, now that he realizes they are overmatched by the shark. As Aristotle notes, individuals who act recklessly in the face of danger are prone to flight once they realize their presumed superiority was mistaken. In particular, Quint may bear out this unflattering description of professional soldiers offered by Aristotle: "When the strain of danger becomes too great, however, and when they are inferior in men and equipment, professional soldiers turn cowards."[22] The two extreme vices of recklessness and cowardice collapse into one another. In the event, Quint's behavior in pushing the boat's engine to its limits is either simple recklessness or recklessness spurred by cowardice. Either Quint is unnecessarily rushing to lead the shark into shallow water, or the threat to his own safety has distorted his judgment and overshadowed the value and probability of defeating the shark.

Ripley's courage comports seamlessly with her vigorous, flawless command of each new situation with which she and the crew are bombarded. Indeed, she is so smart, decisive, quick-witted, strong-minded, and physically adept as to be barely identifiable as a common person of uncommon moral virtue. What keeps Ripley from being overidealized is the fact that she is clearly afraid, does make mistakes, and she would fail without the help of the nonhuman android whom she has peremptorily misjudged. Brody's courage is brought out through his sense of civic responsibility. Ripley's courage is finally animated by her compassion and care.

Once in the Company compound, Ripley discovers a traumatized, orphaned girl. Newt (née Rebecca) is the sole survivor of the human colony. After calming Newt, Ripley tells the lieutenant to quit his fruitless interrogation of her. Excusing his failure to learn anything from Newt, he harrumphs that she has brain lock and that talking with her is a waste of time. We see that the lieutenant's lack of judgment is aggravated by his insensitivity to the girl's condition. Ripley wisely takes a more roundabout approach, sidling up to Newt, offering her hot chocolate, and gently kidding the child as she tends to her. She wins Newt over with generous helpings of succor and humor. Wiping Newt's filthy face, Ripley says, "Uh-oh, I made a clean spot here. Guess I'll have to do the whole thing." As Ripley cleans Newt, she asks her questions and tells the girl how brave she is.

Throughout the hectic action and its lulls, Ripley always has Newt's welfare in mind.[23] Ripley never talks down to the child but tells her the truth and asks for her help. When the two of them are sealed in the medical laboratory with immature alien specimens, Ripley is honest with Newt, acknowledging their predicament, and then tries Newt's idea of breaking the lab window. Following the land vehicle rescue of the Marine crew, and inside the compound, Ripley tucks Newt in for a nap. She has first had to settle down a more unruly child, the hysterical Marine, Hudson (Bill Paxton), and put him and the others to work barricading them in from further alien assault.

Ripley admits to Newt that monsters are real and gives her the locator band she had been given to wear herself. Ripley shows Newt the camera monitoring the child and tells her, "I'm not going to leave you, Newt. I mean that. I promise." Ripley's sincere promise contrasts subtly with Burke's promise not to bring alien specimens back to earth. Burke's plan to return with gestating aliens for profit requires using Ripley and Newt as human incubators, which would cost them their lives.

The film's closing sequences involve Ripley forgoing almost certain safety for a very risky search for the now missing Newt. Ripley is cutting her rendezvous with the android-manned shuttle craft very close in order to rescue the child from the aliens. The goal of Newt's life is so valuable to Ripley that it outweighs running the huge risk of mortal danger to herself, as well as the low probability of being successful in achieving the goal. Ripley will have to find Newt and get her to the shuttle ship before the planet explodes or the alien queen kills them. At one point in fending the queen off, Ripley's roles as warrior and mother are visually fused, as she fights the queen while cradling Newt. Ripley's compassion blossoms into full-blown nurturance in a way that Brody's cannot.[24]

Justice and Avarice

In contrast to Ripley, Brody's compassion is linked to his commitment to justice and civic responsibilities. Brody understands the despair of the mother who has lost her son to the shark and so thinks she is just in holding him culpable. Nothing interferes with Brody's perception of how refusing to close the beaches is to risk the lives of innocent people for the sake of money. Care about his own children and compassion for the families who could suffer loss make Brody vigilant and diligent. On the densely populated beach, the watchful Brody is clearly more caught up in the tension than his police duties alone would require. We identify with him; at the water's edge, we see the beach scene through his eyes. All the children and parents at play look especially vulnerable. When the shark finally attacks a young boy, our stomachs turn as we know Brody's does, yet we also feel a vindication of his judgment that Brody himself never expresses.

When we later see a brooding Brody at home, we know that he has been hard hit by the latest shark attack. Pictures of mutilated shark victims, at which Brody had looked with trepidation, have become part of his violent reality. Drinking and thinking, Brody notices his younger son mimicking his facial expressions. Brody mugs with the boy and asks for a kiss, "because I need it." It is as if this intimate moment with his child can somehow reassure Brody after another parent's comparable loss. Brody's older son is later taken to the hospital, in shock from his proximity to yet another fatal attack during the Fourth of July vacation crush. Brody asks his wife to take their younger boy home. In reply to her question, "To New York?" Brody gently affirms his civic commitment, answering her, "No, home here."

Brody's character illustrates how compassion mitigates against greed by placing the well-being of other people above one's own interests. Compassion augments Brody's unquestioned sense that protecting his fellow citizens is the just thing to do—whether by closing the beaches, ascertaining the true identity of the captured shark, or chartering a boat to stop the killer shark. Brody amply demonstrates concern for the safety of his own children as well as the townspeople, but once the shark pursuit gets under way, he no longer has a parental role to play beyond the indirect one of stopping the shark.

Ripley, however, plays the role of parent only after leaving earth. Ripley informally adopts Newt and must protect her from the monstrous Burke as much as from the alien monsters. The avarice of the merchants of Amity pales in comparison with the wickedness of Burke. His greed prompts an injustice of a vast magnitude and also provides the occasion for Ripley to display the justness of her character in a personal way.

Ripley figures out that Burke had previously ordered the colonists to the egg-infested ship and that he alone is responsible for their deaths. His protests that he wasn't sure that the ship was even there may actually be self-deception, telling himself that he was simply ordering an investigation, or it may be a bold-faced lie. Burke also may be trying to deceive himself by minimizing the deaths of the colonists in calling his decision a "bad call." The rationale he offers for his bad call is economic. After all, if he had not ordered the colonists to investigate the spaceship, there would be "no exclusive rights for anyone." Burke invites Ripley to share in the millions to be made by smuggling gestating aliens through customs, telling her that the two of them can be "set for life."

Ripley is appalled at the injustice of Burke sacrificing the colonists on the chance of making a bundle for himself and the Company. Burke's injustice springs from his greed, his desire for more at the expense of others. He wants more money at the expense of less safety for the colonists. Ripley tells Burke that she will make sure he is punished for this. Her disgust is channeled into the principled administration of retributive justice. Ripley sees her role as ensuring that Burke receives the punishment he deserves.

Ripley is also amazed at Burke's hubris in thinking that he can contain or control the aliens—a more extreme form of the pride that does in Quint in *Jaws*. Both films show an intimate connection between greed and pride. In *Jaws,* the danger of the shark is created by the merchants' greed but is compounded by the pride of Quint. In *Aliens,* the space beasts pose a threat because of the greed and pride blended together in the person of Burke. In both stories, the combination of these self-oriented vices obscures the judgment of the individuals, causing violent harm.

Realizing that Ripley won't play along with his scheme to deliver aliens to the Company's bio-weapons division, Burke plans to use her and Newt to incubate aliens. Burke locks Ripley and Newt in the medical lab with the immature alien specimens (crab-like and tentacled) and shuts off the camera that would alert the crew to their danger. It is one thing to cause the death of anonymous people physically distant from oneself, as Burke has done to the colonists. But he is so devoid of care that he can bring about the death of people he knows without batting an eye—to protect himself and turn a profit in the bargain.

Ripley's response to Burke's death trap is to attend efficiently to her two responsibilities. After telling Newt the truth, that they are in trouble and that, like Newt, she is scared, she sets off the emergency sprinkler system to bring help. Ripley is able to communicate candidly but calmly with Newt while almost simultaneously finding a way out of the calamity. None of our traditional virtues readily reflects this useful ability to deal effectively with very different problems at the same time. It would seem to be a kind of problem-solving dexterity, a plasticity of mind and temperament, that enables exceptional individuals to divide, or shift, their attention without sacrifice of effectiveness. We could think of it as an unusual manifestation of phronesis, since phronesis includes affective and practical facets of the individual, besides his or her intellectual ability. In which case, *Aliens* dramatically extends the classical conception of practical wisdom to include this problem-solving agility.

Burke's treachery is the occasion for Ripley to display a still deeper allegiance to justice. Once out of danger, Ripley explains Burke's plan to the crew: If she and Newt were "impregnated" with larvae by the immature aliens, Burke could have slipped the aliens undetected through quarantine back on earth. This would also have required killing the sleeping Marines, jettisoning their bodies, and manufacturing a believable story. Ripley then keeps the Marines from executing Burke on the spot, telling them, "He's gotta go back." We see no evidence that Ripley must struggle to overcome a desire for revenge. Ripley's dedication to the priority of justice not only extinguishes any promptings she might have for vengeance, but it motivates her to thwart the Marines' unreflective urge to take justice into their own hands.

Each film presents a small exchange involving its protagonist in so offhanded a manner as to risk slipping by us, unremarked. Justice shines so brightly in both Brody and Ripley that they naturally see what it requires and are drawn to do it, without giving unjust options a second thought. When amateur shark hunters descend willy-nilly on Amity, Brody scolds his deputy for not doing more to maintain order and protect "his people." The deputy scoffs that these are hardly his people, as they are out-of-towners and tourists. In a similar vein, after Ripley has pointed out to Burke that Corporal Hicks assumes command of the expedition, with Lieutenant Gorman out of commission, Burke exclaims that Hicks can't make decisions regarding a multimillion dollar installation because he's "just a grunt."

What these two subtle exchanges have in common is this. The deputy discounts the worth of the lives of people who are outside his personal or official sphere of care. He feels no responsibility for the welfare of strangers. Burke believes that people beneath him, the grunts who do his dirty work, don't have the right to make important decisions. Each view conflicts with the deeply held democratic values on which Brody's and Ripley's sense of justice rests. The equal worth of all people, those who may not strictly be fellow citizens as well as ordinary workers, underlies a broader humanitarian perspective on justice.

This wider perspective appropriately contrasts with the communitarian virtues of communication illustrated in *Rob Roy;* the social worlds in which Brody and Ripley fully realize their virtues have been stripped of communitarian values. It is as if Brody and Ripley are battling to maintain some remnant of civic justice in the face of social relations whittled down to the lowest economic denominators.

Ripley and Brody are unusually sensitive to matters of justice and respond to them emotionally and immediately. As with most people, the incidents that arouse the heroes' most intense passions are indicators of their deepest concerns. Recall from the previous chapter that moral character has a strong passional dimension and that passion influences what we discriminate in our surroundings; it shares responsibility for what becomes salient to and for the individual.[25] Aristotle observes that anger is sometimes required of virtuous individuals. Anger should be appropriate to circumstances, offender, and harm, and in particular, virtuous people should feel righteous indignation when they observe or learn about serious injustice.[26]

In both movies, the indignation, consternation, and anger of the reluctant heroes build as the stories progress. Early in *Jaws,* for example, a couple of amateur shark hunters are nearly killed when the shark pulls their dock apart as it swims away with the beef roast the men used for bait. When Brody's deputy fills him in on the episode, joking about his wife's missing supper, Brody snaps, "That's not funny. That's not funny at all." Shark attacks are nothing for the chief of police to laugh at, even when people endanger themselves by their own folly and no one is actually hurt. Brody's anguished exhorting of the mayor to examine the captured shark and then to close the beaches culminates in his indignant insistence that the mayor sign the voucher paying Quint to hunt for the shark.

Brody's final display of anger occurs when Quint destroys the radio Brody is trying to use to call for help. Here Brody is responding to Quint's hubris in putting him and Hooper at the mercy of the shark. It is a reaction to injustice in the derivative sense that Quint is unjust in putting his own vanity above the safety of others and, in doing so, jeopardizing the success of their mission. Since Quint's behavior immediately puts Brody himself at risk, it might seem that Brody's intense reaction is self-regarding. However, Quint's destruction of the radio is irrational and antagonistic to fair play. Quint is increasing the danger to the very individuals who have voluntarily put themselves in harm's way for the sake of protecting the citizens and fortunes of the town. It is like Burke facilitating Ripley's death after she agrees to join the expedition at his behest, partly for the sake of innocent colonists and other potential victims of the aliens.

But before we see Ripley rain her righteous indignation on Burke, *Aliens* portrays her in something less than full dudgeon. During her debriefing for the Company managers, for example, Ripley is miffed at them for slighting her report of alien devastation, at one point sniping, "Did I.Q.'s just drop sharply while I was away?" Ripley is dismayed at the thought of whole families being up on LV426.[27] Once on the planet, Ripley yells angrily at the lieutenant, again because her words are not being heeded. She wants him to pull the Marines out from the installation in which they are being slaughtered by the aliens.

As we saw, Ripley is livid with Burke for risking the lives of the entire colony to investigate the aliens for possible profit and then having the arrogance to assume he can safely get them back to earth. Her antipathy toward Burke peaks when, shortly after his failed attempt to implant her with alien larvae, he closes a bulkhead barricade to save himself from aliens, leaving everyone else at their mercy.[28]

Righteous indignation can easily balloon into self-righteousness. Neither Brody nor Ripley succumb to feeling morally superior to other people, even when they are. Their humility and sense of responsibility keep the pair from allowing themselves to gloat over the demonstrated correctness of their wariness of the horrific beasts and their cautious counsel. Where Brody could just as easily point an accusing finger at the mayor for causing a child's death by keeping the beaches open, Brody focuses instead on his own culpability and on his responsibility in preventing further havoc. And Ripley never lords it over the lieutenant when, first, she elicits a response from Newt after he has failed or, later, saves the Marines after he freezes up. Ripley even refuses the satisfaction of seeing the Marines tear Burke limb from limb, saving him instead for a civil system of justice.

Only the most serious matters evoke the ire of Brody and Ripley. They know what is important and respond appropriately, and their actions are as little governed by their anger at the injustice or obtuseness of other people as they are dictated by their fear at great danger. On the contrary, Brody and Ripley are able to harness their strong emotions to good effect. For instance, Brody uses his frustration with the mayor's refusal to close the beaches to read up on sharks and to surreptitiously assist Hooper autopsy the captured shark. Sublimating his anger over Quint's destruction of the ship-to-shore radio, Brody substitutes the movement of the ship for communication and asks about leading the shark to shore.

Ripley feeds off her strong emotions more dramatically. When the lieutenant responds to her demand to recall the Marines by snapping at her to shut up and then ripping the intercom out of her hands, Ripley's temper pushes her into determined, efficient action. At the movie's climax, Ripley's fury fuels her fighting spirit in the face of the alien mother's assault on Newt. We see, in Ripley especially, how the person complete in virtue enjoys a harmony between thought and passion, which results in crisp action.

Creatures from the Vasty Deep

The wisdom and caution of the protagonists is accentuated by the intelligence, as well as the sheer physical prowess, of the monsters. Their intelligence is also used both to ratchet tension up and to relieve it through humor. In *Jaws,* Quint pays grudging admiration to the shark, saying that he is a "smart, big fish," after the shark disappears under the boat. Bearing out Quint's estimation, the shark proceeds to smash and gobble the boat to smithereens. After Hooper descends inside a shark cage in an attempt to kill the shark with a poison dart, the shark passes in front of him and disappears from view. The shark then reappears behind Hooper, who is poised with the dart-loaded pole but facing in the wrong direction. Slamming into the rear of the cage, the shark knocks the pole from the surprised and stunned Hooper. Shortly thereafter, the great white shark comes looking for Brody in the boat's main cabin. He is indeed smart and not just a big, strong, and fast fish.

In midvoyage, the three men achieve a kind of esprit de corps in the course of drinking and showing shark scars and finally singing.[29] As the men lose themselves in the carefree merrymaking (and we in the audience relax with them), the shark thunderously rams into the boat—no more Mr. Nice Guy, he is going on the offensive. Punctuating periods of invisibility with unpredictable broadsides, the shark keeps the men, and the audience, off balance. Toward the story's end, Quint puts a third barrel on the shark, declaring that he can't go underwater now. We next see a surface shot of the sea, isolated on the three barrels heading away from the camera, toward the boat, and disappearing underneath it. It's funny but also frightening.

In *Aliens,* when the patrol is plunged into darkness inside the compound, Ripley infers that the creatures have cut the power. A befuddled and frightened Marine (the hysteria-prone Hudson) protests that this can't be right because "they're animals." In that moment of quiet tactical advantage, Cameron conveys the intelligence of the aliens and how easily underestimated they are. In pursuit of Ripley and Newt at the film's conclusion, the alien queen takes the elevator several stories up to reach them rather than exert herself. The image of the huge monster stepping out of the darkened elevator to confront the unsuspecting humans is at once comic and terrifying.[30] *Aliens* and *Jaws* cleverly use the very source of the horrific tension to provide momentary relief from it, as if the monsters had intentionally delivered a pun or put over a sight gag.

The intelligence and wiliness of the creatures also add weight to the sagacity and humility of the heroes. Brody and Ripley never underestimate the danger these beasts pose, partly because they have no illusions about their own capacity to deal with them. It is all the more ironic, therefore, that the individual who is not a Marine annihilates the alien queen and the person who is most afraid of water and the shark destroys him. Ripley and Brody succeed, moreover, using the most mundane of weapons. The high-tech firearms of the Marines behind her, Ripley uses the forklift loader to fight the enormous alien queen. After Quint's harpoonery and Hooper's poison dart fail to do the job, Brody finishes the shark off with an old-fashioned police rifle—albeit with the aid of a tank of compressed air.

The climactic face-offs between hero and beast capture the difference between the two films, while demonstrating the essential similarity between Brody and Ripley. As with everything leading up to it, *Aliens* stages the final battle in more spectacular style than *Jaws*. Having staved off the alien queen amidst the collapsing, conflagrating installation, Ripley and the android are talking onboard the main spaceship. Like them, our guard is down, and we receive the last jolt of terror when the queen reveals herself onboard by pole-axing the android and cutting him in two with a thrust of her steely tentacle. The queen stalks Newt, seeking to avenge Ripley's incineration of her eggs. Ripley distracts her, buying time for further maneuvering.

In the manner of a modern knight, Ripley dons the forklift loader like so much motorized armor. Ripley appears on the screen in valorous silhouette, backlit by moon-like beams of light, crowned with a flashing beacon so that she radiates rays of her own. As the queen attacks Newt, Ripley the warrior mother shouts, "Get away from her, you bitch." Reprising the earlier scene in which she demonstrated facility in working the loader, Ripley strikes the queen with a mechanical arm. Ripley raises her mechanized arms in pugilistic invitation, challenging her assailant to "come on!" Contrast this rousing scene with the bedraggled Brody, desperately perched on a spar of the battered, sinking ship, clutching his rifle.

The final showdown in *Jaws* has none of the glamour of Ripley's hand-to-hand grappling—just Brody hoping to get a last shot at his own implacable nemesis. With Hooper missing, Brody has just watched Quint slide down the ship's listing deck, swallowed by the shark—alive and screaming. Instead of becoming unnerved, Brody keeps cool, managing the wry request for the shark to "smile, you son of a bitch," so he can blow up the tank of compressed air nestled in its mouth.[31] Afraid of the shark, the water, and the boat, compelled by a sense of duty, Brody is calm and resourceful as he stares down the predator in what he knows is his last-ditch effort.

Ripley, moreover, has the noble task of protecting her informally adopted daughter, who will seal the relationship by calling her mommy. The movie narratively uses Newt as more than a prop toward which Ripley can display her virtues of compassion, care, and nurturance. We see in Newt a miniature Ripley. She is plucky, direct, resourceful, and never yields to the easy comfort of self-deception. For example, when Ripley tries to bolster her confidence with reference to the Marines, Newt matter-of-factly says that they won't make any difference, and when Ripley apologizes for the destruction of the first dropship, Newt points out that it wasn't Ripley's fault. Newt is the no-nonsense survivor of the aliens' attack, just as Ripley alone escaped from the alien clutches in the preceding movie story. As if recognizing herself in Newt, Ripley confides in her and asks her for directions when they must flee in the closing sequences.[32]

Brody and Ripley are not only technically resourceful, putting to use what they learn about combat and the creatures they battle, but they are socially resourceful as well. They solicit and receive help from the most tractable of their colleagues. Thus, Brody brings Hooper from the Oceanographic Institute, accepts his criticism and advice, and uses his expertise whenever he can. Ripley first elicits instruction in weaponry from Hicks (Michael Biehn) and then establishes his sympathetic authority through her knowledge of military protocol. Ever mindful of the "substantial dollar value" of the installation, Burke balks at Ripley's idea of "nuking" it to be sure they've finished off the aliens. When Burke protests that he can't authorize that extreme action, Ripley cites the chain of command, pointing out that Corporal Hicks is now in charge since this is a military operation. She not only foils Burke's wicked designs with her wits, setting off the alarm sprinkler in the medical lab, but she outfoxes him by employing her knowledge of social structure.[33]

In coping with killers and connivers, animal adversity and human duplicity, Ripley and Brody represent what morally well-rounded people can do. Each character combines virtues needed for success in such diverse domains of life that they are typically found in isolation from one another. Consider how Ripley and Brody exhibit the compassionate understanding of parents as well as the courage and mental toughness demanded in the military. Both also have the scholar's ability to assimilate new information and put it to good use.

Ripley and Brody are able to cooperate in the manner of people who participate effectively in sports or scientific research teams. When lacking control of a situation or frustrated by those in power, both heroes persevere, pitching in as required. The pair of heroic citizens manage to cooperate with individuals who are smarmy and self-serving, such as the mayor and Burke, or who are bellicose and demeaning, such as Quint and the Marines. They can cooperate with people who are themselves uncooperative and don't listen to the counsels of prudence. Thus does Brody work with Quint despite Quint's contemptuous treatment of him and his good ideas. In similar fashion, Ripley persists in being helpful, whether the Marines mock her or the lieutenant rejects her pleas to withdraw the Marines from the fight.

But Ripley and Brody are also able to assume command. Of course, Ripley's command is more dramatic and complete. She literally takes over the task force when the green lieutenant is unable to act. However, Brody also takes charge at the beginning and end of his story. He is responsible for getting the shark hunt off the ground and into the water, and in his final reckoning with the shark, he is at the sinking helm, albeit by default.

The one sphere of human activity for which neither Brody nor Ripley displays any aptitude is business. These model citizens express no interest in money, and they don't possess the businessman's talent for shrewdness, competition, or one-upmanship. By casting the heroics of Brody and Ripley against the backdrop of unprincipled business interests, *Jaws* and *Aliens* intimate that the so-called virtues of business are not virtues at all. Virtues needed to do well in the varied institutions of education, athletics, family, and the military—all but economic entrepreneurship—are embodied in Ripley and Brody.[34]

What enables Brody and Ripley to triumph over such a thicket of obstacles, in a range of situations, are their virtues that promote adaptability: resourcefulness and ingenuity, caution and common sense, humility and courage. What seems most striking, however, is the higher-order virtue they possess. Ripley and Brody share the virtue of being morally independent. They monitor themselves according to their own moral understanding, without external distraction. Both possess a sense of self and self-worth by which they are able to judge their responsibility autonomously.

The films depict the autonomous, moral self-evaluation of Ripley and Brody as forming the core of their integrity. It is woven through their modest self-estimations and their realistic courage, virtues that complement one another. Neither Brody nor Ripley entertain illusions about themselves. Illusions about themselves buttress the bravado of Quint and the Marines, and these illusions obscure their perception and limit their effectiveness when faced with mortal danger. The autonomous moral self-evaluations of Brody and Ripley seem to provide the bedrock for their calm in the face of peril.

Jaws and *Aliens* make thoughtful, parallel connections between the annihilation of the natural predators and the destruction of the man-made environments. Because of the havoc the beasts have wrought, the heroes are simultaneously endangered by the imminent collapse of their human habitats and by the relentless monsters. Although Brody's chances at sea are better than Ripley's during a nuclear explosion, Brody's loss of man-made habitation is directly tied to his threat from the shark. Brody must contend with the voracious shark because the ship it has crippled is itself being swallowed by the sea. Ripley must fend off the alien queen before the meltdown of the nuclear plant, which has been decimated by the aliens. The impending thermonuclear holocaust is added to the threat of the alien queen but does not increase the danger she poses. In truth, the nuclear countdown, with all its sparking, flaming, and hurtling debris, is a bit florid compared to the spare line of the shark's beeline for Brody on the scuttled boat.

Each film further symbolizes the pairing of bestial and artificial destruction in a compelling image. In *Jaws*, the ship is engulfed by the oceanic netherworld as the shark is blown up. *Aliens* portrays the installation on LV426 exploding just before the alien queen is sucked out of the spaceship, into lifeless space. Neither sea nor space, the films suggest, are the proper homes for human beings. Is it a coincidence that the heroes are such down-to-earth people? They are figuratively down-to-earth in their common sense, honesty, and direct approach to everyone with whom they interact. They are literally down-to-earth in their reluctance to quit the sure footing of shore or planet in pursuit of sea demon or space dragon. In the end, Ripley and Brody do combat with a motorized freight loader and a simple rifle, weapons as sturdy and serviceable as the characters who wield them.

Notes

1. Aristotle, *Nicomachean Ethics,* trans. Martin Ostwald (Indianapolis, Ind.: Bobbs-Merrill, 1962), 1123b.

2. Ibid., 1125a. Aristotle notes that these external goods are not the basis of the individuals' greatness but are needed for its full flowering. Following Plato's *Republic* (486), Aristotle appears to include a strictly philosophical species of magnificence, distinct from the more prominent political-militaristic one (*Politics*, 1324). For a good discussion of the two types of magnificence in Aristotle, see Aristide Tessitore, *Reading Aristotle's Ethics* (Albany, N.Y.: SUNY Press, 1996), especially pp.28–35, 110–113.

3. Ron Milo, *Immorality* (Princeton: Princeton University Press, 1984), p.108.

4. Herbert Fingarette, *Self-Deception* (London: Routledge and Kegan Paul, 1969), pp.48–49.

5. Milo, *Immorality,* p.174.

6. Aristotle, *Nicomachean Ethics,* 1152a.

7. Sentimentality fosters a more pervasive, diffuse climate of self-deception. Instead of permitting individuals to do something contrary to their moral convictions, sentimentality creates an unjustified sense of self as noble and sensitive. Sentimentality blocks action, as the self-affirming emotions it cultivates function as a passive substitute for morally beneficial action. See my "The Sentimental Self," *Canadian Journal of Philosophy* 26 (December 1996): 543–560.

8. Richard Sorabji, "Aristotle on the Role of Intellect in Virtue," *Proceedings of the Aristotelian Society* (n.s.) 74 (1973–1974): 107–129, 113.

9. Aristotle, *Nicomachean Ethics,* 1106b. I follow David Pears in his "behavioral" interpretation of Aristotle's ascription of fearlessness to the courageous individual. Such a man has the appropriate amount of fear but behaves like a man who is without fear; see David Pears, "Courage in Aristotle," in *Essays on Aristotle's Ethics,* ed. Amelie Okensberg Rorty (Berkeley: University of California Press, 1980), pp.171–187, pp.178–179.

10. Aristotle, *On Rhetoric,* trans. and ed. George Kennedy (Oxford: Oxford University Press, 1991), 1383a.

11. Pears, "Courage in Aristotle," considers this goal "external" to the act since the internal goal is always the very nobility of the act itself.

12. Ibid., p.181.

13. To see that confidence and fear are not necessarily inversely proportional, or that excessive confidence is not reducible to lack of fear, we need only note that a person who has little confidence in attaining safety might nonetheless feel little fear because he has emotionally assimilated the reasoned understanding that his life is worth sacrificing for the highly probable goal of great value. Conversely, even a person with high expectation of avoiding harm could be deeply frightened because of a disproportionate weight attached to his own well-being.

14. Pears, "Courage in Aristotle," p.181.

15. Aristotle, *Nicomachean Ethics,* 1116b.

16. Ibid., 1130.

17. Bernard Williams writes, "Unjust acts that are not expressions of the vice of injustice can thus stem from other vices." Bernard Williams, "Justice as a Virtue," in *Essays on Aristotle's Ethics,* ed. Amelie Okensberg Rorty (Berkeley: University of California Press, 1980), pp.189–199, p.192. This still leaves open the possibility that to be an unjust person, to actually have the vice of injustice, one must be greedy as well.

18. I prefer discussing *Aliens* over its predecessor, *Alien,* because the sequel gives Ripley a much greater range of obstacles to overcome and things to do, including the nurture of the orphaned girl, Newt.

19. Valerie Gray Hardcastle, "Changing Perspectives of Motherhood: Images from the *Aliens* Trilogy," *Film and Philosophy* 3 (1996): 167–175, 171.

20. For a theoretical discussion of the flexibility essential to phronesis, see the first section of Chapter 6. Later examination of Michael's character and judgment provide another illustration of this aspect of practical wisdom.

21. Aristotle, *Nicomachean Ethics,* p.73, 1143b.

22. Ibid.

23. Among other considerations, Ripley tells Newt to look away from the torch being used to weld doors shut, a small detail that reveals the greatness of Ripley's concern for the child. When images of the aliens attacking the Marines appear on the monitor screen of the land vehicle, Ripley's sensitivity to Newt's feelings flows like an undercurrent in her worry over the plight of the Marines. Ripley asks Newt to leave the room to spare the child a sight that is bound to stir up memories of the massacre of her family and friends.

24. On a feminist interpretation of *Aliens,* Ripley's succor of Newt may not eradicate an equivocal stance on motherhood or reproduction. For example, Valerie Hardcastle points out that the "fear of and alienation from (uncontrolled?) reproduction remains [from the first film]. Ripley has recurring and disturbing nightmares about birthing an alien." Hardcastle, "Perspectives of Motherhood," p.171. Hardcastle notes that the only birth we see in the film is an alien's and that Ripley's destruction of the alien mother's eggs is irrational. For other feminist interpretations of *Aliens* and the *Alien* trilogy, see H. R. Greenberg, "Fembo: Aliens' Intensions," *Journal of Popular Film and Television* 15 (1988): 165–171; and S. Jeffords, "'The Battle of the Big Mammas': Feminism and the Alienation of Women," *Journal of American Culture* 10 (1987): 73–84.

25. See the first section of Chapter 6, as well as Notes 20 and 21 in that chapter.

26. Aristotle, *Nicomachean Ethics,* 1108b.

27. Ripley is also annoyed with Burke for not informing her that an android (Lance Henriksen) is aboard. She had a bad experience with one such synthetic

human in *Alien* and is distrustful. But this scene is more important for hinting at Burke's deceitfulness, as he feigns innocent forgetfulness in failing to tell Ripley that the android, Bishop, was in the crew.

28. The example of Burke fleeing to apparent safety at the expense of the safety of others seems to bear out Bernard Williams's claim that particular cases of injustice need not be the result of economic greed. Here Burke's cowardice leads him to throw other people to the predators while saving himself.

29. The film eases the tension with a bit of light-hearted business. As Quint and Hooper compare war wounds, Brody sheepishly checks his only scar, from his appendectomy. Yet even in this casually comic moment, we are reminded of how much Brody is like us, leading our uneventful, daily lives of upset stomachs, childhood diseases, and appendicitis.

30. As has become her custom, Ripley thinks first of Newt, telling her to close her eyes so as not to look their apparent doom in the face.

31. The shark is thereby affiliated with the alien queen, whom Ripley calls "bitch."

32. The girl's nickname, Newt, might be a metaphor for her survival skills. Like the amphibious lizard, the child can adapt to a variety of circumstances, and we see Newt literally survive in water and on land.

33. In contrast, when Brody early on points out to the mayor that he needs no authority besides his own (as chief of police) to close the beaches, he backs down from his correct political military analysis.

34. In *The Republic of Plato* (346a, 346b), Socrates obliquely raises the question whether moneymaking is an art (techne) like medicine or architecture. If an art, moneymaking is certainly different from other arts, since people can be good at medicine and other arts without making much money. In addition, moneymaking is unique in that it accompanies them all and seems to depend on other arts for its success, whereas no other single art accompanies all the others. Allan Bloom creatively suggests that moneymaking is an ironic trope for philosophy as the "architectonic" art. For Socrates, philosophy is the art that is suited to ordering all the other arts in the state so as to produce justice and happiness. See Allan Bloom's "Interpretive Essay," in his translated and edited text of *The Republic of Plato* (New York: Basic Books, 1968), pp.332–334.

Concluding Angles

We have come to the end of our visions of virtue, having examined seven popular films, most of which are Hollywood productions and were made during the last twenty-five years. Opening with Phil Connors and ending with Brody and Ripley, our films progressively situate their protagonists within an ever-widening web of social relationships until, finally, those relationships break apart. In this body of films so arranged, the central characters are of two distinct types. Characters in the first three movie chapters become virtuous, or embark on their moral improvement, as moral traits supplant their vices or flaws. In the second triad of film studies, the virtues of the protagonists are already in place but are brought to full flowering in the crush of do-or-die crises. This basic division among the films, between virtue acquisition and virtue exhibition, is accompanied by correlative differences in context, content, and tone. Consequently, it seems helpful to examine the films as falling into these two halves of three chapters each.

Consider the three films with which the book begins. *Groundhog Day, The African Queen,* and *Parenthood* are filled with humor, contain almost no violence or death, and have happy endings that perhaps strain our credulity just a bit. In fact, the only film in this set containing overt violence, *The African Queen,* is also the least comedic of the three. Rose's brother, Samuel, dies as a result of being roughly treated by German soldiers; however, the adversary is a nameless, impersonal force, not a character whom the movie invests with a developed personality. Protagonists in these films themselves have a good sense of humor: Phil Connors, Charlie Allnut, and (in *Parenthood*) Gil, Helen, Frank, and Grandma. The movies in the first group all end joyfully. The couples go off to live happily ever after in *Groundhog Day* and *The African Queen,* and *Parenthood* is almost cloyingly reproductive, concluding as it does with a bevy of babies, as the Buchman family sprawls into its fifth generation.

In this set of movies, protagonists undergo radical change. They learn moral lessons and become more virtuous. True, most of the main characters of *Parenthood* have just begun their transformation, with the exception of Helen. In matter of degree of moral melioration, they are not on a par with Charlie, Rose, and Phil Connors. But the focus of the three films is the same—to portray individuals who grow in virtue by recognizing and remedying their moral defects, failings, weaknesses, or vices. None of the characters are confronted by vicious individuals against whom they must struggle or whose wicked machinations they must unravel. Rather, they change because of an inward turn, into themselves and within close relationships. The mood of the films fits the upbeat reformation of the characters. The characters in this first group of films don't possess an exceptional degree of practical wisdom, but they don't have to since they are not faced with complex situations or devious antagonists. Even Helen's astute practical judgment is confined to the small circumference of her children's lives and her relationships with them.

With the second group of films, however, we find central characters who must act within and respond to a virulent, expanded social context. The problems of the protagonists lie outside themselves—in the political economies of city or state, chamber of commerce or megacorporation, gang or gentry. The heroes are not transformed so much as their virtues flourish under the press of these external exigencies. Instead of developing new virtues, they put the virtues they possess into action in the teeth of adversity. These movies are filled with violence and death, requiring a courage and fortitude not found in the films of the first group. Michael, Ripley, and Brody (more or less in descending order) must use their practical wisdom to prevail over the forces arrayed against them. Rob Roy is compensated for his lack of phronesis by his dominating moral and physical strength and by his wife's prudence.

As appropriate to films that conclude with a fight to the death, there isn't much to laugh at. The smattering of humor we find in this set of stories is usually provided by the cinematic telling of the tale, not by the characters themselves. And the scenes or complications we do laugh at tend to the ironic end of the comic spectrum. They are grim (such as Rob and Archie tethered together on the bridge) or self-indicting (Corky telling Michael that he is in over his head), or they afford relief from horror (Brody urging the shark to smile). In these stories, the virtues of the protagonists are fully expressed in their confrontations with human vice and natural danger. Consequently, the humor stems from wrestling with evil and averting disaster and so naturally leans more to severity than levity. Since the tensions are resolved in favor of virtue, however, the films are sanguine. We in the audience feel as though we've triumphed through the bloody battles with the champions of the stories.

Although the films can be divided into the humorous films of virtue acquisition and the violent films of virtue expression, the films are unified as an entire corpus. Common themes and motifs pervade all or most of the movies. In what follows, I discuss a few of the themes I find most interesting or important and conclude with one prominent motif.

Practical wisdom is Michael's defining virtue in *Fresh,* and it is a thick strand in the fabric of the moral personalities of Brody and Ripley as well. A subordinate theme that animates these (and other) films involves the failure of individuals who lack phronesis to heed wise counsel. The foolish person is defined by one of two responses to words of wisdom—ignoring the fine words or disobeying them. Briefly canvasing our films for these responses, then, supplements what we have gleaned about phronesis by illustrating its antithesis. The most blatant responses are, pointedly, those made to the characters most graced with practical wisdom. Thus we have Chuckie disobeying Michael, whether he tells Chuckie to drop the knapsack with drugs or to abort Roscoe's career in dogfighting. Chuckie's inability to hear the wisdom in Michael's directions is of a piece with his machismo aspirations and attraction to superficial finery. *Fresh* proceeds to show that Chuckie's foolishness dooms him to a life that is short, brutish, and nasty.

Driven by his caution, Brody wisely argues, first, for closing the beaches and, later, for seeking help in the pursuit of the shark. The mayor and town merchants disregard Brody's admonitions, and Quint steers angrily away from the prudent course Brody tries to chart for the shark hunt. The business people ashore are foolish in letting financial considerations outweigh concern for human welfare and life. This is a matter of improperly assessing what is worthwhile, as well as putting one's own interests before the needs of other people. Quint's foolishness grows directly from his pride, or hubris. He esteems his own prowess too much and feels himself above listening to the opinions of one so green as Brody.

Less obvious cases of flouting or ignoring practical wisdom occur in *Rob Roy* and *Parenthood.* Although not an especially wise individual, Rob Roy does understand battle, and he orders his brother, Alasdair, not to shoot at Montrose's soldiers. Alasdair's spirited nature prompts him to disobey—spoiling for a fight, Alasdair is filled with animosity toward Montrose and his army. Excessive passion, or the inability to control one's passion, is a different cause of foolishness than either pride or selfishness.

If Alasdair sees the great danger to which firing on the soldiers would expose the MacGregor party, the chance to draw first blood blinds him to it.

Larry's response to his father's thoughtful offer, in *Parenthood*, betrays yet another source of imperviousness to practical wisdom. Whether from self-deception or shortsightedness, Larry turns down Frank's offer to come work with him. Larry thereby refuses a feasible opportunity to pay off his gambling debt and provide a stable life for himself and his son. Larry is self-deceived if he thinks he really will strike it rich in South America or if he thinks he is too good for such mundane work—a possibility suggested by his earlier outburst. However, Larry may simply be incapable of taking a long-range view of his future and so fails to grasp that his best chance at leading a more fulfilling life lies in the prospect his father holds out to him. Larry most resembles Chuckie, afflicted with an obtuseness that perfectly inverts the perspicacity so characteristic of the person with phronesis.

Unlike Chuckie and Larry, virtuous people see the world from a realistic perspective, free from illusion and self-deception. The films portray individuals who are clearheaded about themselves, other people, and about their relationships with these people. For instance, Frank finally sees the truth about his wayward son, Larry, and his role in fostering Larry's irresponsibility. With the help of his wife, Gil realizes that coaching Kevin in baseball and entertaining Kevin's friends at the birthday party won't make his son's anxieties go away. Rob Roy must face how much his honor has cost his family and the clan. And Michael comes to understand that he is the only person capable of saving his sister—not even Aunt Francis's tireless love can keep Nicki from self-destruction.

Another facet of the realism so integral to the virtues is appreciation of the objectivity of values, that they exist independent of ourselves and our particular interests. The films present characters for whom this is an illuminating discovery, as well as individuals whose abiding recognition of objective worth is what elevates them above their peers. The moral transformation of Phil Connors, for example, is accompanied by his sensitivity to the beauty of music and his apprenticeship to its discipline. Charlie Allnut discovers the value of committing himself to a cause that is greater than his own mean little appetites, whereas Rob Roy has long understood that it is this very commitment—to honor, family, clan—that serves our interests best by keeping us whole.

Jaws and *Aliens* concentrate on characters for whom justice, even for strangers and enemies, is the star by which they unhesitatingly take their bearings. And Michael, in *Fresh,* shows his appreciation for his sister's beauty and for Roscoe's uncorrupted and affectionate animal nature. Brody and Michael also demonstrate a respect for the independently existing world in which these objective values are embedded. Just as Brody devotes himself to learning about the timeless nature of sharks, so does Michael apply himself diligently to studying the vagaries of human nature. As a result of their respective educations, Brody and Michael realistically assess the animal and human predators they confront.

The films we have surveyed illustrate a variety of obstacles to realistic perception. Some characters, such as the drug dealers in *Fresh* and Quint, are led by excessive pride to overestimate their abilities or underestimate what they are up against. Still others—Gil, in *Parenthood,* for example— feel unreasonably responsible for the success or happiness of other individuals. As a result, their perception of problems, or solutions to them, is distorted. For many of us, nothing more subtle than striving to satisfy our desires or gratify our appetites keeps us from perceiving the truth. So it is with the mayor in *Jaws* and with Nathan in *Parenthood,* neither of whom sees the harm they are subjecting others to because their desires obscure their vision. In addition to detracting from realistic perception of our circumstances and other people, the force of desire can stand more squarely in the way of virtue.

Taken collectively, our movies thoughtfully balance the many ways unruly desires block virtue with the proper place of pleasure in a virtuous life. A host of characters suffer from not being able to keep their appetites in check. Larry can't control his desire for the quick buck or the excitement of gambling, and everything Burke *(Jaws)* does serves his avarice. Archie *(Rob Roy)* lives solely to satisfy his appetite for women, money, and martial victory. We can even see Nathan's life as emptied of meaning by his consuming desire for Patty's brilliance. On the other side of the ledger, *The African Queen* offsets its criticism of Charlie's initial egoistic hedonism by insisting on the importance of bodily pleasure to the good life. This is why Rose must be awakened to the delight of pure sensation—the hurtling of the boat, the roar of the rapids, the cool water spraying her face.

Better off than Rose are those characters whose virtues don't prevent them from enjoying life's happy moments in the first place. No matter how Spartan a life Rob Roy is capable of leading, he knows how to enjoy the pleasures of sexual intimacy, camaraderie, and a festive bonfire. Even the austere and serious-minded Michael enjoys chatting with the cute young girl, playing with the friendly Roscoe, and developing his skills at chess. Although Chief Brody unsparingly broods over the continuing shark attacks, he can still take solace from the kiss his son plants on his cheek. And the message that floats like a child's balloon above the growing pains of *Parenthood*'s parents is that no matter how conscientious and caring we are in our child-rearing, we must, after all, enjoy our children.

Most interesting of all are the protagonists who learn to curb their original desires and subsequently receive pleasure from virtuous activities and from giving pleasure to others. Phil Connors and Charlie Allnut are paradigms of this pleasant reversal. Both stop worrying about the immediate satisfactions of the flesh and learn to enjoy acting for more noble goals, such as helping other people in need or defending one's country against its enemies. More personally, Phil and Charlie take pleasure in pleasing the women they love, and Phil makes beautiful music for the enjoyment of the entire community. We see how deprived of joy people like Larry and Archie must be because they are incapable of delighting in bringing happiness to people who care about them. This is why Newt plays such a pivotal role in *Aliens*. She gives Ripley someone on whom to personally bestow her abundance of moral riches.

The intimate friendship that Newt and Ripley form brings us to the motif with which I want to round out this conclusion. Despite the relative isolation of the characters in the second group of films and the individual emphasis in the transformation of Phil Connors, all the films examined stress the social nature of human existence. In particular, the conclusions of the films depict their protagonists in close personal relationships with one other person. The marriages of the characters in *Parenthood* are strengthened, or at least shored up, and Rob Roy and Chief Brody return to the safe haven of their mates, having survived harrowing combat.

In parallel fashion, unmarried protagonists are coupled or paired with a worthy character to mark the story's finale. Moreover, the pair embark on a new beginning, filled with hope, as we in the audience are similarly lifted with optimism for the renewal their life together seems to portend. Skipping over the obvious—the romantic relationships of Phil and Rita, Rose and Charlie, and Helen and Mr. Bowman *(Parenthood)*—notice the more interesting, because unromantic, coupling of characters in the films of the second group.

In *Fresh*, for example, Michael and his sister will try to live on their own together, as a remnant of what was perhaps never a nuclear family, intact. After all, we never see their mother, who is completely out of the picture (presumably dead), and we are told that Michael is not supposed to be visiting his father. Michael maintains the legalistic fiction that playing chess with his father is not really being with him—they just bump into each other in the park, at regularly scheduled times! Michael initiates the intimacy with Nicki and masterminds the plan that results in their paired escape from the oppressive, degrading world in which they have been surviving. In addition to trying to save his sister from the men who narcotize and eroticize her, Michael seems to intuitively realize his own need for emotional companionship. The odds on the pair's success may not be great, but they are a considerable improvement over the chances the siblings would have had in the bleak alternative.

At the conclusion of *Aliens*, Ripley and Newt have become mother and informally adopted daughter. What began as Ripley taking a frightened, dirty little girl under her protective wing has developed into a loving relationship, filled with mutual respect, trust, and shared humor. Just as Newt elicits the latent virtues of care and nurturance in Ripley (hitherto lavished on her cat, Jonesy), so Ripley provides Newt with a luminous example of womanhood and hope. Newt is smart, quick-witted, pretty, and startlingly free of illusions about people or predicaments. In short, a miniature version of Ripley herself. The universe of interplanetary capitalism to which they return is not a friendly one, but Ripley and Newt will support and care for each other as they make their way in it. Following our skein of stories, we proceed from couples comprised of two adults in the standard romantic mating, to a pair of children, thence to an adult-child relationship. These various generational combinations of intimate union are represented in our films, conspicuously, at the close of their narratives.

The central characters are already coupled in marriage in the other three films—*Parenthood, Rob Roy,* and *Jaws*. However, even here, intimations and echoes of the motif of new pairing appear. For example, the father of the Buchman brood, Frank, teams up with his grandson, Cool, at the end of *Parenthood*. Since Frank's wife, Marilyn, is virtually invisible throughout the movie, we are strangely left with a stronger impression of Frank and Cool as a pair than we had of Frank and his wife. With the return of Rob Roy to his family, we are reminded that Mary is pregnant, giving Rob another man's child to make his own. As with Frank and Cool, this future pairing will be nested within the larger family and clan, drawing us away from the romance of the insulated couple, toward the supportive structures of family and community.

Recall how happily Rose and Charlie swim out of the picture frame at the conclusion of *The African Queen*. As with Michael and his sister, and

Ripley and Newt, we don't see where they are headed. Considering our films together, we realize that a couple alone is a fragile thing indeed. Part of what makes the conclusion of *Groundhog Day* such a happy one is that Phil and Rita have a gentle, responsive community in which to settle. Of course, the town is revealed to Phil as a caring community only when he penetrates its surface by doing virtuous deeds for its inhabitants. Perhaps it is fitting that I end my concluding angles with a return to Punxsutawney, since the return Phil so dreaded as an egoistic hedonist appears so wonderful to him as a virtuous individual. At film's end, remember, Phil is granted a new, post–Groundhog Day day. He exclaims that he and Rita should live in Punxsutawney—though at first they'll just rent. I hope that reading about *Groundhog Day,* and its companions, provides impetus for readers to revisit these visions of virtue on video, whether buying or renting.

Index